C000125133

CHRIS BUSH

Chris Bush is an award-winning playwright, lyricist, theatre-maker and an Associate Director at Sheffield Theatres. Past work includes *Jane Eyre* (Stephen Joseph Theatre/New Vic Theatre), *Fantastically Great Women Who Changed The World* (Kenny Wax, UK tour), *Hungry* (Paines Plough), *Kein Weltuntergang/ (Not) The End of the World* (Schaubühne, Berlin), *Standing at the Sky's Edge* (Sheffield Theatres – Best Theatre: South Bank Sky Arts Awards, Best Musical: UK Theatre Awards), *Nine Lessons and Carols: Stories for a Long Winter* (Almeida Theatre), *Faustus: That Damned Woman* (Headlong/Lyric Hammersmith/ Birmingham Rep), *The Last Noël* (Attic Theatre/UK tour), *The Assassination of Katie Hopkins* (Theatr Clwyd – Best Musical: UK Theatre Awards), *Pericles* (National Theatre: Olivier), *The Changing Room* (NT Connections), *The Band Plays On*, *Steel*, *What We Wished For, A Dream, The Sheffield Mysteries* (all Sheffield Theatres), *Scenes from The End of the World* (Yard/ Central School), *A Declaration from the People* (National Theatre: Dorfman) and *Larksong* (New Vic, Stoke-on-Trent). Awards include a South Bank Sky Arts Award, two UK Theatre Awards, the Perfect Pitch Award, a Brit Writers' Award and the Theatre Royal Haymarket Writers' Award.

Other Titles in this Series

Mike Bartlett
THE 47TH
ALBION
BULL
GAME
AN INTERVENTION
KING CHARLES III
MRS DELGADO
SCANDALTOWN
SNOWFLAKE
VASSA *after* Gorky
WILD

Chris Bush
THE ASSASSINATION OF KATIE HOPKINS
THE CHANGING ROOM
FAUSTUS: THAT DAMNED WOMAN
HUNGRY
JANE EYRE *after* Brontë
THE LAST NOËL
STEEL

Jez Butterworth
THE FERRYMAN
JERUSALEM
JEZ BUTTERWORTH PLAYS: ONE
JEZ BUTTERWORTH PLAYS: TWO
MOJO
THE NIGHT HERON
PARLOUR SONG
THE RIVER
THE WINTERLING

Caryl Churchill
BLUE HEART
CHURCHILL PLAYS: THREE
CHURCHILL PLAYS: FOUR
CHURCHILL PLAYS: FIVE
CHURCHILL: SHORTS
CLOUD NINE
DING DONG THE WICKED
A DREAM PLAY *after* Strindberg
DRUNK ENOUGH TO SAY I LOVE YOU?
ESCAPED ALONE
FAR AWAY
GLASS. KILL. BLUEBEARD'S FRIENDS.
    IMP.
HERE WE GO
HOTEL
ICECREAM
LIGHT SHINING IN BUCKINGHAMSHIRE
LOVE AND INFORMATION
MAD FOREST
A NUMBER
PIGS AND DOGS
SEVEN JEWISH CHILDREN
THE SKRIKER
THIS IS A CHAIR
THYESTES *after* Seneca
TRAPS
WHAT IF IF ONLY

debbie tucker green
BORN BAD
DEBBIE TUCKER GREEN PLAYS: ONE
DIRTY BUTTERFLY
EAR FOR EYE
HANG
NUT
A PROFOUNDLY AFFECTIONATE,
    PASSIONATE DEVOTION TO
    SOMEONE (– *NOUN*)
RANDOM
STONING MARY
TRADE & GENERATIONS
TRUTH AND RECONCILIATION

Chris Hannan
CRIME AND PUNISHMENT
    after Dostoyevsky
ELIZABETH GORDON QUINN
THE GOD OF SOHO
SHINING SOULS
WHAT SHADOWS

Branden Jacobs-Jenkins
APPROPRIATE
GLORIA
AN OCTOROON

Cordelia Lynn
HEDDA TESMAN
after Ibsen
LELA & CO.
LOVE AND OTHER ACTS OF VIOLENCE
ONE FOR SORROW
THREE SISTERS *after* Chekhov

Lucy Kirkwood
BEAUTY AND THE BEAST
    with Katie Mitchell
BLOODY WIMMIN
THE CHILDREN
CHIMERICA
HEDDA *after* Ibsen
IT FELT EMPTY WHEN THE HEART
    WENT AT FIRST BUT IT IS
    ALRIGHT NOW
LUCY KIRKWOOD PLAYS: ONE
MOSQUITOES
NSFW
TINDERBOX
THE WELKIN

Winsome Pinnock
LEAVE TAKING
ROCKETS AND BLUE LIGHTS
TAKEN
TITUBA

Stef Smith
ENOUGH
GIRL IN THE MACHINE
HUMAN ANIMALS
NORA : A DOLL'S HOUSE
REMOTE
SWALLOW

Jack Thorne
2ND MAY 1997
AFTER LIFE
BUNNY
BURYING YOUR BROTHER IN
    THE PAVEMENT
A CHRISTMAS CAROL *after* Dickens
THE END OF HISTORY…
HOPE
JACK THORNE PLAYS: ONE
JUNKYARD
LET THE RIGHT ONE IN
    after John Ajvide Lindqvist
MYDIDAE
THE SOLID LIFE OF SUGAR WATER
STACY & FANNY AND FAGGOT
WHEN YOU CURE ME
WOYZECK *after* Büchner

Phoebe Waller-Bridge
FLEABAG

Joy Wilkinson
ACTING LEADER
FAIR & FELT EFFECTS
THE SWEET SCIENCE OF BRUISING

Chris Bush

ROCK
PAPER
SCISSORS

Three Plays

NICK HERN BOOKS
London
www.nickhernbooks.co.uk

A Nick Hern Book

Rock / Paper / Scissors first published in Great Britain as a paperback original in 2022 by Nick Hern Books Limited, The Glasshouse, 49a Goldhawk Road, London W12 8QP

Rock / Paper / Scissors copyright © 2022 Chris Bush

Chris Bush has asserted her right to be identified as the author of this work

Cover image: Chris Bush

Designed and typeset by Nick Hern Books, London
Printed in Great Britain by Mimeo Ltd, Huntingdon, Cambridgeshire PE29 6XX

A CIP catalogue record for this book is available from the British Library

ISBN 978 1 83904 107 5

For Rob.
Happy 50th.

Introduction
Chris Bush

This is a very silly idea.

We first started dreaming up these shows in February 2021. Directors Rob Hastie and Anthony Lau, designer Ben Stones and myself were making *The Band Plays On* at the Crucible and going slightly insane through the pressures creating work during a global pandemic, trying to imagine a brighter future while struggling to navigate the strange new realities of the day to day. The fiftieth anniversary of the Crucible was coming up in November, and who knew how we were going to mark it, or even if the theatre would be open at all by then? While I went home to work on rewrites and do deep dives into lesser known Sheffield Britpop acts, the directors were putting together funding applications and drawing up bold new seasons with a combination of blind hope and bloody-mindedness that all theatre professionals know only too well.

One morning, Rob met me outside my digs to walk with me to the theatre. He had an idea. What if we threw caution to the wind and thought big – even bigger than usual? What if we tried to do something never attempted before – something that could more or less only be done here, within a complex of three world-class stages all only a few metres from each other? What if we took over every inch of Sheffield Theatres with three brand-new standalone shows with a shared cast, playing simultaneously in the Crucible, Lyceum, and Crucible Studio? Alan Ayckbourn's *House* and *Garden* had done the same thing with two plays, but no one had ever tried it with three (arguably for good reason). The concept was absurd. Would we even be open in a year's time? What was the story? How do you even begin to plan something like this? I had no idea. Of course I said yes immediately.

We started kicking ideas around straight away. What was the hook, beside the sheer audacity of attempting it? What if each show had a distinct genre – one farce, one murder mystery, one musical, all linked by the same set of characters? What if we showed the same character at different points in their life? A christening, a wedding, a funeral (*Birth, Marriage* and *Death* as your three titles)? Time travel was definitely discussed at one point. Then for a while we settled on the idea of two weddings, one in the Crucible, one in the Lyceum, and the caterers in the studio (working titles of *Bride, Groom* and *Cake*). What if two childhood sweethearts were now getting married on the same day to different people, next door to each other, and hilarity ensued? This concept evolved into one real wedding in the Crucible, and a local am-dram production of a wedding-themed musical in the Lyceum, with all the potential for mistaken identities that might entail. I even came up with the fake show-within-a-show, *Wits 'n' Weddings*, a 1980s mega-flop based on the works of Philip Larkin with a book by a young Richard Curtis… alas, it was not to be.

As fun as some of these ideas were, I was never quite sure *why* we wanted to tell any of these stories, beyond the technical challenge they presented. We all agreed some kind of 'farce engine' felt useful, but then a lot of the comedy in farce comes from the audience knowing more than the characters onstage – this is difficult when any given audience might only be getting a third of the overall story at any given time, and these shows needed to be entirely self-contained, as well as forming part of a greater whole. We were all enjoying ourselves, but I felt like I needed to go back to the dramaturgical drawing board.

What makes good drama?

All drama fundamentally revolves around conflict. All stories are about a hero (protagonist) who wants something (a goal) but there's something or someone (an obstacle) in their way. Sometimes that obstacle is physical, or psychological, or elemental, but often it takes the form of an *antagonist* – a villain – a character whose dramatic function is to stop our hero from getting what they want. This might be because the antagonist despises the hero, and wishes them to suffer, but equally it could just be because they have goals of their own, and those goals are incompatible. The crucial takeaway is this: we are all protagonists in our own stories, but we could very easily be antagonists in someone else's, whether we're trying to be or not.

'Main Character Syndrome' is a contemporary term for a timeless condition. It describes someone who believes that they are the centre of the universe, and anyone else is of little or no significance. It's a twenty-first-century form of solipsism, and something we can all be guilty of. Three standalone plays with a shared company – three distinct viewpoints on a common event – is the theatrical antidote to this. Each play would have its own protagonist(s), but said protagonist might become a primary or secondary antagonist when they step off one stage and onto another. It doesn't mean any of these people are monsters, they just want different things. Theatre, at its best, is a machine for generating empathy – it can transport us to strange and unfamiliar worlds and populate them with characters we'll come to care deeply for, and learn to understand, despite the fact that they might appear to be nothing like us. This simultaneous-trilogy structure offers a unique opportunity for further experiments in empathy: we can watch villains become heroes and vice versa when we watch the same events from a different angle. Our sympathies may shift entirely depending on what order we watch the shows in. A traditional 'hero's journey' three-act saga can often get a bit black-and-white in terms of its morality, in part due to the necessary primacy it places on the hero's perspective – here we can gently remind an audience, through the theatrical form, that life is messy and complicated and we rarely have the full picture.

However, I still didn't know what the plays were about. I wanted to write about intergenerational conflict, and how each generation might have a legitimate reason to feel uniquely hard done by. The next trilogy concept was *Work, Rest* and *Play* – a young generation of school-leavers facing an uncertain future, their parents representing the squeezed middle, and their grandparents in retirement. Was this a family saga of three spaces within the same house? The granny annex, the grown-up dinner party downstairs, the teenagers getting high in the garage? What event would throw them all into crisis? 'No one wants to see a play called *Work*,' said Rob Hastie. And a play called *Play* felt a little sub-Beckett. Fair enough. Keep thinking. What about a properly Sheffield trilogy, using local placenames as generational markers? *Intake* (the youth), *Halfway* (middle-aged), and *Endcliffe* (for the OAPs)? Was that a bit niche?

Furthermore, I felt like we'd explored intergenerational family dynamics in the domestic realm quite thoroughly in *Standing at the Sky's Edge*, so maybe this should move into the world of work. At this fiftieth anniversary moment of reflection, it was a chance to think about what cities are for, what civic/public spaces are for, who owns our heritage, who owns our future? Where have we come from and how does that inform where we're going?

For all this intellectualising, we also just brainstormed a lot of three-part lists. What words went together and did any of them mean anything? How about...

Hop, Skip, Jump
Stop, Look, Listen
Ready, Set, Go
Red, Yellow, Green
*Faith, Hope, Charity**
*Snap, Crackle, Pop***

Then, on 3 September 2021, with time rapidly running out and a season announcement due very soon, Rob and I had the following exchange over WhatsApp (edited only for clarity).

Chris Bush, 17:29

'I feel like *Rock, Paper, Scissors* could be a good name for something (and hints at three competing forces of equal strength) but I don't know what they mean by themselves.'

Chris Bush, 17:30

'*Scissors* = stainless steel, Sheffield history etc etc, *Paper* = office work? Or press? *Rock* = rock music? Teenage rebellion? Dunno...'

Rob Hastie, 17.31

'Oo that's quite fun'

Chris Bush, 17:37

'Could be something in whatever they're competing over – an inherited building, for instance – could it stay testament to

* The National Theatre got there first.
** Almost definitely trademarked.

industrial heritage (scissors), become a cool music venue (rock), or just bland but commercially lucrative office space (paper)?

Rob Hastie, 17:44

'Oh that's VERY good'

Chris Bush, 17:46

'I wonder if then (another rethink) do we want our stages to all be different parts of the same building/complex – the factory floor, the old manager's office, the break room or something? And lean into that idea of everyone milling around the same space in real time?'

And that was that. Of course this was still only the sketchiest of ideas, but in just over fifteen minutes something had crystalised. It now felt like we had the bones of a story (or multiple stories) worth telling. Something that spoke to intergenerational conflict, about heritage, about legacy, about autonomy, and how much any of us are in control of our destiny at any given time. What has been done here, and how does that inform what we should do next? How can we work together when no one really has enough? No heroes, no villains, just a group of people trying to survive in difficult circumstances. An exercise in empathy – which is, after all, the best reason to make theatre in the first place.

I'm incredibly thankful to have been such a big part of Sheffield Theatres' fiftieth anniversary season. They have the best people, the best stages, the best ideas, and I owe them everything. Particular thanks to Rob Hastie for his flawless leadership under impossible circumstances, to Anthony and Elin, and all our fearless cast, crew and creatives for signing up to such a patently absurd idea. To my agents, Matt and Alex, to all at Nick Hern Books, to my family, for raising me in the best city in the world, I'm very, very grateful. What an adventure.

June 2022

Rock / *Paper* / *Scissors* were first performed at Sheffield Theatres (in the Crucible, Lyceum and Studio Theatres respectively) on 16 June 2022 (with *Paper* on 18 June). The cast was as follows (in alphabetical order):

SUSIE	Denise Black
MEL	Natalie Casey
LEO	Andrew Macbean
MOLLY	Daisy May
BILLY	Alistair Natkiel
FAYE	Samantha Power
OMAR	Guy Rhys
ZARA	Lucie Shorthouse
AVA	Dumile Sibanda
MASON	Jabez Sykes
LIV	Maia Tamrakar
TRENT	Joe Usher
COCO	Chanel Waddock
XANDER	Leo Wan

For *Rock*

Director	Anthony Lau
Designer	Ben Stones
Lighting Designer	Richard Howell
Sound Designer	Annie May Fletcher
Assistant Director	Alexandra Whiteley
Production Manager	Steph Balmforth
Stage Manager	Kate Schofield
Deputy Stage Manager	Linnea Grønning
Assistant Stage Manager	Blue Merrick

For *Paper*

Director	Robert Hastie
Designer	Janet Bird
Lighting Designer	Johanna Town
Sound Designer	Sam Glossop
Assistant Director	Callum Berridge

Production Manager	Luke Child
Stage Manager	Sarah Gentle
Deputy Stage Manager	Sarah Greenwood
Assistant Stage Manager	Sarah Longson

For *Scissors*

Director	Elin Schofield
Designer	Natasha Jenkins
Lighting Designer	Jai Morjaria
Sound Designer	Tingying Dong
Assistant Director	Grace Cordell

Production Manager	Hamish Ellis
Stage Manager	Ros Chappelle
Deputy Stage Manager	Jasmine Davies
Assistant Stage Manager	Alizee Butel

Composer	Richard Taylor
Movement Director	Tom Herron
Vocal and Dialect Coach	Anita Gilbert

Company Manager	Andrew Wilcox
Casting Director	Christopher Worrall
Casting Consultant	Stuart Burt CDG
Assistant Sound Designer	José Guillermo Puello

Musicians

Guitar	Tom Woodhouse
Drums	Natasha Rose Allen
Bass	Philipe Alexandre Clegg

Characters

SUSIE, *sixties, female. Sister of the recently deceased Eddie*
LEO, *sixties, male. One of her oldest friends*
XANDER, *twenties/thirties, male. A corporate design consultant*
ZARA, *mid-twenties, female. A PhD student. Daughter of:*
OMAR, *forties/fifties, male. The current factory manager*
BILLY, *thirties/forties, male. A music photographer*
MASON, *late teens, male. An apprentice*
AVA, *late teens, female. An apprentice*
LIV, *late teens, female. An apprentice*
TRENT, *late teens, male. An apprentice*
FAYE, *early forties, female. Eddie's adopted daughter*
MEL, *early forties, female. Faye's partner*
COCO, *early/mid-twenties, female. One half of a pop act*
MOLLY, *early/mid-twenties, female. The other half*

This text went to press before the end of rehearsals and so may differ slightly from the plays as performed.

ROCK

ACT ONE

The former main factory floor of an old scissor factory. Back in its heyday, hundreds of workers would have had stations here. Now operations are run on a much smaller scale with a skeleton staff, and this space isn't used at all, mostly because it's draughty, high-ceilinged and too expensive to heat. Grimy brick walls, large windows that haven't been cleaned in decades. Anything useful has been moved or sold. Anything left has gone to rust. Somehow it's still magnificent.

SUSIE *and* LEO *enter. They take it all in.*

SUSIE. It's really something, isn't it?

LEO. The light, it's –

SUSIE. I know.

LEO. Phenomenal.

SUSIE. Did I ever take you round here, back in the day?

LEO. I don't think so.

SUSIE. I used to sneak boys in when no one was looking and have my way with them in the storage rooms.

LEO. Now I would've remembered that.

SUSIE. You missed out.

LEO. Absolutely. (*Beat.*) It's those windows. Don't ever let them clean those windows. That's what's doing it.

SUSIE. Hmm?

LEO. The light. Places would kill for that depth of grime.

SUSIE. You think?

LEO. There's an art director somewhere right now going round a, um, some warehouse somewhere in London, or New York, or San Francisco, with a little, a tin full of gravy browning – that's what they'd use – an old bean can and a shaving brush, dabbing at his windows, trying to recreate this exact quality of light. But you can't, because that right there is history.

SUSIE. Well I'm glad you like it.

LEO. It must have been magnificent, back in the day. When did your father buy it?

SUSIE. Seventy… Seventy-one, it was – fifty years ago last winter. On its last legs even then, so he got it for a song – paid cash – never even had a mortgage. Handed it over to Eddie to see what he could make of it. And as you can tell, that was a roaring success.

LEO. For everything there is a season.

SUSIE. Oh don't you start.

LEO. I thought it was a lovely service.

SUSIE. Some of us don't believe in seasons. Some of us never go out of style.

LEO (*beginning to take something out of his pocket*). I found something that made me think of you, actually. It was –

SUSIE (*cutting him off*). But you can see the potential?

LEO. I can see daylight through the roof.

SUSIE. Excellent for ventilation. I like it. It's raw. If it were up to me, I'd just push everything to the corners and wheel some speakers in, but it does need to be comfortable – and warm. We should look at insulation – conservation – ways to keep the heat in.

LEO. Everything okay?

SUSIE. Yes, fine. Silly. 'Conservation' – it's nothing. It's thermodynamics. One of those very clever conversations Dad and Eddie would have that I was never a part of. Anyway.

LEO. Uh-huh.

SUSIE. Anyway, you just need bodies, don't you? Enough bodies will always generate enough heat. Much greener. It just goes on and on. We can open everything up in stages, but bodies in the space – that's the priority. We can have practice rooms, recording studios – imagine if we set up our own little indie label here!

LEO. But one thing at a time?

SUSIE. Yes, yes. But we need a flag in the sand. The stage up at this end, I thought, and the bar over there. Cloakroom, toilets, a little green room up on the mezzanine, or a VIP space for entertaining. VIP toilets. It's where you want to spend the money, believe me. With shagpile seats so it's harder to snort coke off them.

LEO. You've really thought of everything.

SUSIE. I've been planning this for fifty years.

LEO. Really?

SUSIE. This is my moment. There's more office space across the yard. That's where we'd put the studio, I think, in the end. And the yard itself – it's all ours – it only needs a few picnic tables, some space heaters, or, or just blankets, why not? Little outdoor bar, makeshift stage, food trucks – all independent. Maybe that's step one. We don't start inside at all, a little outdoor festival over the summer.

LEO. This summer?

SUSIE. Take advantage before the weather changes.

LEO. But *this summer*?

SUSIE (*ignoring this*). And I want… you know that man who does the cutlery sculptures? Forks and spoons and… kinetic – they move about. I want to commission something like that, but with scissors.

LEO. Uh-huh.

SUSIE. As a centrepiece – a celebration of what we did here. Put it over the gates – the first thing you see as you walk in. High enough that it won't put someone's eye out. Running with scissors. What do you think? 'Running With Scissors' as the name of something? A club night? Something for the lesbians?

LEO. Susie –

SUSIE. What?

LEO. Do you think perhaps you want to slow down?

SUSIE. Absolutely not.

LEO. Okay, but –

SUSIE. I'll tell you the same thing I told Johnny – there is only one way to live, one way to love, and one way to play rock and roll, and that's fast, imprecise and with enthusiasm.

LEO (*ignoring this*). Who else do you have on board?

SUSIE. You don't think I can do it by myself?

LEO. I didn't say that.

SUSIE. Everyone's going to want a piece of it, believe me.

LEO. It just sounds like a lot of work.

SUSIE. Good. Work is good. Work keeps you young. This is a legacy project, y'know? My legacy. My family's legacy – the city's legacy, right here.

LEO. What do you need?

SUSIE. Money.

LEO. Right.

SUSIE. Lots of it.

LEO. Okay.

SUSIE. You still know some rich people, don't you?

LEO. One or two.

SUSIE. All my rich friends are now either dead or responsible, which is worse than dead. And both sets have children who disapprove of me.

LEO. Have you had a survey done yet? Any engineers in?

SUSIE. These places were built to last. Good bones. Any damage is just cosmetic.

LEO. And you know that for a fact?

SUSIE. Just like me.

LEO. Susie –

SUSIE. All it needs is a fresh lick of paint.

LEO. And permissions – licensing?

SUSIE. The thing is, Leo – the thing you seem to be forgetting – is that once I get my teeth stuck into something, nobody is able to say no to me – not once I'm determined. You tell me 'no' and I just hear 'try harder'.

LEO. Yes, that is one of your more irritating qualities.

SUSIE. So I can count on your support?

LEO. Some people slow down, you know, when they start to reach the twilight of their years.

SUSIE. Reach the what now?

LEO. Some people take up cross-stitch, or flower arranging, or golf.

SUSIE. Yes – start with those suckers.

LEO. Susie –

SUSIE. Some people are boring fuckers, Leo, I don't know what to tell you. Here – let me paint you a picture.

SUSIE *fishes out a portable Bluetooth speaker from a bag, switches it on and puts it down somewhere.*

LEO. You don't need to sell me on –

SUSIE. Shut up and listen. You're going to love it.

SUSIE *finds the right track on her phone. Music starts to play out of the speaker. It's a live recording, rough and ready, of some old-school rock and roll, the kind of thing that might've come out of the Cavern Club in the sixties. As she talks, some magic happens. The sound travels out of the little speaker and starts to gradually fill the whole space. It could be that the music itself changes – from rock and roll to psychodelia to punk and beyond. She's filling the space with her personal history. It becomes almost shamanic – a call to arms, an invocation.*

Do you remember this? We're both too young, but this is the world we were born into. Listen. They can't play for shit. The charm is that they can't play for shit. Fast, imprecise and with enthusiasm. Words to live by. Popular music – and I mean this – popular music only becomes culturally significant once any old idiot can play it. It only happens after the war. Because take swing music – big band – the sort of thing our parents would listen to. What do you need for that? You need a *big band*. You need trained musicians, and a raised stage, or an orchestra pit, you need a dance hall, you need all that jazz. But rock and roll doesn't need anything. It needs youth and energy and imperfection. And the punks took all that and ran with it. Punk perfected imperfection. Three chords is plenty. Anything above five is masturbation. Of course we're not going to clean the windows. This place should feel *raw*. And we won't play *this* – but the spirit of it… Too much music nowadays is made on computers. I want this to be a place where everything happens live. Because it was alive once – it was on life support by the time my father bought it, but there was a time… Alive, with industry. Alive with *life*. With calloused hands, with metal on metal, with hammers and tongs that echoed up and out of the valley. Alive with sweat and steel and bodies generating their own heat. Can't we have all that again? Dance with me, Leo. I'm sorry I never brought you here back in the day, but we can make up for it now. Are you embarrassed? Everyone's embarrassed by me nowadays – they used to be outraged, but now they're just *embarrassed*. If you won't dance just close your eyes and listen. No, keep them open and look up at that light. Imagine this building alive again – imagine feeling alive again. The stage goes up at that end, the bar over there. Dance floor, booths along that wall. Bodies against bodies against bodies, now all that's allowed, now we've had a chance to remember what we were missing. Come on. You need this as much as I do. Your reluctance to dance has been noted, but I haven't given up on you yet. I've still got my teeth in you too.

At this point, SUSIE *notices* XANDER (*and ideally we notice him for the first time too*), *stood quietly to one side, watching them. He's well-groomed and wears a slightly shiny suit. The soundscape drops out, and* SUSIE *turns off the Bluetooth speaker. She refuses to be embarrassed by this.*

Can I help you?

XANDER. Mrs Spenser?

SUSIE. Miss.

XANDER. I'm sorry?

SUSIE. *Miss* Spenser.

XANDER. Oh, I'm sorry.

SUSIE. Doctor Spenser, actually. But as it was honorary it feels like an affectation.

XANDER. Whatever you –

SUSIE. Susie. You must be the man.

XANDER. Uh…

SUSIE. From the agency?

XANDER. That's right.

SUSIE (*to* LEO). You see – it's all coming together. Billy's who I was telling you about on the drive over. He's going to help us sell, sell, sell. (*To* XANDER.) It was Billy?

XANDER. Xander.

SUSIE. Oh. I wasn't very close.

XANDER. Don't worry about it.

SUSIE. Are you sure you're not called Billy?

XANDER. Fairly sure.

SUSIE. Shame. I think it'd suit you. If we get along, maybe I'll have you re-baptised. (*To* LEO.) I did that once, in Nepal. Actually it was California, but the decor was Nepalese. Beautiful.

LEO (*to* XANDER). Don't mind her.

SUSIE. No, don't mind me. Nobody minds me. (*Beat.*) Xanthus, you said?

XANDER. Xander.

SUSIE. Short for Alexander?

XANDER. That's right.

SUSIE. But not Alex?

XANDER. No.

SUSIE. Or Al?

XANDER. I –

SUSIE. Or maybe just Der?

LEO. Don't bully him.

SUSIE. Xander. Fascinating. Good for you. (*Beat.*) Xander, I'd like you to meet Leo. He's very taken by the dirty windows.

LEO. A pleasure.

XANDER. Yes, the quality of light in here –

SUSIE. Yes, we're all hugely excited by the light. You see we're of the generation who were raised several dozen feet underneath the South Yorkshire Coalfield, so the possibility of natural daylight remains extremely thrilling.

XANDER. I –

SUSIE. Hashtag-sarcasm, if that wasn't clear. (*Aside, to* LEO.) I find you have to verbalise your subtext for the under-thirties. (*Back to* XANDER.) You're much younger than I was expecting.

XANDER. Right.

SUSIE. Now you say it back.

XANDER (*choosing to move past this*). Yeah, um, the light is… Light's always going to be your secret weapon somewhere like this – it's transformative. I'd treat it like a church, or a cathedral.

SUSIE. Yes – yes, I like that. A holy space. For secular worship.

LEO. Like, um, like the Union Chapel.

SUSIE. Magnificent. I knew I liked you, Billy.

XANDER. Xander.

SUSIE. For now. Carry on.

XANDER. Right. So, uh, so I'd want to show off as much of the original character as you can – even the imperfections – especially the imperfections –

SUSIE *nudges* LEO *approvingly.*

And you're right – it does all start with the windows – with light. So many church conversions butcher the windows – they block them in, cover them up, slice them in two. But you could consider false walls, light wells, mezzanines –

LEO. You seem like a very knowledgeable young man.

XANDER. Thank you.

LEO. And how long have you been in photography?

XANDER. Photography?

LEO. Yes. (*To* SUSIE.) Isn't he here for photographs?

SUSIE. Yes.

XANDER. No.

SUSIE. No? (*Beat.*) Oh – you know what? That must be Billy.

LEO. So who's this?

SUSIE. It's a good question. (*To* XANDER.) Who are you?

XANDER. I'm Xander.

SUSIE (*to* LEO). He's Xander. I spoke to an agency, they put me in touch with Billy –

XANDER. You're expecting a photographer today?

SUSIE. Yes. Get something we can show investors – get a buzz going.

XANDER. Oh.

LEO. Not your department?

XANDER. No.

SUSIE. Are you work experience, or – ?

XANDER. No, I'm –

SUSIE. Well look, I'm sure he's on his way. In the meantime why don't we just have a poke around?

XANDER. Uh. Yes, that's... I'm sure... Do we have access to the whole site?

SUSIE. Absolutely.

XANDER. Okay.

SUSIE. In a manner of speaking.

XANDER. I'm sorry?

SUSIE. We're just going to tread lightly, try not to get under anyone's feet.

LEO. Whose feet?

SUSIE. They know we're here. Up to a point. They know that at some point I might be here.

LEO. Who's they?

XANDER. Is this still a working facility?

SUSIE. It's… *Barely.* Technically –

LEO. You told me they'd gone bust.

SUSIE. Gone bust, going bust, it's the same difference. (*To* XANDER.) Yes, it's conceivable there are still one or two – a skeleton crew of… But it really doesn't matter. They don't use this part of the factory, anyway.

XANDER. Maybe I should clear this with the office.

SUSIE. It's fine. I'm his sister! I'm family.

XANDER. You're his sister?

SUSIE. That's right.

XANDER. I thought you were the daughter.

SUSIE. Oh Xander, you old flatterer.

XANDER. It's just I have down –

SUSIE. No, I'm the daughter of… Yes, my father, Thomas Spenser – (*To* LEO.) I'm sorry, I'm repeating myself – (*Now back to* XANDER.) He bought the site originally. My brother Eddie ran it for fifty years. He passed away a short while ago and now here we are.

XANDER. And you are the owner? You are now in possession of – ?

SUSIE. What are you getting at?

XANDER. I just have a note on your file –

SUSIE. I hired a photographer, not the Spanish Inquisition.

XANDER. I'd just like to clarify –

SUSIE. Yes! Alright, yes. There has been some confusion surrounding… We still haven't found a will. My brother was colossally disorganised. It doesn't mean anything. Of course it all passes to me. I'm the only Spenser left standing.

XANDER. I see.

SUSIE. No, no, I don't think you do see. This is *ours*. That isn't in question. This building has been ours for the past fifty years –

LEO. He's only doing his job.

SUSIE. What do you know about his job? What even is his job? Who is he? (*To* XANDER.) Look at that suit – you look like an estate agent.

XANDER. Is it possible that we're actively trespassing?

SUSIE. Don't be so dramatic. I grew up here – how can I trespass? Wet blankets, both of you. Billy's on his way, and the band will be here soon, and then we can start getting somewhere.

XANDER. The band?

SUSIE. Yes, the band! I've arranged for a band – that's why we need a photographer! Very young, very hot – they're going to bring this place alive! I would volunteer myself, but I'm a fossil now, I'm not going to get any pulses racing. (*Beat.*) Feel free to jump in and contradict me any time you like.

LEO. Susie –

SUSIE (*to* XANDER). I *did*, for the record, back in the day – Leo can testify – but I know how this industry works. So I found this girl – beautiful. Voice is beautiful. And she has a friend – a sister? This double-act – very *now*, very contemporary. Gorgeous.

XANDER. I think I'm a few steps behind.

LEO. You and me both.

SUSIE. Well who needs either of you? I'll just wait here for Billy. We talked it all through – We're going to sell people a vision. We shoot the girls in the space, the old and the new, the beauty and the brickwork, proud heritage and a bold new future.

XANDER. I might just step out and make a call.

SUSIE. Okay.

XANDER. Just to –

SUSIE. If you must.

XANDER. Check in with…

SUSIE. Yes, yes, off you go. Do what you've got to do.

XANDER. I'll be right back.

   XANDER *goes*.

SUSIE (*to* LEO). Alex is a perfectly acceptable abbreviation of Alexander.

LEO. What is all this?

SUSIE. I'm trying to get some pictures taken, that's all. I didn't realise I'd need permission from the Queen.

LEO. And you're sure he's not the man you spoke to?

SUSIE. Of course he isn't.

LEO. Okay.

SUSIE. Of course I… I want David Bailey, not some prepubescent compliance manager.

LEO. Then I'm sure it'll get cleared up.

SUSIE. I have arranged – I have organised – a band, a very fashionable band, and a photographer, and I have a fully realised vision for… Stop looking at me like that!

LEO. Like what?

SUSIE. Like you're wondering if I've finally lost it. I know who I spoke to.

LEO. You found a band?

SUSIE. Why shouldn't I have found a band? They're students, I think. Very arty. Describe themselves new-new-wave. You like that?

LEO. Is that what you do now? Spend your evenings hanging out in student bars?

SUSIE. So what if I do?

LEO. Reliving a misspent youth?

SUSIE. I found them online. We've been corresponding.

LEO. You haven't sent them any money, have you?

SUSIE. Right – I'm going to show you the emails. (*She starts fiddling with her phone.*) Coco, her name is. Astonishing girl. Beautiful. She reminds me of me.

LEO. Okay.

SUSIE. You believe me, don't you? You don't think I'm making this up?

LEO. I think… With love, I think that Susie Spenser has a great track record in willing things into existence, but perhaps –

SUSIE. This isn't some whim. I've planned this to the letter.

LEO. I'm just saying is it possible you've been a little optimistic in – ?

ZARA enters. She's casually dressed and has a backpack with her. She spots LEO and SUSIE and stops.

ZARA. Oh. Hello.

SUSIE laughs in delight.

Um…

SUSIE. Welcome! Welcome, welcome, welcome.

ZARA. Hi.

SUSIE. I'm Susie, this is my very old friend Leo.

LEO. Nice to meet you.

SUSIE. Don't talk with your mouth full, Leo. (*To* ZARA.) I'm sorry, Leo is just finishing up eating his words.

ZARA. Hi. Right. Sorry, I didn't think anybody –

SUSIE. Don't worry, you're not late. We're actually still waiting on the photographer.

ZARA. Photographer?

SUSIE. Yes, there's been a little confusion, but we're getting to the bottom of it now. Please – put your bags down, make yourself at home. I'm Susie. Did I say that?

ZARA (*with a flash of realisation*). Oh! Oh, are you the newspaper people?

LEO. Newspaper?

ZARA. For the article – the feature?

SUSIE. Yes.

LEO. Really?

SUSIE. In a manner of speaking. For the publicity images, yes?

ZARA. Right. Brilliant. My dad didn't really tell me much about it.

SUSIE. Your father?

ZARA. Yeah, he's the one who set it all up.

LEO. Is he your manager?

ZARA. He's the manager, yeah.

SUSIE. Got it. I've been speaking with Coco.

ZARA. Who?

SUSIE. Coco – don't I have that right? We've been having some difficulty with names today. The other one. Your sister? Friend? Girlfriend? I didn't want to presume.

ZARA. Um. I'm Zara –

SUSIE. Zara! It's a pleasure.

XANDER *returns*.

XANDER. Mrs Spenser – ?

SUSIE (*to* ZARA). Hold that thought. (*To* XANDER.) *Miss* Spenser, as we've established.

XANDER. Yes, Miss Spenser, sorry for –

SUSIE. Or how about Doctor Spenser after all? Perhaps it'd help if you skipped straight to the honorific.

XANDER. I've just spoken with –

SUSIE. Xander, Zara – Zara, Xander. Xander is… Well no one's quite sure what Xander's here for. Zara – Zara is who I was telling you about – well she's a piece of the puzzle, anyway. Zara is here to have her photograph taken, and generally be brilliant and look gorgeous and help us turn this place around. (*To* ZARA.) Sound good to you?

ZARA. Uh…

SUSIE. Problem?

ZARA. You want me in the photos?

SUSIE. Well of course we do, darling.

ZARA. Right. It's just… I'm not sure I'm necessarily the right person.

SUSIE (*to* LEO). There's always the shy one. Just wait until Coco gets here.

ZARA. I am really happy to help out. I didn't know you'd be doing photos at all, actually. I thought it was more of an interview thing.

SUSIE. Oh.

ZARA. Yeah, you know, just talking about what we do, and –

SUSIE. Oh, absolutely. Yes, absolutely. We'll do a Q&A, make sure we cover all of that, but we need the visuals to sell it. A picture's worth a thousand words, after all. (*Beat.*) Is that what you think you'll be wearing?

ZARA. Is this not good?

SUSIE. No, it's charming.

ZARA. I don't have anything else with me. I really wasn't…
I could try to nip home. Most of my nice stuff is still at uni.

SUSIE. Ah, right, of course.

ZARA. Is that a problem?

XANDER *tries to get a word in.*

XANDER. Miss Spenser – ?

SUSIE (*ignoring him, still to* ZARA). No, no, no. It's perfect.
Wonderful. Very real. Not entirely what I was expecting, but –

ZARA. Did you want the uniforms? The overalls?

SUSIE. Is that what they are?

ZARA. Yeah. The thing is I don't really wear them though.
Because I'm not an official –

SUSIE. Then this is gorgeous. You're gorgeous.

XANDER *interjects.*

XANDER. Doctor Spenser. Can I clarify something?

SUSIE. Oh, you're still here. (*To the others.*) He's still here.

XANDER. You're Susan Spenser?

SUSIE. It's Susie, and I don't do autographs.

XANDER. Yes – I spoke to the office, and I don't think you're
the person I'm here to see.

SUSIE. Excellent. Why are you still here then?

XANDER. I'm meant to be talking to the daughter.

SUSIE. Yes, I explained –

ZARA (*to* XANDER). Oh. Sorry – hi – I'm the daughter.

LEO. You are?

ZARA. Are you not all together?

LEO. Whose daughter?

XANDER (*to* ZARA). You're the daughter? (*To* SUSIE.) And
you're the sister?

LEO (*to* SUSIE). I thought she – (*Meaning* ZARA.) was the sister?

SUSIE. The friend or the sister. Or the girlfriend.

XANDER (*to* ZARA). You're Faye?

SUSIE. No, she's Coco.

ZARA. No, I'm Zara.

SUSIE. That's right. Coco is the sister.

LEO. Or the friend. Or the girlfriend?

SUSIE (*to* XANDER). Did you say Faye?

XANDER. Yes.

ZARA. Who is it you're looking for exactly?

XANDER. The owner's daughter.

ZARA. Right. Yes. That's me.

SUSIE. What?

XANDER (*to* ZARA). I'm very sorry for your loss.

ZARA. What?

OMAR *enters*.

OMAR. What's going on in here?

LEO (*to* SUSIE). Is this him?

SUSIE. Billy?

OMAR (*to* ZARA). Who are all these people?

ZARA. You're here! They're from the paper.

SUSIE. Just to clarify, that isn't strictly –

LEO. Did you promise them press?

SUSIE. No, I never said –

OMAR. The paper?

ZARA. You know – the feature in *The Star* – you said you'd been trying –

OMAR. Oh!

LEO. *The Star*?

ZARA. This is my dad.

SUSIE. Oh! You're the manager!

OMAR. That's right.

SUSIE. Right, right! Finally! (*To* XANDER.) Not the *owner*, the manager. (*Back to* OMAR.) And is the other one on her way?

OMAR. The other one?

SUSIE. The sister.

LEO. Or the friend. Or the girlfriend.

SUSIE. The bandmate.

OMAR. I don't follow.

XANDER. You're her father?

OMAR. Yes.

XANDER. I thought the father was dead.

OMAR. Excuse me?

XANDER (*to* ZARA). You said you were the daughter.

ZARA. Yes – his – (*Meaning* OMAR.) daughter!

LEO. Is anyone else getting dizzy?

SUSIE. No, now listen – you're confusing things. It's all very simple. We're going to take Zara's picture – Zara and Coco, as soon as she arrives. Billy is the photographer –

OMAR (*referring to* XANDER). Is this Billy?

LEO. That's an easy mistake to make.

SUSIE. Billy's whereabouts remain a work-in-progress.

XANDER (*offering his hand to* OMAR). Xander MacIntyre, Claybourne-Harris.

SUSIE. Now who needs that many names?

XANDER. It's not… I'm *from* Claybourne-Harris. We're –

OMAR (*shaking* XANDER*'s hand*). Omar Sarbani.

SUSIE. Yes! Now that is familiar.

OMAR. And who's Coco?

SUSIE. Coco! Am I going mad? The other one. The one I've been emailing. The sister!

LEO. Or the friend.

XANDER. Or the girlfriend?

OMAR (*to* SUSIE, *with a flash of revelation*). Wait – I know you.

SUSIE. Finally!

OMAR. You're the sister.

LEO *groans*.

(*Still to* SUSIE.) You're Eddie's sister.

SUSIE (*thrown*). I… Yes, that's right.

OMAR. I saw you at the memorial service. I remember your reading. Ecclesiastes.

SUSIE. Oh.

OMAR. Why do you want to take a photograph of my daughter?

SUSIE. Why were you at my brother's memorial?

OMAR. Why wouldn't I be?

Beat. Realisation.

SUSIE. Oh! Omar! Mr Sarbani!

LEO. Susie?

SUSIE (*still to* OMAR). You're the *manager*!

OMAR. Yes, I –

SUSIE. He's the manager! Of here – you're the manager of *here*.

OMAR. Didn't I just say that?

SUSIE (*referring to* ZARA). Not of her.

OMAR. Well, technically –

SUSIE. And she's your daughter?

OMAR. Yes.

ZARA. Hi.

SUSIE (*to* LEO). This isn't Coco.

LEO. No.

SUSIE. Or the sister. Or the friend. Or the girlfriend. (*To* ZARA.)
You're not in a band.

ZARA. Um. No.

SUSIE. And this is your father. (*To* OMAR.) You're Omar
Sarbani.

OMAR. That's right.

SUSIE. I got one! I never forget a name. You were Eddie's
number two. You've been working here, what – ten years?

OMAR. Thirteen.

SUSIE. Thirteen! So okay, so we're getting somewhere, so as of
right this moment I'm still short one band and one
photographer, but let's not worry about that, let's move with
the momentum. (*To* XANDER.) Now, as for you – who are
you, exactly?

XANDER. Xander MacIntyre, Claybourne-Harris.

SUSIE. Well isn't that illuminating.

XANDER. I'm here to meet a Mrs Faye Spenser. Um. She's…

LEO. Oh!

SUSIE *and* OMAR. She's the daughter.

ZARA. What?

SUSIE. She's Eddie's daughter.

OMAR. Yes.

SUSIE. Stepdaughter, as it happens. For the record.

LEO. And she's here?

XANDER. She's supposed to be.

OMAR. Meeting her for what, exactly?

XANDER. I think I should probably be discussing that with her.

SUSIE. But who are you? What are you?

LEO. Is he an architect?

ZARA. Or an estate agent? He looks like an estate agent.

SUSIE. Yes! I said that too. It's the suit.

XANDER. Claybourne-Harris provides a range of bespoke solutions for urban redevelopment.

SUSIE (*another revelation*). Oh! Oh, I see. Now I understand it! The nerve of her!

ZARA. So is no one from the paper? Nobody from *The Star*? (*To* OMAR.) Is that even happening today?

OMAR. I don't know.

SUSIE. So she's making a land-grab! Faye, and Mr MacIntyre over here, with his original features and his cathedral windows – she thinks it's all coming to her.

OMAR (*to* XANDER). Is that true?

SUSIE (*also to* XANDER). What's her plan then? What has she hired you for?

XANDER. I should really only be discussing that with Mrs Spenser.

SUSIE. There isn't anything for you to discuss.

XANDER. Actually I agree. Until all legalities are cleared up –

ZARA (*to* XANDER). She's trying to sell it out from under us, is that what you're saying?

XANDER. As I say –

SUSIE. For shame. Scandalous. I knew he wasn't rock and roll.

ZARA. But she can't. It isn't hers to sell.

SUSIE. Exactly.

ZARA. The site belongs to us.

SUSIE. Excuse me?

OMAR. Now we don't entirely know that.

ZARA. But he told you –

XANDER. To you?

OMAR. Eddie wanted the work here to continue. He told me he would place ownership of the factory in a trust that I would control.

SUSIE. He did?

OMAR. However there's been some difficulty in locating the paperwork.

XANDER. So I understand.

OMAR. His filing systems were a little opaque – and obviously we're all still coming to terms with the loss. (*Beat – a new thought*.) I'm sorry, Miss Spenser – Susan –

SUSIE. Susie.

OMAR. What is it that brings you here?

SUSIE. Hmm?

OMAR. Of course you're always very welcome. I don't think there's much left by the way of personal items, if you were –

SUSIE. No, no.

OMAR. And I'm still a bit confused about this whole photographer business.

SUSIE. Ah, yes. A few wires crossed. Perhaps now isn't the best time.

OMAR. I've been writing to the local papers for months, trying to get us some coverage – that's a world you're probably far more familiar with than I am. Perhaps I could pick your brain?

SUSIE. Uh. Yes, of course.

ZARA. Did you say something about a band?

SUSIE. Yes. Yes, that was…

ZARA. Why are you bringing a band in here?

SUSIE. Just a little bit of fun. Nothing important. You don't actually use this space though, do you? Nothing happens in here.

ZARA. Are you after it too?

SUSIE. That's a shame, isn't it? Because the light in here is just extraordinary. Don't get Leo started about the light. Did everyone meet Leo?

ZARA. Do you think you're getting it?

SUSIE. Of course I understand why – you just don't have the capacity to work in here any more. Sunrise, sunset. Fifty years since my father bought this place. You all know that. And back then – well, I was just a girl – I didn't get a say in anything. Eddie, much older than me, of course – a great deal older.

OMAR. Miss Spenser –

SUSIE. So he was gifted it. Eddie did his thing in here for fifty years, but now as the only true family left – the only blood relation –

ZARA. Unbelievable.

SUSIE. But it does get cold, doesn't it? Even in the summer. Beautiful, but cold. That's why you need more bodies, to heat it up. That's the solution. (*To* OMAR.) Perhaps there's somewhere a little more private we could talk?

ZARA. Not a chance.

OMAR. Zara –

ZARA. Is she for real?

OMAR (*to* SUSIE). I have an office across the courtyard – I'd be delighted to discuss this further.

SUSIE. Wonderful.

ZARA (*to* OMAR). Did you want me to come with you?

OMAR. No, you carry on – you can give us some space.

SUSIE. Yes, everyone give us some space. Leo, you can entertain yourself?

LEO. Certainly.

SUSIE (*to* XANDER). Mr MacIntosh Claypipe-Hamburger – you stay out of trouble.

OMAR (*to* ZARA). Keep an eye on the others. You know where to find me. (*To* SUSIE.) It's this way.

SUSIE. I know the way.

SUSIE *and* OMAR *go. A beat.*

LEO. Well, maybe I should –

ZARA. You can't just go wandering off anywhere. This is still an active worksite.

LEO. Just how active are we talking?

ZARA. Highly active! Highly. There's a lot of...

LEO. Really?

ZARA. We don't use the whole building any more, but we're still going.

LEO. I'll be careful.

ZARA. You'll keep your nose out.

LEO. Yes ma'am.

ZARA *softens.*

ZARA. There's, um, there's actually a nice café just round the corner, actually – if you go out of here and turn left. It's sort of Scandi – cinnamon buns and stuff.

LEO. Really?

ZARA. They do these knotted black pepper and cardamom things – they're really good.

LEO. I can investigate.

ZARA. I'm not being horrible, it's just...

LEO. Of course, I understand. (*To* XANDER.) Pleasure to meet you, Bill.

LEO *goes.*

XANDER. I shouldn't stay either.

ZARA. Right.

XANDER. Are you okay?

ZARA. Yeah, I'm fine.

XANDER. You're sure?

ZARA. It's going to be fine.

XANDER. Good. (*Beat*.) Sorry about all the –

ZARA. Because it's ours. Eddie was really clear about what he wanted. You could probably just go home now, actually – save yourself a bit of time.

XANDER. Right.

ZARA. It's all going to get sorted out. We just need to find the papers.

XANDER. Okay.

Beat.

I don't get any say in… I just get called up, and told there's a client, and I look into… I'm not really a part of –

ZARA. Yeah, I get it.

XANDER. Right. Good.

ZARA. So Eddie's daughter hired you – to do what? To redevelop the site?

XANDER. Something like that.

ZARA. What do they want to do with it then?

XANDER. I shouldn't really discuss it.

ZARA. It's not gonna happen though, so it doesn't matter. (*Beat*.) Fine – what would you do, if you did have a say? Not whatever it is they've asked for, but if you got given the keys and a million pounds? (*Beat*.) Actually a million probably wouldn't go very far, would it?

XANDER. It'd get you started.

ZARA. Five million then. Ten. Blank cheque.

XANDER. That's very generous.

ZARA. Let me guess – big bachelor pad. Lots of bare brick. I'm seeing a big neon jukebox, Union Jack cushions everywhere, bowling alley down the middle.

XANDER. You reckon?

ZARA. Definitely.

XANDER. Like you're reading my mind.

ZARA. Nah. I think you're actually more of a classic Disney
princess – full-on floor-to-ceiling wall-to-wall bookcases with
a big wheelie ladder to go between them like in *Cinderella*.

XANDER. *Beauty and the Beast*.

ZARA. What?

XANDER. That's the library from *Beauty and the Beast*.

ZARA. That was a test. You've passed the test.

XANDER. Right.

ZARA. Or failed, depending on how you look at it.

XANDER. So what would you do?

ZARA. I'd use it to make scissors.

XANDER. Really?

ZARA. That's what it was made for.

XANDER. So you'd carry on the family business?

ZARA. I won't be the one making them, I'll just let them have it.

XANDER. Very selfless of you.

ZARA. I'm a very selfless person.

XANDER. Right.

ZARA (*a new thought*). Reckon you could put a pool in? Like
a classy one – old-fashioned, Turkish baths-style, all
beautiful tiles and a bit Victorian?

XANDER. Could get expensive.

ZARA. Blank cheque. And then – if I'm going full-on Barbie
Dreamhouse – I'd want one of those retractable glass floors
to slide out over the top.

XANDER. 'One of those retractable glass floors'?

ZARA. Yeah, you know what I mean.

XANDER. That's not a thing.

ZARA. Yes it is! So I've got a giant swimming pool underneath, then you flick a switch and out pops a dancefloor for any time I need it. For all my galas.

XANDER. You throw a lot of galas?

ZARA. I would do, if I lived here. And it's clear glass, so you can still see all the fish swimming underneath.

XANDER. Fish in your swimming pool?

ZARA. Only on gala nights. Like koi carp – those fancy ones.

XANDER. No more scissors then?

ZARA. No, only in the... Yes, in the real world, first choice is let them keep making scissors, and if it can't be that, then a... a soup kitchen, food bank, homeless shelter, but in the hypothetical, purely selfish, money-no-object –

XANDER. Got it. I'm with you.

ZARA. Might even stick that bowling alley in too, just for a laugh. And a bendy slide between each floor.

XANDER. Classy.

ZARA. It is. They put slides in once at the Tate Modern. Everyone loved them.

XANDER. Right.

ZARA. I used to do this thing when I was little. Mum and Dad would take me for walks in the country, in the woods, over the moors, round reservoirs, or whatever. And I'd always point out the nicest, most spectacular bit of scenery, and tell them that's where I'd put the roller coaster. Like a runaway mine train weaving through the forest, log flume off the aqueduct. And to begin with I just did it cos I thought it was funny, but then I kept going because I could see how much it wound them up – Mum, especially. She'd be all 'can't you just appreciate the natural beauty?', and I'd be like 'nah, dodgems.'

XANDER. And that's the vibe you're going for in here?

ZARA. You know there's a shopping centre in America that actually has a theme park inside it? Saw it on a documentary.

Minnesota, I think. And that's like a full-on mall, so it's much bigger than this, but I reckon you could still squeeze something in. I mean if you've got space for stairs, you've got space for a helter-skelter, right?

XANDER. Oh, hundred per cent.

ZARA. Okay, you've had enough time to think. I want your real answer now. You've got the keys, and the sky's the limit. What're you going to do with it?

XANDER. Other than the wheelie bookcases and the bowling alley?

ZARA. Yeah, I'm taking them as a given.

XANDER *thinks*.

XANDER. Okay. See up there? That'd be the old supervisor's office, right?

ZARA. Uh-huh.

XANDER. So build out from that level, extend a mezzanine running right the way around. Have that as office space. Small units, but great light. Could be really tiny – could be cubicles even – hot-desking for freelancers – and I'd have mine up at that end – that's your prime spot – that's the best one. Then down here, clear it out and keep the floor plan really open. Retail. Freestanding plots for… for craftspeople, artisans, makers – all high-end stuff. Not pretentious, just proper. Not tat. Fit in two dozen pitches, easy, just in here. Independent – expert –

ZARA. Like us?

XANDER. Dunno. They any good, your scissors?

ZARA. The best.

XANDER. Okay. So you've got your plot, your little stall, or shack, or cart, or… something. But you make them elsewhere. Cos you don't even use this big space, do you?

ZARA. Can't afford to heat it.

XANDER. Right. So it's all made and stored somewhere else, or – or okay – or you've got a little workshop up on the

mezzanine where you can finish things off, just the final
touches, so people can see the process. Like the little mesters
back in the day, but revitalised. Master craftspeople. Strip
everything back, clean it up, show off the bones of it. You
make it a destination – make it somewhere people will come
to from all over, because they know they're getting
something special. Some permanent pitches, some always
changing, so there's always something new to come look at,
and in the winter, I want a Christmas tree that touches the
ceiling, and… and every year every business has to make a
new decoration for it – but – yes – but has to be made from
stuff that was going for scrap, so you have to keep coming
back every year, to take a look – like a tradition – a ritual.
That's your USP.

ZARA. And the dodgems?

XANDER. Yeah, squeeze them in somewhere.

ZARA. Sounds nice.

XANDER. Cos the high street is dead, yeah? And it's not just
one thing that's killed it. It's the pandemic but not *just* the
pandemic, austerity but not *just* austerity, Amazon but not
just Amazon. So you've got to up your offer. Cos if I see –
you show me two pairs of scissors online, and one costs
three ninety-nine, and the other is – what's the most
expensive pair you sell?

ZARA. Everyday, or – ?

XANDER. No, really special. Top-end.

ZARA. I mean you could spend hundreds.

XANDER. Wow. Okay, right.

ZARA. But that's for shears, or for big, specialist –

XANDER. Right.

ZARA. Handmade. Last you a lifetime.

XANDER. Okay, but that's it – however you describe it, that's
never going to convince me shopping online. But maybe if
I'm here – if I can hold them, feel the weight, see where
they've come from – you see what I'm saying?

ZARA. Maybe.

XANDER. The high street's dying because there's no good
reason why I'd leave the house for something I can get just
as easily – more easily – from my sofa. So you've gotta give
me more than that. You've gotta make this a temple, a
cathedral, an emporium that only sells the sort of thing you
have to come see for yourself – properly special things.
(*Beat*.) You know Picasso visited here once?

ZARA. That's an urban legend.

XANDER. No, I was reading an article. In 1950, back when it
was the old-old owners. He was in Sheffield and they took
him here, and he said what they did here was art.

ZARA. Yeah? That's because it is.

XANDER. Right – yes – right. But you need to find a way to
show people… Picasso comes, and he draws two women
making scissors – two random women hunched over a
grinding wheel – and suddenly it's art – not just his drawing,
but what they're doing *becomes art*, because Picasso
watches them do it – it's transformative, right?

ZARA. Right?

XANDER. You'll never get the art from a website. Websites are
fucking pointless for something like this. People need to be
able to see the process, feel involved, know the story. If you
were to let people come here, pick them up, wander around,
then they'd get it. They'd get an experience. Better than
dodgems. Better than a helter-skelter. They'd understand
what they were paying for. Cos Picasso saw it, but even he
had to come see it for himself. That's what you need to do.
If you build it, they will come.

ZARA. Wow.

XANDER. I'm right though, aren't I?

ZARA. Do you actually know what you're talking about or are
you just confident?

XANDER. Makes no difference if you can't tell.

ZARA. Ah, right – you're a dickhead. I forgot. There was a
    moment there when I thought you might not be a dickhead,
    but then I remembered you're still an estate agent, so…

XANDER (*laughs*). You don't think I'm right?

ZARA. Eighty per cent of the global population shop online.

XANDER. And are eighty per cent of the global population
    buying your scissors?

ZARA. You should talk to my dad.

XANDER. Yeah?

ZARA. Yeah. He enjoys arguing with younger men.

    XANDER *chuckles*.

XANDER. What's it like, working for your dad?

ZARA. Oh, I don't – I mean not officially. I just help out
    sometimes over the holidays.

XANDER. Doing what?

ZARA. Fixing the website.

XANDER. Oh.

ZARA. Yeah.

XANDER. That's cool. I wasn't…

ZARA. That's okay.

XANDER. I didn't mean to… No reason why you can't have
    both.

ZARA. Yeah.

XANDER. Holidays from what?

ZARA. University. PhD.

XANDER. So you're properly clever?

ZARA. Don't sound surprised.

XANDER. I wasn't.

ZARA. Why else do you think my dad has to find young men to
    argue with?

XANDER. You're not going to take over from him then? He's not training you up?

ZARA. No chance.

XANDER. No?

ZARA. What do your parents do?

XANDER. Oh. Mum's a nurse. Dad works for the fire service.

ZARA. Wow.

XANDER. What?

ZARA. Really?

XANDER. What's the matter with that?

ZARA. Nothing. They're just like cartoon-character-parent jobs. Like something out of a children's book.

XANDER. Is it?

ZARA. They must be so disappointed in you.

   ZARA *laughs*. XANDER *doesn't*.

   Sorry, that was –

XANDER. No, it's –

ZARA. Just trying to be funny, not –

XANDER. Yeah.

ZARA. Sorry.

XANDER. I'm not an estate agent.

ZARA. Right.

XANDER. I'm a corporate design consultant.

ZARA. Okay.

XANDER. It's a very –

ZARA. I'm sorry.

XANDER. It's fine.

ZARA. I'm sure they're really proud.

An awkward beat. Then BILLY, *a photographer, enters.*
He's laden down with gear, including a fairly obvious
camera. ZARA *jumps up.*

Billy! He's real. You're Billy. (*To* XANDER.) He's Billy –
bet you anything.

BILLY. Now that's a welcome.

ZARA. Sorry. We've just heard a lot about you.

BILLY. Oh?

ZARA. Prodigal son.

BILLY. Right.

ZARA. Sorry.

BILLY. Are you the band? Are you Coco?

XANDER (*to* ZARA). Can we avoid doing all this again?

BILLY. What's that?

ZARA. No, we're not the band. Sorry.

BILLY. Okay.

ZARA. Doesn't seem like they've turned up yet. Are you
looking for… (*To* XANDER.) What was her name?

XANDER. Susie – Susie Spenser.

BILLY. The one and only.

ZARA. You've just missed her.

BILLY. Right.

ZARA. Who is she? Is she someone?

BILLY. What do you mean?

ZARA. She talks like she's someone – like someone who's used
to people knowing who she is. (*To* XANDER.) Do you know
her?

XANDER *shrugs.*

BILLY. Really?

ZARA. What?

BILLY. Susie Spenser! The G-Clamps? Hammer and Tongs?

ZARA (*still blank*). Right.

BILLY. Crazy Susan? Ran Bessemer Beats, used to play with the Mappin Street Band.

ZARA. Yeah, you're really just saying words at me.

BILLY. Really? (*To* XANDER.) You too?

XANDER. I think she said she was a doctor?

BILLY. What? No, she's... Susie Spenser wasn't just part of the scene, she *was* the scene for a while.

ZARA. What scene?

BILLY. *The* scene! She never really had a massive hit herself, but she worked with everyone. And if you ever saw her live... She'd blow the roof off.

ZARA. Like a singer?

BILLY. Yeah, in part. Singer, songwriter, played a bit of everything. Managed a few acts too, back in the day. Got everywhere, knew everyone. She was wild. Force of nature.

XANDER. Yeah, that tracks.

BILLY. You know when Jarvis fell out of that window on Division Street? Guess who he was trying to impress? (*Beat – off their blank looks*.) Really? She's a living legend! And this is what her brother did? Different world, in't it?

ZARA. Sounds like it.

BILLY. It's a beautiful space though. I can see the appeal. I take it we're shooting in here?

ZARA. Great question. Shooting what, exactly? We never really figured that one out.

BILLY (*checks a name on his phone*). Hold on. (*Reads*.) 'Co-Codamol. Retro-futurist art-pop provocateurs forged in steel.'

ZARA. Right. Great.

BILLY. Heard of them?

ZARA. Can't say I have.

BILLY. Me neither. Can't wait.

XANDER. Right. I feel like I'm sucked into this now too. Why exactly are there art-pop provocateurs having their photo taken in an old scissor factory?

BILLY. It's for the *Mojo Queen*, isn't it?

ZARA. The what now?

BILLY. Isn't that what she's calling it? Y'know, after the King Mojo Club out Pitsmoor way.

ZARA. Calling what?

BILLY. Cos rumour has it the old King Mojo only shut down because she broke Stringfellow's jaw in the ladies' loos when she was fifteen.

XANDER. Really?

ZARA. Broke what?

XANDER. Is that true?

BILLY. Who's to say? (*Beat.*) No actually, it's impossible, the timelines don't match up, but half of Sheffield would still swear they were there when it happened. And that's what you call infamy. (*Beat.*) Stunning light in here.

ZARA. Sorry, can we go back? What's a Mojo Queen?

BILLY. The club she's opening in here. You've got to use your imagination, but it's got the bones.

ZARA. What, like a nightclub? She wants to turn it into a nightclub?

BILLY. What do you reckon?

ZARA. Fucking hell.

XANDER. I can see it.

ZARA. That is ridiculous. Today is completely ridiculous.

BILLY. I am in the right place?

ZARA. Um. I don't know. I honestly don't know any more.

BILLY. Right.

ZARA. She's not here. She was, but she's gone. She's still with my dad, maybe? You haven't missed her by much.

BILLY. No worries. I'll give her a bell – see if she's around.

ZARA. Great.

BILLY *goes. A beat.*

A club?

XANDER *shrugs.*

I really was just making a joke before. I was being silly, I wasn't... Just because everyone hates estate agents, don't they? (*Beat.*) But you're not an estate agent, so that's okay. You're a... a...

XANDER. Corporate design consultant.

ZARA. Right. Really impressive. Sounds really important.

Beat.

Anyway, I should probably get on.

XANDER. Right. Yeah.

ZARA. I've still got quite a lot to do on the website. These scissors aren't going to not-sell themselves.

XANDER. Sure.

ZARA. We're really busy at the moment, actually. We're doing really well.

XANDER. Okay.

ZARA. And you probably need to go and find what's-her-name, his daughter, don't you – so you can plan how you're going to turn us into a Morrisons, or whatever.

XANDER. Right.

ZARA. Waste of your time, but –

XANDER. I'm not –

ZARA. It's okay.

XANDER. Yes. Yeah, I should probably see if she's arrived yet.

ZARA. Yeah.

Beat. XANDER *starts to awkwardly leave.*

Do you think I could be in a band?

XANDER. I…

ZARA. Not even that I could, but that I look like someone who could? Could you picture me in a band?

XANDER. Um. Sure.

ZARA. You don't have to say that if you don't mean it.

XANDER. No, absolutely.

ZARA. Thanks.

XANDER. Right then. (*Beat.*) You know some of these old factories, they'd have their own little train tracks built into the floor to move things about, like for goods deliveries and stuff.

ZARA. Right?

XANDER. Clean them up, start of your roller coaster right there.

ZARA *smiles.*

ZARA. Nice.

XANDER. I'll, um, I'll try to stay out of people's way.

XANDER *goes.*

ZARA *takes a breath, then puts her backpack down somewhere. She pulls a laptop out of it, and a pair of wireless headphones, which she puts on. She gets some music going, which at first we hear only just audibly, tinnily leaking out of the headphones. She switches on the laptop. She starts to get into the groove of the music, first tapping her toes, gradually shifting into full on air-drumming/ physicalised response, and as she does so, the music shifts and fills the whole auditorium again, so we can hear it clearly. Just as she's reaching maximum expression, MASON enters. He's one of the young apprentices who keeps the factory limping on. He watches ZARA with amusement.*

MASON. Working hard, are you?

ZARA pulls her headphones off and the music stops.

ZARA. Oh, hi.

MASON. Were you having some sort of seizure, or – ?

ZARA. What is it?

MASON. Do you need me to call an ambulance?

ZARA. Did you need something, Mason?

MASON. Do you know where your dad is?

ZARA. In his office.

MASON. Right.

ZARA. But he's in the middle of something.

MASON. Has he only just gone in there?

ZARA. I don't know. About ten minutes ago, maybe?

MASON. Have you seen the lesbians yet?

ZARA. What?

MASON. Doesn't matter. You'd know if you had.

ZARA. What's happening?

MASON. There are two lesbians running around somewhere, and we think they broke into the office, and we're not sure if it's a sex thing or industrial espionage, but Liv reckons they're trying to steal the factory.

ZARA. Right.

MASON. Been a bit of a funny morning to be honest.

ZARA. Wait, two… Were they in a band?

MASON. You what?

ZARA. The two women – did it look like they were in a band?

MASON. Fair play, because that is not the follow-up question I was expecting.

ZARA. Doesn't matter.

MASON. You're mental, you know that?

ZARA. Was that everything?

MASON. Are we getting shut down?

ZARA. I don't know.

MASON. So maybe?

ZARA. No! I mean I don't think so.

MASON. Has your dad said anything?

ZARA. I'm just trying to work on the website – honestly.

MASON. At least Eddie used to tell us stuff. Mostly about how shit everything was, but at least he told us.

ZARA. I promise – as soon as I know anything –

MASON. Yeah, whatever.

ZARA. I'm just trying to get on.

MASON. Why did you ask about a band?

ZARA. No reason.

MASON. Really?

ZARA. It's… There's a possibility… I think maybe there might be a band coming in today, who may or may not be lesbians – I don't think that's relevant – and I don't fully understand why that's a thing that might be happening, but apparently it is.

Beat.

MASON. So you're having a weird day too then?

ZARA. Yeah.

MASON. Why though?

ZARA. Can you please just stop asking me things I clearly don't have the answers for?

MASON. Right. I'll go ask your dad then.

ZARA. Just… No. Please, just… You've got loads to do, yeah? We actually have a big order for once, and we've fallen behind on it, so –

MASON. Why do you keep saying 'we'?

ZARA. What?

MASON. You don't work here.

ZARA. No, but you do, don't you, so can you just go back to the workshop? Please. I'll talk to Dad in a little bit and then I'll come and find you. I promise.

Beat.

MASON (*shrugs*). Whatever.

ZARA. Thank you.

MASON. You're still full of shit though.

ZARA. Thanks, Mason.

MASON. And the website's still crap.

ZARA. I'm working on it.

MASON. Good. Cos otherwise we're busting our arses for nothing.

MASON goes. As soon as he's left, SUSIE reappears from a different entrance. She's been watching them for a little while.

SUSIE. I did not care for that young man's tone.

ZARA jumps.

ZARA. Jesus!

SUSIE. Sorry.

ZARA. No, you're alright.

SUSIE. Does he work here?

ZARA. Yeah.

SUSIE. For how long?

ZARA. Uh, almost a year? It'll be coming up to a year soon.

SUSIE. If a man ever spoke to me like that, he certainly wouldn't have been employed for almost a year.

ZARA. It's fine.

SUSIE. Especially not if my father was paying his wages.

ZARA. That's not really how the power structure around here works.

SUSIE. No?

ZARA. He's alright. (*Beat.*) I mean he's a prick, but he's harmless.

SUSIE. Have you always had problems with asserting yourself?

ZARA. That… that isn't accurate.

SUSIE. It's not uncommon amongst young women.

ZARA. How did you get on with my dad?

SUSIE. But it does suggest certain issues with your self-worth.

ZARA. Did you clear things up with him? Are you off now?

SUSIE. Of course the relationship a daughter has with her father creates the blueprint for how she allows all future men to treat her –

ZARA. Right.

SUSIE. So maybe I need to go back and speak to him again.

ZARA. Please don't.

SUSIE. No?

ZARA. It isn't… Mason's not… He's called Mason.

SUSIE. And is that standard behaviour for him?

ZARA. It doesn't matter.

SUSIE. Interesting.

ZARA. He doesn't matter. I let Mason talk to me however he wants because he doesn't matter to me in any way. He isn't important.

SUSIE. I see.

ZARA. That's not low self-esteem. That's actually me managing my emotional labour. I don't need to expend my energy trying to improve him.

SUSIE. Attagirl.

ZARA. Did you see Billy – the real Billy – the photographer?

SUSIE. No.

ZARA. He was just in here – you didn't pass him?

SUSIE. I'm sure I'll catch him up later.

ZARA. Only I do have quite a lot to be getting on with.

SUSIE. Oh, am I being rude? I'm being terribly rude, aren't I? Do you forgive me?

ZARA. Um. Yeah, sure.

SUSIE. And very quick to forgive as well – also very interesting.

ZARA *sighs*.

ZARA. Is there something else you need?

SUSIE. What is it that you're studying? He said – your father mentioned you were studying. A postgraduate something.

ZARA. A PhD. Political Science.

SUSIE. Oh, Lord help us.

ZARA. Excuse me?

SUSIE. I saw the brightest minds of my generation destroyed by the civil service, starving, hysterical, naked. (*Beat.*) So is that why you're like this?

ZARA. Like what?

SUSIE. Why you won't give me a straight answer on anything.

ZARA. I'm just trying to get on with my work.

SUSIE. Which is what, exactly?

ZARA. Whatever Dad needs help with. Computer stuff mostly.

SUSIE. Secretarial?

ZARA. No. He just doesn't like computers, that's all.

SUSIE. I see.

ZARA. It's not –

SUSIE. Does he pay you – your father? Do you get paid for the work you do here?

ZARA. I don't need to be.

SUSIE. But I imagine the others do? That young man – does he get paid to work here? Does he get paid to talk to you like that?

ZARA. It's really not a big deal. It doesn't take up much of my time.

SUSIE. Why do you allow your father to take advantage of you?

ZARA (*pointedly*). I was taught to be polite to my elders. (*Beat.*) Was there anything else?

SUSIE. I just find it interesting –

ZARA. Aren't you a little old to be opening a nightclub?

SUSIE. Oh, so you've heard?

ZARA. Do you think that's wise?

SUSIE. No, I think it's the best kind of foolish. You see I've had to wait quite a while for my moment. *My* father never tried to get me involved in operations. He did say that once I was married, Eddie and my husband could run the place together.

ZARA. Really?

SUSIE. Suffice to say he died disappointed.

ZARA. That man here earlier – Leo – he's not – ?

SUSIE. My husband? Oh no. No, I like Leo far too much to think of him romantically. (*Beat.*) You see for men of my father's generation, giving a woman such a responsibility would've been unthinkable. Whereas now in this brave new world a manager's daughter can look forward to a lifetime of unpaid labour.

ZARA. Not if you come in and steal it from us.

SUSIE. This is a family business. I can't steal what's already mine.

ZARA. We're a family too.

SUSIE. Oh, so you want to take over?

ZARA. That's not –

SUSIE. Of course you don't – Little Miss PhD. You can't be interested in all this?

ZARA. That's not the point.

SUSIE. Isn't it?

ZARA. It's not like you go back centuries. Do you think people
realise that? Because I didn't at first. You see 'Spenser and Son'
and you presume it's been called that forever, which is exactly
how you want it, but no – the Hallamshire Scissor Company,
founded when – eighteen-something? Seventeen-something?
Dad would know. And then fifty years ago the Spensers buy it
up and start rewriting history. Fifty years. That's nothing.

SUSIE. It's a long time to wait.

ZARA. My dad saved this place. It was circling the drain –

SUSIE. Still is, as I understand it.

ZARA. No –

SUSIE. No?

ZARA. He's turning things around. We're working on this huge
new order – the start of a new relationship – it could change
everything.

SUSIE. Really?

ZARA. With some gigantic Chinese firm. It was one of the last
things Eddie set up before he died. We're making it work.

SUSIE. For how long?

ZARA. For now.

SUSIE. How many people work here? (*Beat.*) Indulge me.

ZARA. Five.

SUSIE. Not including you?

ZARA. No.

SUSIE. Your father – and that rude boy? Who else?

ZARA. There's Trent, and two girls as well – *women* – Liv and
Ava.

SUSIE. How very modern.

ZARA. They're all here on apprenticeships. We're training up a
new generation.

SUSIE. And that's sustainable, is it?

ZARA. We don't need another club. We've got plenty of bars already. This place is doing something special.

SUSIE. What brought your father here?

ZARA. He needed a job.

SUSIE. This isn't the first place you'd come looking.

ZARA. Aren't many places that do this. (*Beat.*) He used to work in the city. He was a commodities trader – metals, mostly. He was brilliant. He was amazing at it, actually, but he'd had enough. He wanted to do something with his hands.

SUSIE. And that was it?

ZARA. He had a friend – an old uni friend, this really intense Norwegian – who talked to him about Heidegger. Do you know Heidegger?

SUSIE *shrugs blankly.*

Me neither. German philosopher. Actual genuine Nazi, but we don't like to talk about that. Anyway, Dad needed a change, and this guy Erik – the Norwegian – Erik talks to him about Heidegger, and meaning, and existence, and *authenticity*, right? How most humans live wildly inauthentic existences – but the craftsman, the person who knows how to make things with his hands – he's the only person who's living properly. One conversation, eight or nine pints, and the rest is history. He finds your brother, they end up talking about Einstein –

SUSIE. Of course they did.

ZARA. Einstein and thermodynamics and –

SUSIE. Conservation?

ZARA. Yes!

SUSIE. They must have been insufferable.

ZARA. Because conservation, it's –

SUSIE. Our father's favourite topic.

ZARA. Right – not just heritage, not preservation, but –

SUSIE. The conservation of energy.

ZARA. How does it go? Nothing created, nothing destroyed, only reused, right? Which is beautiful. Which is important – and that's at the heart of everything he's trying to do here – old techniques handed down, products that last forever –

SUSIE. That's the sales pitch.

ZARA. And he just fell in love. Head over heels in love with all of it.

Beat.

SUSIE. He could take the equipment, if he wanted. I'd make him a very reasonable offer.

ZARA. It wouldn't be the same.

SUSIE. Why not?

ZARA. This is where they're made.

SUSIE. Sentimentality. You don't need to be here.

ZARA. This is a place for making things.

SUSIE. It was. This was once a very good place for making things. Purpose built. Precision engineered. And it made things well. It served its purpose. Served its time. But now... Look at you! Hidden away in the bowels, clustered around the remnants of a dying star. It's a parody of the thing it was. The Playmobil, Fisher-Price version. It's sad. Things passing away once they've had their time isn't sad, but stretching things out towards grotesquery is undignified. Surely you must see that? (*Beat.*) Did you know my brother well?

ZARA. Fairly well, I suppose. I'd always say hello when I came in here.

SUSIE. And you were at the memorial service too?

ZARA. Yes. I should've recognised you sooner.

SUSIE. Ecclesiastes. It wasn't my first choice of reading, but –

She recites.

'For everything there is a season,
and time for every matter under heaven:
A time to be born, and a time to die;
a time to plant, and a time to pluck up what is planted;

A time to kill, and a time to heal;
a time to break down, and a time to build up;
A time to weep, and a time to laugh;
a time to mourn and a time to dance.'

ZARA. I remember now.

SUSIE. For everything there is a season. We've planted, we've wept, we've mourned. Now it's time for dancing. The steel age is over – it is here, at least – within these walls. And Eddie never understood Einstein – nor did my father. Nor do I, not entirely, but I know when a metaphor doesn't hold true. The first law of thermodynamics, young lady, is about the *transfer* of energy – nothing created, nothing destroyed, but *transformation*, nonetheless. Not stasis. Not decay. The baton is passed on. I'm doing this for you – the next generation – the ones who come after. I would bequeath to you a living, breathing, cathedral of music rather than this mausoleum. And it'd be much kinder – much better to say goodbye now, to draw a line under it, now that Eddie's gone – rather than drag it out, gasping and wheezing to the bitter end. Finish this big order, tie up any loose ends, and get out with your heads held high. Look at you – you're a politician. You're a pragmatist. I know you know I'm right.

ZARA. Dad would never agree to it.

SUSIE. You'd be doing him a favour. (*Beat*.) You said Billy showed up?

ZARA. Yeah, he's around somewhere.

SUSIE. We should still have him take a few pictures of you while he's here. His work really is wonderful. Very expressive, very dynamic – he has a way of cutting right to the heart of someone. I wonder what'd happen if you allowed yourself a moment in the spotlight. I wonder if you'd like it. Maybe you'd surprise yourself. What do you say?

SUSIE *and* ZARA *regard each other for a moment. Music builds and builds then cuts out suddenly.*

End of Act One.

ACT TWO

The space is empty. Then, after a few moments, BILLY *leads in the two female apprentices,* AVA *and* LIV, *dressed in overalls/boiler suits – they might have made some effort to adjust/improve them, tying the sleeves around their waists, etc. They seem a bit nonplussed by what's going on, but aren't too interested in questioning it.*

BILLY. That's right, come on through, watch your step.

LIV. Which paper did you say this was for?

BILLY. Oh, I can't tell you that, love.

AVA. Why not?

LIV. Cos my gran's gonna need a copy.

BILLY. Sorry – I'm just the shutter monkey.

LIV. But when will it come out?

BILLY. It'll all just be for syndication. Could crop up anywhere.

LIV. They didn't tell us that.

BILLY. Don't worry, you're in good hands. The light in here – something special, in't it? We'll set up at this end. Now then, what's happened to your fella?

> TRENT, *another apprentice, similarly dressed, now follows on. He's holding a mop, a bucket, a broom, general stuff you might find lying around in a factory.*

That's it – you got a bit laden, didn't you? Watch your step.

LIV (*to* BILLY). What do you mean, 'crop up anywhere'?

BILLY. Don't worry about it.

AVA. And you're sure they wanted us in here?

BILLY. Hundred per cent. This is what we're selling, right? All this glorious space. And you guys, of course. (*To* TRENT.) Nice one. Easy does it. Just pop 'em down for a second.

LIV. And they want all of that in it?

BILLY. You've gotta trust me, guys. We're gonna paint a picture.

TRENT. Okay.

BILLY. Right. I'm going to put you up under that big window to begin with, and we'll get some nice side light from that corner too.

LIV. Yeah, but why is there a broom?

BILLY. Well, there's no proper kit in here, is there?

AVA. Kit?

BILLY. Yeah, you've not got any of your gear with you?

TRENT. Like equipment?

BILLY. Yeah.

LIV. It's not exactly portable.

BILLY. Right. We don't want all that anyway. We don't need to pretend it's real, because you're real, yeah? So unreality is the order of the day. (*Beat.*) Okay, yes, I heard that out loud too. You're just going to have to trust me.

LIV (*to* AVA). Do you trust him?

TRENT. I do.

BILLY. Okay, so here's the vision. We need to let the space tell the story, yeah? Empty space, stripped back, glorious light. We're going guerrilla-style, really playful – just bodies in space, and movement, and *life*, yeah? Got to have that life. So no artifice. If we're pretending, it's because it's fun to pretend. And still keeping a real sense of the band, the energy of it, all of you just grooving together, keeping time, even when you're empty-handed – alright? (*Beat.*) Where did I lose you?

AVA. It's just not really what we're used to.

BILLY. Don't worry – I'll ease you in nice and gentle.

AVA (*to* LIV). Do we need to talk to the boss about all this?

BILLY. Who's that – your manager?

LIV. Yeah.

BILLY. Hasn't he gone through it all already?

AVA. Sort of. He knew it might be happening, but –

BILLY. Is he around then?

TRENT. Somewhere. I've not seen him yet today.

AVA. He's about. He's in a mood.

BILLY. Okay, well look, with your blessing, let's just get a few shots while the light's good, and I'll make sure you all get to look through everything before it goes out – sound okay? (*Beat.*) It is only a camera – it doesn't bite.

LIV (*to* AVA). What do you reckon?

TRENT. I say we just do it.

    AVA *shrugs an agreement.*

BILLY. Thank you very much! Right, now let's try to breathe some life into you! Kinetic energy – that's what we're after. A hundred years of honest labour surging through the three of you. (*To* TRENT.) Now then, mop or broom – pick your weapon.

TRENT. Um, broom?

BILLY. Great choice. Now wield it with pride. Gonna push you back towards that window a little, got you framed nicely. (*To* LIV *and* AVA.) So – drums – which one of you is my drums?

    Beat – neither responds.

    Honestly ladies, sooner we start, the sooner we finish.

    LIV *steps up.*

LIV. Sure. Why not?

BILLY. Lovely. So you come sit yourself over here –

    BILLY *pulls over a box/crate and places it back and centre beneath a window.*

    Just got you a little off-centre. And now you need…

He glances around, picking up some metal files, scrap bits of wood, whatever is to hand.

Your sticks, madam. Which just leaves –

AVA. I'm Ava.

BILLY. Ava. Beautiful. Saved the best till last.

LIV rolls her eyes. BILLY fishes out a large pair of scissors and offers them to AVA.

Your microphone, my lady. Gonna pop you up here beside her. Just a little shuffle to your left – balancing the space. Lovely.

LIV. What're we doing?

BILLY. We're making music. Now we're flying.

BILLY positions TRENT.

So, Mr Broom, I'm sure you've got the idea. You're mirroring vocals, giving me some bass, some guitar, whatever feels natural.

TRENT. Right. On it.

BILLY. Drums – self-explanatory. Ava looking great.

BILLY steps back and starts checking the composition through his camera.

Okay, let's see what we're working with. (*To* TRENT.) Pretty boy. Brush down, handle up – that's the one. Just inch in a little closer together. (*To* LIV.) Sorry, love, missed your name.

LIV. It's Liv.

BILLY. Okay, Liv – don't be afraid to give it some welly. The dafter you feel the better it's going to look. Same rule for all of you. If it's not working I'll let you know and we'll try something else. Fantastic.

He starts taking some test shots.

LIV. What if I was over with Trent?

BILLY. Nah, you're my centrepiece. (*To* TRENT.) Keep the handle nice and high, if you can.

AVA (*to the others*). Mason's never going to believe this.

LIV. Oh God, and Zara would be loving it.

AVA. Do you think we should've told them?

BILLY. Who's that?

TRENT. Oh, just –

LIV. No one. Doesn't matter.

BILLY. Not missing someone, are we?

LIV. No one who matters.

BILLY. Okay. Eyes front, if you can, guys. Energy towards the camera.

AVA. This feels so weird.

BILLY. Looking great. Now why don't we try to get some kind of rhythm going? Liv, was it? How about you count us in?

LIV. Um… Right. (*She hesitates for a moment, then appears to find confidence.*) One, two, three, four!

Music kicks in again, and incredibly, magically, for a few moments they actually are a band. The space is transformed. Lights and sound and life everywhere. They're enjoying themselves too. It's joyous, uninhibited, giggly. Then the moment comes to an end, and reality resumes.

BILLY. Wow. Phenomenal. Got some cracking shots there. Now, I want some singles and some doubles. I might shuffle you about a bit, change up the background –

He's interrupted by the return of OMAR.

OMAR. What's happening now?

BILLY. Sorry, mate. We're not in your way, are we? I thought you didn't use this space.

OMAR. What are you doing with them?

AVA. He's taking our pictures.

OMAR. Yes, I can see that.

LIV. He's the photographer.

BILLY (*to* OMAR). I'm Billy. It's a pleasure. Won't be much longer now.

OMAR (*utterly bewildered*). What is…?

BILLY. We'll be out of your hair in a minute.

OMAR. But you can't –

BILLY. Listen, mate, I know there's been a bit of confusion this morning, and everyone's been mucked around a bit, but I've just been hired to shoot a band. Here's the band, here's my camera, they're looking brilliant, so if you can just give us a bit of space to finish up, I'll get the shots I need, they can get off, and we can all carry on with our days, alright?

OMAR. They're not a band.

BILLY. Now no need to be rude.

OMAR. No they're not.

BILLY. Of course they are! Who are they then?

OMAR. They're the apprentices.

BILLY. Right. Great name. Feels a bit early two thousands but I dig it.

OMAR. No –

BILLY. Much better than Ibuprofen, or whatever it was before.

OMAR. They're not… They work here.

BILLY. Don't be daft.

OMAR. They do! (*To the apprentices.*) Tell him!

TRENT. Um, yeah, we do.

LIV. Of course we do.

AVA. Didn't you know that?

BILLY. As what?

AVA. As apprentices.

BILLY. What?

OMAR. Thank you!

LIV (*referring to* BILLY). So who's this guy then?

BILLY. No – because – no, now just hang on –

AVA. Is he not from *The Star*?

TRENT. Should I put this broom down now?

OMAR. Yes!

BILLY. Actual apprentices?

OMAR. Yes!

BILLY. Who work here?

OMAR. Yes!

BILLY. Not a band called The Apprentices?

TRENT. No, sorry.

BILLY. Why did you get me to take your photos then?

LIV. Er, you asked us, mate. You came and rounded us up.

BILLY. You said –

AVA. No, but the article! (*To* OMAR.) You said someone was coming in.

OMAR. Not this again!

AVA. You said *The Star* were going to run a big feature on us. You asked us to help out.

LIV. I've already texted my gran.

OMAR. That isn't… Yes, that might still happening, but –

AVA. So who is he then?

BILLY. I'm Billy.

OMAR. Don't worry about it. Let's all just –

LIV. Nah – I am worried now. I'm worried cos I've been playing air-drums for the last five minutes and I thought it was for a good cause – team-player Liv, the people's champion – but actually I've just been posing for some complete random off the street – probably for some sexual fetish or something –

BILLY. Steady on.

LIV. Which strikes me as something I might legitimately worry about, yeah? (*Beat*.) Why am I still holding these!?

LIV *throws down her makeshift drumsticks*.

TRENT. He's not a random.

LIV. Who is he then?

TRENT. He's a music photographer. (*To* BILLY.) You are, aren't you? You're Billy Gunderson.

BILLY. That's me.

AVA. How do you know that?

TRENT. He's famous.

LIV (*to* BILLY). Are you?

TRENT. He's shot everyone. Arctic Monkeys, Jarvis, did that series with Self Esteem down in The Wicker.

LIV. So why did you think he wanted to take your picture?

TRENT. Cos he came and asked us.

LIV. Jesus Christ.

TRENT. Decided not to question it. (*Beat*.) What? It's not the sort of thing that happens every day.

AVA. Are you serious?

TRENT. I've been trying to say yes to the universe.

LIV. But you didn't think to tell us?

TRENT. Cos then you wouldn't have done it. I bet we all look great. He said we looked great.

OMAR. Can you all just get back to work and do something constructive – please!

AVA. We thought we were – we thought this was what you wanted.

OMAR. And I appreciate that, I really do.

AVA. Fine. Come on then.

They start to leave.

LIV. I actually was great, for the record.

TRENT (*to* BILLY). You got everything you need?

BILLY. Yeah, mate, I reckon.

TRENT. Sweet.

Before they can go, SUSIE *appears from a different direction.*

SUSIE. I thought I heard voices – Billy! That must be you!

BILLY. Miss Spenser. At last!

SUSIE. Oh, Susie – I insist. Apologies for any confusion. And this must be my band – finally! My beautiful band! Let's get a look at you.

OMAR. No!

SUSIE. No to what?

TRENT. No, we're not a band. Sorry.

SUSIE. What do you mean?

OMAR. I thought you'd left us, Miss Spenser.

SUSIE. No such luck.

TRENT. I feel bad now – like I've misled people.

SUSIE. Billy – what's going on?

BILLY. It seems we're still missing a band.

SUSIE. What do you mean?

LIV. We're not a band.

SUSIE. You're not?

OMAR. No!

SUSIE. Then why on earth are they…? Look at them! Why are they dressed as a band if they're not a band?

BILLY. That's what I thought.

SUSIE. I mean just look at those uniforms.

OMAR. They're work uniforms.

SUSIE. Are they?

AVA. Yeah. Sorry.

SUSIE. Well they're fantastic.

LIV. Thanks.

OMAR. Go – out – back to work – all of you.

SUSIE. Hang on a minute – maybe we could make this work. If they look the part –

OMAR. They have actual jobs to be doing. We have a very large order to catch up on.

BILLY (*to* SUSIE). I've got plenty of shots already.

LIV. Um – you can't use them – they were taken under false pretences.

AVA. Absolutely.

LIV. But is it for something cool?

SUSIE. Very cool.

LIV. Okay, you can't use them unless I look really hot.

OMAR. I haven't okayed any of this.

SUSIE. And you don't have to. It's a free country – anyone can have their photograph taken. This might be better actually – more authentic. (*To* BILLY.) They looked good?

BILLY. Oh yeah, top. Took a little encouragement, but they're naturals.

SUSIE. Well then. (*To the apprentices*.) You do all look wonderful – now let's see… (*To* TRENT.) You must be Trent.

TRENT. Hi.

SUSIE. I'm Susie. And I must have a Liv here somewhere?

LIV. That's me.

SUSIE. Which only leaves Ava. I've always been very good with names. A pleasure to meet you all. Thank you for giving so much of yourselves today – both your talents and your time – it means the world, honestly.

AVA. Who are you?

TRENT. She's Eddie's sister. (*Beat.*) I'm good with faces.

SUSIE. That's right. I'm Susie, and I'm very honoured.

AVA. Sorry for your loss. Are you here to help us?

SUSIE. You're good kids – and wonderful craftsmen –
cra   craft*people* – honestly, it's exquisite. It warms my heart.
He was so proud of you all. Whatever the future holds, you
should always remember that.

LIV. So what are the pictures for?

SUSIE. All in good time. I've kept you far too long, and Mr
Sarbani here is about to pop a blood vessel. Off you go –
keep up the good work. I'm so glad to have met you.

OMAR *gives a nod, and the apprentices leave.* SUSIE *waves
them off rather grandly.*

OMAR. I didn't realise you were still on site, Miss Spenser.

SUSIE. Where else would I be? (*To* BILLY.) Thank you again,
Billy, I can't tell you what a relief it is to have you here.

OMAR. I really must insist –

SUSIE. As long as it still says Spenser on the building I don't
see any reason why I should go anywhere. (*Back to* BILLY.)
Now how did you get on? Tell me honestly.

BILLY. They had some spirit.

SUSIE. Okay. Well look, we're still expecting the real band any
minute. Of course it's wonderful to have captured something
so authentic, but it seems to me that the safest thing is just to
start over – we can double everything up with the
professionals and see where we get to.

BILLY. Understood.

OMAR. I can't just have you and your entourage parading
through here all day.

SUSIE. Mr Sarbani, as far as either of us can prove, you might
now be the one trespassing, so until we know exactly where
we stand, I suggest the best thing is just for us to keep out of
each other's way. Is this an operational space?

OMAR. No, but –

SUSIE. Then don't be a dog in the manger.

BILLY. Can I get a few of you while we're waiting?

SUSIE. No, no.

BILLY. Just one or two? Something for the press release?

SUSIE. There's really no need for that.

BILLY. You sure?

SUSIE. I'm not the focus here – this isn't about me.

> OMAR *scoffs*.

> Believe it or not, I am trying to give something back. I am trying to leave something behind for the ones who come after.

OMAR. And what do you think I'm trying to do?

SUSIE. Lord only knows.

OMAR. Everything I do here –

SUSIE. I had an enlightening conversation with your daughter.

OMAR. Really?

SUSIE. Bright girl, isn't she? Beautiful girl. Far too good for this place.

OMAR. I don't think anyone's too good for this place.

SUSIE. No?

OMAR. I think this place is as good as anywhere. Just the way it is.

SUSIE. Why don't you pay her for her labour?

OMAR. That isn't…

SUSIE. Who else are you taking advantage of? Just the way things are?

OMAR. No one.

SUSIE. You're sure?

OMAR. We provide opportunities.

SUSIE. Really?

OMAR. We're preserving something – a way of life – a philosophy –

SUSIE *rolls her eyes*.

Billy, was it?

BILLY. That's right.

OMAR. I could show you around. We have a workshop space, where everything's still made.

BILLY. I think I've been that way already.

OMAR. Beautiful, isn't it? There's not a machine in this building any less than fifty years old – and there doesn't need to be. Things were built to last back then. Italian motors – precision engineering. I could show you.

BILLY. I'm not really –

OMAR. You could make a, uh, a photo essay, couldn't you? Something that forges a connection.

SUSIE. Billy's here on my dime.

BILLY. I've actually got to be over in Doncaster this afternoon.

OMAR. Another time then?

BILLY. Maybe.

OMAR. Because I do think if people could see… I worked in finance before I came here, all day, every day, people buying and selling things that will never actually exist, but this is *real*. I can show you moulds we still use that were made a hundred and fifty years ago, hammers where the wood of the handle has moulded to the maker's hand. That doesn't take years, it takes decades. You can't rush this work. It centres you. It slows you down. And we have clients – customers – who still send their scissors back to us to be resharpened – that's a service we provide. Customers who've had the same pair for decades, who've inherited them from a relative, maybe, who come to understand what we do and they fall in love. How could you not fall in love here?

SUSIE. A lot of those customers left, are there?

OMAR. More than you'd think.

SUSIE. Really?

OMAR. Even if there was only one –

SUSIE. How does that grab you as a business model, Billy?

OMAR. We are on the cusp of a renaissance, I guarantee it. We're building new relationships in Asia, we're making headway. (*To* BILLY.) You'll come back and see?

BILLY. If I can. (*To* SUSIE.) If your lot don't turn up soon I'm going to have to make some calls. I've only got another half-hour or so.

SUSIE. Of course.

BILLY. We can always rearrange –

SUSIE. No – no need. It shouldn't be long. I've asked Leo to chase them. This place is such a warren.

OMAR. Why are you bringing a band here?

SUSIE. I want this place to sing again.

OMAR. What does that mean?

SUSIE (*not directly answering, to* BILLY). The stage up that end, I thought. Space for a green room above. Bar against that wall.

BILLY. Yeah?

OMAR. I see.

SUSIE. This building deserves to sing. I'm sure we could find jobs for them all – all your charming young workforce. Something on the bar, perhaps. We'll need staff and I don't see why they shouldn't have first refusal.

OMAR. They have jobs already.

SUSIE. But for how much longer? Forgive me, Mr Sarbani, but I remain unmoved. If I was being direct, I'd say what you're doing here is parasitic. You aren't rebuilding anything, you're draining the last of its life force. Leeching off your beautiful daughter, and your beautiful apprentices, so full of promise.

OMAR. You're right – we should try to stay out of each other's way. Just clear up after yourselves when you're done.

OMAR *starts to leave*.

SUSIE (*changing tack*) Why is she so necessary – your daughter? Because she doesn't make things, does she? She's brilliant, I'm sure, but what exactly do you need her for? She said computers, but you worked in the city, so you must be capable of using them. Are there just certain jobs that you deem to be beneath you?

OMAR. No!

SUSIE. So it's about control then – keeping tabs on her?

OMAR. Why shouldn't she be here?

SUSIE. Because she should be running the world!

OMAR. She volunteers. I don't make her.

SUSIE. Oh, I'm sure. That looks good with the politics, I suppose. Just how much of her life does she get a say in?

OMAR. You don't know anything about it.

SUSIE. I know a thing or two about daughters. I know a thing or two about that. Set her free, Mr Sarbani! Set them all free! Oh, that craftsman, and his authentic existence. The former banker and the future leader, and their little Disneyland version of the simple life. You're playing! It's a holiday for you, isn't it? It's a corporate retreat. You think this is serving a community? You think this benefits anyone other than yourself, preserving us in aspic, placing us behind glass? You think operating like this offers anyone any kind of future? You don't get to dictate what our future looks like.

OMAR. There is no future here without me!

SUSIE (*scornfully*). Oh! And thus spoke the voice of God!

They're interrupted by the return of XANDER, *showing around* MEL *and* FAYE, *a lesbian couple in their early forties*.

XANDER. So this is your largest open space – lots of options in here.

MEL. Wow. The light is incredible.

SUSIE *groans*.

BILLY (*to* SUSIE). Not your band?

SUSIE. Not my band. Much worse.

XANDER. Hello again.

SUSIE. Hello, Xanthony. (*To* FAYE.) Hello, Faye.

FAYE. Hello, Auntie Sue.

SUSIE (*to* XANDER). So you tracked them down?

XANDER. Yes, I think we've resolved any confusion now.

FAYE (*to* SUSIE). You remember Mel?

SUSIE. Yes, we caught up earlier.

MEL. We shan't be here much longer. We've got most of what we came for.

OMAR. I presume you haven't found anything conclusive?

MEL. No, not yet.

SUSIE. You're wasting your time here, you know.

MEL. We'll wait and see what the lawyers say.

FAYE (*to* XANDER). Am I okay to take some pictures?

SUSIE. Why are you asking him?

FAYE. Who should I be asking?

OMAR. Go ahead – everybody else seems to be.

SUSIE (*to* FAYE *and* MEL). So go on – how did you get on with young Alexander here? Has it changed your grand vision? Luxury penthouses? Corporate office space? Small-scale nuclear reactor?

FAYE. Does it matter?

SUSIE *and* OMAR (*together*). It matters.

MEL. Whatever happens we'll preserve the character. Xander has some great ideas.

SUSIE. I'm sure he has.

BILLY (*to* SUSIE). Who are these two then?

SUSIE. Nobody important.

FAYE. Charming as always.

SUSIE. Eddie's stepdaughter, and her wife Melanie, who are
    somehow under the misapprehension that all of this might be
    coming to them.

BILLY (*to* FAYE *and* MEL). Billy Gunderson – pleased to meet
    you.

SUSIE. There's really no need.

MEL. I'm sorry if this has all become a bit unpleasant. It wasn't
    meant to. We really are trying to do this in the best way we
    know how.

SUSIE. I'm sure you'll use a very polite wrecking ball as well.

OMAR. It doesn't strike me that you're doing any different,
    Miss Spenser.

SUSIE. Three options, as I see it – they'll kill it off entirely, you'll
    let it die of natural causes, I'm going to make it to live again.

FAYE. That's really unfair.

MEL. Eddie would want to provide for his family – I think we
    can all agree on that.

SUSIE. You are not his family!

OMAR. His family are the people who work here!

FAYE. Oh bollocks!

SUSIE. Yes, that really is fantastically convenient bollocks.

MEL. But we need to take a cold hard look at the numbers – at
    the most viable –

SUSIE. Now hold on –

MEL. As the only ones with a serious business plan –

SUSIE. I am serious – I am deadly serious –

FAYE. You're a fantasist, Auntie Susie.

BILLY. Right – if nobody here needs me –

Another entrance – COCO and MOLLY, the band, finally arrive. They are unmistakably pop stars, dressed up to the nines – we immediately know who they are. They carry a few bits and pieces with them, including an old battered briefcase.

COCO. Oh my God, finally.

MOLLY. Are we in the right place? Please tell me we are.

SUSIE. Girls!

MOLLY (*to* SUSIE). Are you in charge?

OMAR (*in unison*). No.

SUSIE (*in unison*). Absolutely.

BILLY. So is it safe to assume…?

SUSIE. Please – please for the love of God tell me one of you is Coco.

COCO. Yeah, I'm Coco – this is Molly.

MOLLY. We're Co-Codamol.

SUSIE. Hallelujah!

MOLLY. Are you Sophie Slater?

SUSIE. Susie Spenser.

MOLLY. Oh.

COCO. Literally written on the walls, Mol.

MOLLY. Right. Sorry.

SUSIE. Close enough. Names are hard.

COCO. So we are in the right place?

SUSIE. Without question.

COCO. Wow, this is a bigger team than I expected. (*Spotting* FAYE.) Oh.

SUSIE. Yes, great point. (*To the others.*) Maybe we could thin out the space a little?

MOLLY (*to* COCO). I thought you said 'faded grandeur'.

COCO. And?

MOLLY. It's pretty fucking faded.

FAYE*'s phone rings.*

FAYE (*to* MEL). It's Joni's school – I should take it.

MEL. Okay.

FAYE. You just keep going here – I'll catch you later.

FAYE *kisses* MEL *on the cheek and goes.*

MOLLY (*to anyone else*). Is there anywhere I can put anything down without it getting filthy, because most of this is dry-clean only?

SUSIE. It's not dirt, ladies, it's character.

COCO. No, it's definitely dirt.

SUSIE. It's both. Look at those windows – look at the light!

MOLLY. Is that a dead pigeon up there?

COCO. Is it?

MOLLY. Coco –

COCO. Yeah, but it's all the way up there.

MOLLY. That is a biohazard. That is literally how pandemics get started.

OMAR. Please, feel free to leave if the surroundings aren't to your liking.

MOLLY. Er, who are you?

COCO. Who is he and what's with his attitude?

SUSIE. No one.

MOLLY. Okay, so is it possible for him not to be here? Because today has already been really stressful.

COCO. Is one of you hair and make-up? We need hair and make-up like yesterday.

SUSIE. This is really more of a grassroots operation.

MOLLY (*picking at something on a wall*). Oh, I thought it was moss.

BILLY *intervenes. He turns on the charm.*

BILLY. Molly, was it?

MOLLY. That's right.

BILLY. And Coco? I'm Billy – I'm the lucky one who's gonna be taking your picture today.

COCO. Oh. Okay.

BILLY. So we're aiming for a really kinetic, guerrilla-style –

MOLLY. That's not really our aesthetic.

BILLY. Right.

COCO. I actually put a mood board in the email.

BILLY. Amazing. Thank you for that.

MOLLY (*to* COCO). What are we doing here?

BILLY. Now I can definitely answer that. Do you know how old this place is?

MOLLY *shrugs.*

Nor do I. Anyone?

SUSIE. A hundred and fifty years.

OMAR. A hundred and forty-eight. On this site.

BILLY. A hundred and forty-eight. Incredible. And sure, she's starting to show her age, but you can't hold that against her. Now – either of you know the most important thing about any picture?

COCO. Go on.

BILLY. It's balance. Contrast. Light and shade. Negative space. So if I've got age, I need youth. If I've got ugliness, I need beauty. This here is history, so where's the future? Do you see what I'm getting at?

COCO *and* MOLLY *look at each other blankly.*

If the backdrop is giving me ramshackle, I've got to pair it with something flawless. So – what do you think you two are doing here?

They finally get it. They're flattered. MEL *lets out an audible groan.*

MOLLY. Well okay then.

COCO. It's just nice to know we're not the only artists here.

BILLY. Don't worry, ladies, there's always method to the madness.

COCO *and* MOLLY *are now thoroughly onside with* BILLY, *still less certain about* SUSIE.

MOLLY. We still need to talk to someone about the dressing-room situation.

SUSIE. Yes, now you see –

COCO. Honestly, we're not being divas, but that office has been a nightmare.

OMAR. What office?

COCO. The little room across the yard.

MOLLY. The one that smells of death.

OMAR. Have you been in my – ?

SUSIE. Let's just get on, shall we? Make hay while the sun shines.

OMAR *sighs.*

MOLLY. Does anyone have a steamer?

COCO. And some sage? I know we're on a schedule but I would really love to cleanse the space if we can.

MOLLY *(to* SUSIE*).* And so who are all these people?

SUSIE. Don't worry about all that. Billy and I are the only people you need to know. Everyone else is… superfluous.

COCO. Ooh. Oh now I don't want to be a bitch but I'm actually quite uncomfortable with you talking about other people like that.

MOLLY. Yeah, you actually can't.

SUSIE. No, I wasn't –

COCO. We actually have an ethical working manifesto.

MOLLY. It's rooted in mutual respect.

COCO. Again, it was in the email chain.

SUSIE. Of course.

COCO (*selecting* XANDER, *more or less at random*). Hiya, I'm Coco.

XANDER. Xander MacIntyre, Claybourne-Harris.

MOLLY (*whispers to* COCO). Oh my God – I think they represent Charli XCX.

COCO. Really?

MOLLY (*to* MEL). Namaste.

MEL. Hi.

SUSIE. So Melanie here is Faye's wife – she's the woman who just left. And Faye's stepfather used to own this factory.

COCO. Oh. Okay.

MOLLY. It's just so sad now, isn't it? Bet you can't wait for them to do something useful with it.

MEL. That's what we're hoping.

SUSIE. And this here's Omar – he's been keeping things ticking over.

COCO (*to* OMAR). Bless your heart.

MOLLY. Big respect for that. Scissors. So random!

COCO. But so much respect.

OMAR. Thank you.

BILLY. Shall we get a few test shots now – see what we're working with?

MOLLY. In here?

BILLY. Yep. You want to come over this side? I've got a few bits and pieces for you to play with.

MEL (*to* SUSIE, *out of their earshot*). Where did you find these
people?

SUSIE. Don't you like them? They're the future.

BILLY (*still talking to* COCO *and* MOLLY). Who wants the
broom? And you're gonna give it a bit of guitar – then we'll
get the other one of you on scissors microphone.

COCO. No.

BILLY. No?

COCO. No, I don't think so.

MOLLY. We don't mime.

BILLY. No, but –

MOLLY. We're musicians? People need to know we're real
musicians.

BILLY. Yes, but unreality is –

COCO. I think we just need to move on from the concept.

OMAR (*to* SUSIE). Was this really worth derailing my day?

SUSIE. Let him work his magic.

BILLY. Why don't we try a couple for fun?

COCO. I'm just not sure I'm following the narrative.

MOLLY. Why am I singing into scissors?

BILLY. Because that's what they... they make scissors, they –

COCO. So do they make brooms as well?

BILLY. Okay – tell you what – let's leave the props for now.
Just try to give me something dynamic in the space, yeah?
Something with a bit of life in it.

> BILLY *takes some test shots while the others talk.* COCO
> *and* MOLLY *provide artful, extremely low-energy poses.*
> *There's nothing of the fun or excitement there was when the*
> *apprentices were posing. It's all very dead.* COCO *uses the*
> *briefcase to stand on.*

MEL (*to* XANDER). So how many units are we looking at in here?

XANDER. All depends on how you want to divide it. Office space on the ground floor will give you more security than retail. Then –

MEL. Uh-huh.

BILLY (*still directing the shoot*). Okay, just try to lift your head a little.

XANDER (*to* MEL). Or you keep the whole thing residential. Ground-floor flats if you want to maximise the number of units, but they won't go for as much. If you're going high-end you could use that for your reception, onsite gym, pool even.

MEL. Pool?

XANDER. You do have the space for it.

BILLY. Come on, ladies – a little bit more.

OMAR (*to* SUSIE). And this is what you want, is it?

SUSIE. It's a start.

OMAR. And you say I'm playing?

SUSIE. It's a means to an end.

OMAR. We've been doing something special here. We're offering something special.

SUSIE. To who? Those children you employ?

As this conversation continues, BILLY *now has* COCO *and* MOLLY *posing with two large pairs of scissors. It's started to get a bit silly and a bit sexy. They peer through the handles, pretend to lick the blades, perhaps even 'scissor' the two pairs together. This should get increasingly distracting.*

OMAR. Nobody else is – nobody else is investing in them.

SUSIE. Trust me – bar work would serve them better. How long did you say you'd been here?

OMAR. Thirteen years.

SUSIE. Thirteen – and how far have you really come?

OMAR. Remarkably far.

SUSIE. But is it enough? Do you know enough to take over their training, now it's only you left to do it? And if you do – and if you succeed in the impossible and keep things limping on for another thirteen years, what will you have achieved beyond thoroughly preparing a handful of apprentices for a life that no longer exists? And what then?

OMAR. Then it'll have been a good thirteen years.

SUSIE. For who?

OMAR. For all of us.

SUSIE. You're delusional. And it's damaging, your delusion – it's damaging to those around you, to suck people into your obsession, to pretend there's a career out there waiting for them, it's not – (*She is finally too distracted by the photography antics and screams across to them.*) It is not a toy – will you take them out of your mouth!

BILLY, COCO *and* MOLLY *are startled and stop.*

They are sharp! They are precision-engineered, hand-crafted, highly effective cutting instruments! Are you out of your minds? Give them here!

She takes the scissors off them. A pause.

Gosh, they're heavy. I'd forgotten how heavy. I don't even keep a pair out any more.

MOLLY. Uh, what the fuck?

BILLY. Everything okay?

SUSIE. I think we're done here.

COCO. Excuse me?

SUSIE. Thank you for your time. I think we have everything we need.

MOLLY. Already?

SUSIE. I've got your contact details. I'll be in touch soon. Thank you for your patience.

COCO. Are you kicking us out?

SUSIE. I'm sure everyone has somewhere else they'd rather be.

MOLLY. For real?

COCO. Fine. (*To* MOLLY.) Come on.

MOLLY. But –

COCO. We won't beg – we're better than that. Come on.

> COCO *and* MOLLY *go, a little huffily, taking their things with them, but leaving the briefcase behind.*

BILLY. Is that a wrap then?

SUSIE. Yes, yes. You can get off as well. Wind it up, shut it down. (*To the others.*) Show's over, everyone. Thank you for your patience. It's been an unusual day.

> BILLY *starts packing some things away.*

MEL. Are you alright?

SUSIE (*still holding the scissors*). Do you have a pair of these at home?

MEL. We've got three.

SUSIE. I really had forgotten the weight of them. They feel exactly the same.

OMAR. That's the idea. A little constancy in the universe.

SUSIE. But it's impossible, don't you see? You have to see it's impossible. Things can't stay the same way forever – that's physics, that's thermodynamics, that's… evolution. Life goes on. (*Beat – then, to* XANDER.) You want to put in a *swimming pool* – did I hear that right?

XANDER. It's one idea that came up today.

MEL. This site has value – that value needs to be optimised.

SUSIE. And there is a value beyond money! There is –

OMAR. I have a responsibility to my employees –

MEL. We have dependents too. Children. I need to provide for –

SUSIE. Yes, yes, I understand –

MEL. No, I'm not sure you do.

SUSIE. I do.

MEL. I have to provide.

SUSIE. Money can't always be your bottom line.

MEL. We're just trying to do right for our family.

OMAR. Everyone's trying to do right.

XANDER. I think – if I may? – I think Mr Sarbani's right. Until you have a legal paper trail, I'm not sure there's much point in going any further.

SUSIE. I have family too. Just because I haven't… Just because mine are buried –

MEL. I'm sorry.

SUSIE. I have just as much a right. I'm trying to leave something behind.

MEL. I appreciate that. (*To* OMAR.) Do you think we might have one more look through your office together? Just to see if we can't get to the bottom of this?

OMAR (*checks his watch*). Alright, but not for long. I need to check in on the others. We have a huge order to complete. We're in demand.

SUSIE. I'm sure.

MEL. I just think everyone would benefit from some clarity, one way or another. (*To* SUSIE.) Are you coming?

SUSIE. No, I think I'll stay here a moment – but I won't cause any trouble, I promise. No more surprises.

MEL (*to* XANDER). Mr MacIntyre, I don't suppose there's anything else we'll need you for today.

XANDER. Oh, right.

MEL. But thank you for your time.

XANDER. Not at all.

MEL. I'll be in touch.

OMAR (*to* SUSIE). If we discover anything, we'll come straight back.

MEL *and* OMAR *go.* XANDER *is still lingering.*

BILLY (*to* SUSIE). You have to let me get a couple of you before I go.

SUSIE. What on earth for?

BILLY. Just in case. For my portfolio.

SUSIE. You're very kind.

BILLY. You're Susie Spenser.

SUSIE. And who's that, exactly?

BILLY. My first ever gig. The G-Clamps at The Boardwalk. Fifteen years old and with the best fake ID money could buy. Magic.

SUSIE. Is that true? But you're a child!

BILLY. Swear on my life.

SUSIE. Next you'll be telling me you had a poster of me on your wall.

BILLY. Maybe I did.

SUSIE. No one has ever produced a poster of me.

BILLY. Maybe I made my own. Over there – in the good light.

SUSIE *reluctantly budges over a bit.* BILLY *takes a few candid shots as she looks down at the scissors still in her hands. Then she lifts her head to face the camera – defiant, the hint of a smile. A few more snaps.*

I'll get these over to you as soon as I've had a look.

SUSIE. Thank you. And invoice too – and add for any extra expense –

BILLY. No bother – just get me back when you're up and running.

SUSIE. I will.

He starts to go.

Billy?

BILLY. Yep?

SUSIE. You don't know any rich people, do you?

BILLY. No, I only know musicians.

SUSIE. Good for you. Take care now.

BILLY. It's been a pleasure. I'll put these back where I found them.

BILLY *picks up the briefcase, mop, broom, and any other bits and pieces, smiles and goes. A beat.*

XANDER. Doctor Spenser?

SUSIE. Ah, you're still here. He's still here, everyone! (*Glancing around.*) Oh, it's only us.

XANDER. Yes.

SUSIE. Can I do something for you, Xander MacIntyre from Claybourne-Harris?

XANDER. We offer a range of bespoke solutions for urban redevelopment.

SUSIE. Yes?

XANDER. I think residential units would present a missed opportunity.

SUSIE. Do you now?

XANDER. The market for city-centre living is getting oversaturated. We don't really know what city centres are for at the moment. The rules are being rewritten, so it's unstable, unpredictable, but I think there's an appetite for destinations. Uh. I think that will always be true. I don't know exactly what you had planned for this space, but...

SUSIE. A destination?

XANDER. That's the only way it makes sense to me.

SUSIE. Go on.

XANDER. Uh… Right. Yes. Um. A cathedral of making – whatever making means. An emporium for… Let the light in. Strip everything back. You know Picasso came here once?

SUSIE. I did.

XANDER. A place for artistry. For creation. And a Christmas tree that touches the ceiling.

SUSIE. Really?

XANDER. Just a thought.

SUSIE. Well aren't you just full of surprises? Take that jacket off.

XANDER. Excuse me?

SUSIE. It's beneath you. You deserve better. (*Shrugging off her leather jacket.*) Here.

XANDER. What's happening?

SUSIE. I'm giving you a little rock and roll. Didn't I say I'd re-baptise you? Go on.

Baffled, XANDER *slips off his own jacket and puts on Susie's. She takes him in.*

Okay, well you look ridiculous. It was a nice thought. Give it back.

Beat.

Quickly now, it's chilly.

XANDER *gives the jacket back.*

Ah, Mr MacIntyre. If only I was five years younger.

Now LEO *enters. His own coat/jacket is covered in gunk. He holds a small paper bag.*

Leo! I was starting to think you'd abandoned me.

LEO. Never. Not disturbing, am I?

SUSIE. Not jealous? (*To* XANDER.) I release you, Mr MacIntyre. It's been an unexpected pleasure. Go well.

XANDER. Thank you. Likewise.

XANDER *smiles a little awkwardly and goes.*

SUSIE. Have you been staying out of trouble?

LEO. Have you?

SUSIE. Never.

LEO. I just passed your musicians – they didn't seem too happy.

SUSIE. No, I don't expect they were.

LEO. Big day?

SUSIE. Big day. What happened to you?

LEO. A little mishap with some office supplies.

SUSIE. I see.

LEO (*offering the bag*). Cardamom knot?

SUSIE. No, I couldn't.

LEO. Suit yourself. (*Going for the piece of paper in his pocket again.*) I've been thinking –

SUSIE (*cutting him off, handing him the pair of scissors*). Here – with love, from Spenser and Son.

LEO. Did you steal these?

SUSIE. I can't steal what's mine. (*Beat.*) They can't see it.

LEO. No?

SUSIE. No. I couldn't sell it to them.

LEO. That's okay.

SUSIE. I've lost it. Doesn't exactly bode well.

LEO. You've had a hard day.

SUSIE. I seem to be having an awful lot of hard days lately. (*Beat.*) I thought the girls might help – you know, Coco and… but they were the worst of all.

LEO. Yes, in hindsight they might have been a misstep. What were they in the end?

SUSIE. Hmm?

LEO. Friends, sisters, or – ?

SUSIE. You know I'm still not sure.

LEO. Well isn't that the youth of today?

SUSIE. Very true. (*Beat*.) Do you remember Slag?

LEO. Who?

SUSIE. Slag. They were this girl group, early punk group from around here. And they were all the daughters of steel workers, that was their thing. You know, *slag*, it's the… the detritus, the run-off, from, um… It's a waste product. So they all thought that was very clever, because we were a waste product – all of us, up in the post-industrial north, and *they* were a waste product, the useless progeny – the unwanted daughters of men who only wanted sons. And I thought: 'Sign me up! That's me! I fit that bill.' They were a little bit older than I was, but that shouldn't matter. I was young, I was keen, I was gifted. So I wrote to them – pleaded my case, offered my services. You know what they did? They wrote a manifesto against me. They did! They actually did – this photocopied pamphlet that they handed out at gigs. I was eighteen, nineteen, maybe. But their dads were all workers, you see – salt of the earth – whereas mine had bought the factory – and fired one of their dads, in one instance. Unfortunate. So I wasn't one of them. I was the enemy – the bourgeoisie – the first to be lined up against the wall. And that's who I was – I was the daughter, and then the sister, and once I'd succeeded in distancing myself from all that I was the muse, the inspiration, the hanger-on. I was the girlfriend, the Yoko, the distraction, only ever existing in relation to the problematic men in my orbit. But this – I could do this. I could make it work. Risky – risky because music is always risky, all live entertainment is inherently… But I could make it work. Start with the bar, build word-of-mouth, smaller gigs, rehearsal space to bring in income during the day. Then get the recording studio set up, sponsorship, fund bursaries and residential retreats for emerging artists – I could do this!

LEO. I know you could.

SUSIE. Not because it's mine – although it is – it is rightfully mine – but because I'm the one with the ideas – I'm the one with the expertise. How many bands have I founded? How many nights have I put on? And I keep up. I put in the hours.

LEO. No question.

SUSIE. A cathedral of music – you like the sound of that? I think we've had a real impact on the young Mr MacIntyre. There's hope for him yet.

LEO. Really?

SUSIE. And Billy – the genuine Billy – he was a sweetheart. I struck gold with him.

LEO. Good.

SUSIE. He came to a G-Clamps gig, back in the day.

LEO. Did he now?

SUSIE. And he knows everyone – shot everyone – he's an asset – we need to keep him onboard.

LEO. And he was keen?

SUSIE. Oh yes – he saw it. He got it straight away.

LEO. Well there you go – hope for us yet.

SUSIE. Here – let me show you something else.

She finds a picture on her phone and shows it to LEO.

LEO. What am I looking at?

SUSIE. You like it?

LEO. Are you going on holiday somewhere?

SUSIE. I had an offer accepted on the house last week.

LEO. What?

SUSIE. Still got to finalise all the paperwork, but…

LEO. What are you telling me?

SUSIE. It's my new digs for a little while.

LEO. Susie –

SUSIE. It's only temporary.

LEO. No –

SUSIE. Just until –

LEO. No, absolutely not – categorically not. You need to call…
whoever it is you call in this situation and undo all this.

SUSIE. It'll be fine.

LEO. You can't sell your house and live in a caravan, to… to
what end, exactly?

SUSIE. To get things moving.

LEO. Moving how?

SUSIE. A little injection of capital. It won't cover everything,
but it will get us started. And it helps to let investors know
you're serious – you're putting your money where your
mouth is.

LEO. I won't let you do this.

SUSIE. Oh yeah, how are you going to stop me?

LEO. You don't even know if the building's yours.

SUSIE. I do. Of course it is. It's got my name on it.

LEO. You and Eddie hardly left things on the best terms.

SUSIE. He's my brother! What, I'm supposed to be *nice* to him?

LEO. You can't gamble everything on this.

SUSIE. He should've come to me sooner. He should've sought
me out. You know I read the wrong Ecclesiastes at the
funeral – 'for everything there is a season – a time for this,
a time for that.'

LEO. You hate Ecclesiastes.

SUSIE. I do. It's bland. Funeral-bland – comforting-bland.

LEO. So you've told me.

SUSIE. Smug. Self-righteous. And you know the worst thing
about it?

LEO. I do.

SUSIE. I've told you before?

LEO. You can tell me again.

SUSIE. It's thermodynamics. Ecclesiastes is fucking
    thermodynamics. 'There is no new thing under the sun.'
    Nothing created, nothing destroyed, nothing new in the
    entire sorry universe. What kind of horseshit is that?

LEO. I'll take it up with the big man.

SUSIE. Einstein or God?

LEO. Whoever I meet first.

SUSIE. That's what I should've given them – the part that's too
    depressing for funerals – the bit you never hear in full. 'What
    profit hath a man of all his labour which he taketh under the
    sun? One generation passeth away, and another generation
    cometh: but the earth abideth for ever.'

LEO. Yes –

SUSIE. 'Is there any thing whereof it may be said, See, this is
    new? It hath been already of old time, which was before us.
    There is no remembrance of former things; neither shall
    there be any remembrance of things that are to come with
    those that shall come after. The thing that hath been, it is that
    which shall be; and that which is done is that which shall be
    done: and / there is no new thing under the sun.'

    LEO *joins in on the final line*.

LEO (*with* SUSIE). There is no new thing under the sun.

SUSIE. Fucking Ecclesiastes. Horseshit.

LEO. Susie –

SUSIE. I create.

LEO. What?

SUSIE. I create. Of course I create.

LEO. I know.

SUSIE. Twelve notes – that's all you get. And what – nothing
    ever created again once you have those twelve? No – infinite
    – *infinite* variations. Infinite possibilities. Textures, flavours,
    reimaginings. Einstein was a musician. He understood. But
    Dad didn't, Eddie didn't. Just drop a little thermodynamics
    into your quarterly sales evaluations to show everyone

you're an intellectual – you're cut from a different cloth. There is nothing new under the sun, so on we go, quarter after quarter, year after year, same old same old, and we don't change because the universe doesn't change, not really, and that's something to be proud of somehow – we tell ourselves it's good if we don't change, because what we make will last forever. Fashions come and go but we'll stay the course. But things break down – that's the second law, the bit they never got to – a hot thing will always eventually become cold, and as things approach absolute zero… I have a finite supply of energy in my system I want to *do something* with it.

LEO. Will you promise me something?

SUSIE. What?

LEO. Promise me you're not going to live in a caravan.

SUSIE. I'm a tough old bird. I'll be fine.

LEO. Promise me.

SUSIE. I have a finite supply of energy in my system, Leo. And so many chances – so many times I was so certain that this was it – I'd found my breakthrough – and each time I got knocked down on my arse it got a little bit harder to get back up again.

LEO. You have been magnificent.

SUSIE. I've lived my life in the shadow of magnificence – it's not the same thing.

LEO. No.

SUSIE. Yes.

LEO. You cast a long shadow yourself, Doctor Spenser.

SUSIE. You old flatterer.

LEO. But you have to be sensible.

SUSIE. That isn't very rock and roll.

LEO. Please.

SUSIE. I'll fight for this. I'll fight to leave something behind.
Tell me you can see it. Tell me you can *hear* it. Close your
eyes and it just comes pouring out of the walls.

A shift in light as ZARA *enters. She brings on a microphone
and stand, and sings. This is not happening in reality, but
everyone hears it all the same. What might perhaps start as
an unaccompanied folk ballad could rattle through rock and
roll, punk and into a contemporary sound as the verses
progress.*

ZARA (*sings*). The Sheffield grinder's a terrible blade.
Tally hi-o, the grinder.
He sets his little 'uns down to trade
Tally hi-o, the grinder.
He turns his baby to grind in the hull
Till his body is stunted and his eyes are dull,
And the brains are dizzy and dazed in the skull.
Tally hi-o, the grinder.

He shortens his life and he hastens his death.
Tally hi-o, the grinder.
Will drink steel dust in every breath.
Tally hi-o, the grinder.
Won't use a fan as he turns his wheel.
Won't wash his hands ere he eats his meal.
But dies as he lives, as hard as steel.
Tally hi-o, the grinder.

At whose door lies the brunt of the blame?
Tally hi-o, the grinder.
Where rests the heavier weight of shame?
Tally hi-o, the grinder.
On the famine-price contractor's head,
Or the workman's, under-taught and -fed,
Who grinds his own bones and his child's for bread?
Tally hi-o, the grinder.

*The song ends and lights shift. We're now back in the real
world, as if* ZARA *has only just entered (although it's
possible she still talks awkwardly into the microphone).*

Um. Sorry. Dad asked me to come talk to you. Uh. It isn't
good news – not for any of us. We got into his records –

Eddie's records. Um. I should just say it. That big order – you know there's this big order from China that everyone's been working on, and it's been the only thing keeping them afloat? He made it up. Eddie made that up. He was just trying to buy them some time, we think. So he remortgaged everything, took out loans too. Basically… Basically what we think is none of us own the site, the bank does. There's nothing here but debt. Anyway. I don't know what happens now, but it's out of our hands. I'd steer well clear of it, I reckon.

ZARA *steps down.*

SUSIE. Okay.

ZARA. Maybe you'll do your club somewhere else.

SUSIE. Oh. Right.

ZARA. I don't think it was a bad idea, for what it's worth.

SUSIE. Thank you.

ZARA. Anyway. Got a bunch of people next door who aren't going to have jobs for too much longer. Dad's gone to speak to them now. I should be there for him.

SUSIE. Yes, of course. Don't let us keep you.

ZARA. I'm sorry.

SUSIE. So am I. I'm sorry you never got the chance to take the reins. Even if you didn't want them, I'm still sorry you'll never have the chance.

ZARA. I'll be okay.

SUSIE. I'm sure you will.

ZARA. My dad does try. He believes. He's a good man.

SUSIE. Yes. Perhaps you might apologise to him for me?

ZARA. Okay.

SUSIE. Does Faye know what's happened?

ZARA. Yeah.

SUSIE. I wasn't very kind to her – to her or her wife. I know they have children. I'm sure they have struggles of their own. I should do better. How did she take it?

ZARA. I think everyone's still processing.

SUSIE. Yes. Thank you, Zara, and good luck. You're going to be magnificent.

ZARA. It was really nice to meet you. And you too, Leo.

LEO. Look after yourself.

ZARA goes. A pause.

SUSIE. Well. That's that then.

LEO. Susie –

SUSIE. If you were ever going to tell me you've been in love with me all these years, now would be the time to do it. Not to place any pressure, but now might be the only time.

LEO. I…

SUSIE. Don't worry about it.

LEO. I have something for you. I would very much like to share something with you. I came across it months ago, and I was going to send it to you, but then I wanted to wait and read it to you instead. Hold on.

He produces a creased piece of paper from his pocket.

Sonnet 59. Do you know it?

'If there be nothing new, but that which is
Hath been before, how are our brains beguiled,
Which, labouring for invention, bear amiss
The second burden of a former child!
O, that record could with a backward look,
Even of five hundred courses of the sun,
Show me your image in some antique book,
Since mind at first in character was done!
That I might see what the old world could say
To this composed wonder of your frame;
Whether we are mended, or whether better they,
Or whether revolution be the same.
O! Sure I am, the wits of former days
To subjects worse have given admiring praise.'

SUSIE. Is that your answer?

LEO. This is my answer.

He kisses her.

SUSIE. Is there anything new under the sun?

LEO. Of course there is.

SUSIE. Shall we go looking for it?

LEO. Call your solicitor. Go get your house back.

SUSIE. Why? You've got plenty of space, haven't you?

LEO. One thing at a time.

SUSIE. Or you could sell yours too – there's space in the caravan – space on the open road.

LEO. As tempting as that sounds –

SUSIE. What's stopping us? I'm a woman of finite energy, Leo.

LEO. I don't believe that. (*Beat.*) There's a little Danish pastry place just round the corner – it has some of the most uncomfortable bar stools I've ever come across, but the coffee was excellent.

SUSIE. I know where you mean.

LEO. Or if you'd rather go for something stronger?

SUSIE. No – no, that sounds wonderful. Can I meet you there in just a minute? I feel like I should say goodbye.

LEO. Of course. Take all the time you need.

LEO *goes*.

SUSIE. So, that's that then.

You always were the stupid one.

What in God's name were you playing at? Remortgaging? Fabricating orders? How long did you think you could keep this up? How did you imagine this would end? Or didn't you care, just so long as you weren't around to deal with the fallout? What an abdication of responsibility. Jesus! Fuck! Grow up, Eddie! I was going to do something. Not just for me – it wasn't just for me. I was going to give something back. I was going to establish a *legacy*. I was looking towards the future, not like you and Dad, always clinging on to the past. It could've worked.

Okay, okay, sure, not with those two I brought in – that was a mistake – but the idea is sound. There are plenty of acts out there, plenty of young talent, plenty of people who could benefit from my expertise.

One generation passeth away, and another generation cometh, but the earth abideth forever.

Fucking Ecclesiastes. I'm still here, aren't I?

Why didn't you tell me you were in trouble? Why didn't you come to me *before* you were in trouble? Why didn't I get a say in any of this? Why didn't I get handed the keys fifty years ago, while we're at it? I could've done something with it back then. I wouldn't have made scissors, that's for sure. I could've made music. I could've made something. But it's no good crying about all that now.

There is no remembrance of former things, neither shall there be any remembrance of things that are to come by those that shall come after.

And 'twas ever thus. So we just give up, do we? We just dig our graves and wait for the sun to go down – wait to be forgotten?

Fuck you, Eddie! And fuck Einstein, while we're at it. I create! I bring new energy into the universe! I'm not just recycling the same shit round and round, circling the drain, closing in on absolute zero.

How dare you? How dare you leave me with nothing?

How dare you leave me?

There is nothing.

And Dad would say 'No – no, silly girl, no, you don't understand it. Ask old Albert. Nothing has been lost. Nothing is now missing that was once there before. The energy has just transferred, that's all.'

Which is, I think, quite Buddhist actually. I'm not an expert, but it definitely sounds Buddhist. Only then he wouldn't have liked it. Give him science. Give him the philosophy of the atom, none of that mysticism. This world of ours is a closed system, even if we can't see into all the corners, so nothing can ever leave it.

Where are you then?

Where are you?

I should've come round more.

She picks up the pair of scissors again.

They're just like I remember them, I'll give you that. You trained them well. Nice to have something to leave behind.

Leo's waiting. You remember Leo? You never liked him. So I'm off to practise the transfer of energy. I'm off to enjoy what little heat I have left, until I cool completely. If I leave it any longer, he'll really start to feel like the consolation prize, and that'd be unkind to him. It isn't enough, but it's something.

It's never enough, is it?

I create.

Fucking Ecclesiastes.

I create.

Goodnight.

She places the scissors down carefully and leaves.

End.

PAPER

ACT ONE

A musty, unloved manager's office. A large desk with a fairly ancient desktop computer on it, several filing cabinets, archive boxes littered all over the floor. Perhaps some general detritus that definitely doesn't belong here – spare machine parts, cleaning supplies, bits and bobs. At least one electric heater. Probably some pest control boxes. It's certainly not derelict, but absolutely gets a little cold and a little damp. A small area of the room appears to be in semi-regular use – a patch of free desk space, a clear path through to it – but generally it's clear that this space is used as much for storage as work.

Along the back wall, a door leading to a corridor and a frosted-glass window, through which figures could be seen passing, but not easily identified. To one side, a door leading to a storage cupboard, and to the other, a fire door leading straight outside. The lights are off, but there's enough daylight that we can see it fairly clearly.

FAYE *and* MEL *enter from the corridor.* FAYE *turns on the lights.*

FAYE. Oh. Oh, okay. This is it.

MEL. Yeah?

FAYE. Yeah.

FAYE *breathes in deeply, taking it all in.*

MEL. You okay?

FAYE. Yeah, fine – I'm fine – it's just weird.

MEL. Right.

FAYE. Not *bad*-weird, just… I don't know.

MEL. Do you need a minute?

FAYE. No, no. (*Beat.*) Do you remember it?

MEL. I've not been here before.

FAYE. Yes you have!

MEL. Have I?

FAYE. Yes, I took you back in... God. Super-early days. Like decades ago.

MEL. Right.

FAYE. I snuck you back here, just the two of us, and...

MEL. Did you?

FAYE. You really don't remember?

MEL. Sure it was me?

FAYE. Who else would it have been?

MEL. I don't know – another of your conquests?

FAYE. I'm very sure!

MEL (*with a shrug*). Okay. So where do you think we should be starting?

FAYE. No idea.

MEL. Next door looks like it's just materials, and a bunch of stuff waiting to ship out.

FAYE. Uh-huh.

MEL. Didn't think there'd be so much of it. And it's all just scissors?

FAYE. Scissors, shears, that sort of thing.

MEL (*taking it in*). Wow, it is... not nice in here. (*Beat.*) Sorry. That sounded –

FAYE. It's okay.

MEL. I don't know what I was expecting. No – you know, maybe it is coming back to me. In my head it was a bit more opulent.

FAYE. Used to be.

MEL. And the site's massive, isn't it? Do you know the square footage?

FAYE. No idea.

MEL. We should look for plans too – blueprints – as well as –

FAYE (*still distracted*). Yeah. (*Spotting something.*) God – that lamp. That lamp's been here since I was five.

MEL. Do you want it? (*Beat.*) You could probably just take it.

FAYE. Where would we put it?

MEL. I don't know, but if –

FAYE. I don't want it.

MEL. Do you think it smells funny?

FAYE. No. Maybe.

MEL. Not damp, just funny?

FAYE. You think?

MEL. A bit funky, definitely.

FAYE. It smells familiar. I think I recognise it.

MEL. Yeah?

FAYE. Maybe.

MEL. I could prop a door open.

FAYE. No, can you leave it?

MEL. Yeah?

FAYE. Just for a bit of privacy?

MEL. Okay.

FAYE. They say, don't they, that smell's the most nostalgic sense? I quite like it. Because I haven't been in here for decades – literal decades – but one sniff and… Actually I did come in here quite a bit when I was little. In the holidays, or weekends sometimes when Mum was busy. Used to think it was a treat.

MEL. And as the boss's daughter –

FAYE. Oh yeah, very powerful.

MEL. Bet you had them waiting on you hand and foot.

FAYE. Definitely.

MEL. Tugging their forelocks as you pass.

FAYE. Is that a role-play scenario you're wanting to play out, or – ?

MEL. You're alright.

FAYE (*adopting the persona of a flustered southern belle*). 'I don't know what you're doing busting in here, mister, but if my daddy hears…'

MEL. And it always smelt like this?

FAYE (*dropping it*). Yeah, I think so. Sort of. Sort of the same, only there's more of it now, y'know? It's concentrated.

MEL. Lovely.

FAYE. I like it. It's the stink of history.

MEL *rolls her eyes*.

This was your idea.

MEL. What?

FAYE. You were pushing to do this today. I said I could do it by myself.

MEL. I know.

FAYE. I am capable.

MEL. I know. I'm just here for moral support. Practical guidance.

FAYE. I don't need supervision.

MEL. I know that.

FAYE. I mean it. You could go get some air, get a coffee –

MEL. I'm fine.

FAYE. Do some shopping, maybe?

MEL. Do we need anything?

FAYE. What?

MEL. From the shops?

FAYE. No. I don't know. That's not the point. You could just browse. Bit of retail therapy.

MEL. Buy myself something pretty?

FAYE. Or buy me something pretty.

MEL. Ah, I see.

FAYE (*teasing*). Interesting that the first place your mind went was –

MEL. Shall I go buy you something pretty?

FAYE. You could buy yourself some underwear that doesn't have holes in.

MEL. I need the holes. For my legs.

FAYE (*ignoring this*). Or there's that hardware store, isn't there, by the arches?

MEL. Now we're talking.

FAYE. No – because you said you needed to look for… whatever it is you need for the kitchen units? Brackets? Hinges?

MEL. Yeah, right.

FAYE. If you're still thinking of doing it yourself? (*Beat.*) Which you don't have to – we can get someone in – but let me know if –

MEL. No, I'm going to do it. I'll get it done.

FAYE. Okay. (*Beat.*) When do you think you'll – ?

MEL. It's on my list.

FAYE. There's a new bakery, as well – did you see? Looked sort of Nordic – had some seats in the window.

MEL. Uh-huh.

FAYE. Nothing like that when I was little.

MEL. It's good though, isn't it? Shows the area's improving.

FAYE. Yeah.

MEL. Real Estate 101 – get a loaf of bread in the oven.

FAYE. Well, maybe you could go and sample the produce.

MEL *takes* FAYE*'s hands gently.*

MEL. Dearest. Honey muffin. Love of my life. Would you like me not to be here?

FAYE. I didn't say that.

MEL. Strictly speaking that's not an answer, is it?

FAYE. I'm not saying I don't want you here, I'm just saying it isn't *necessary* for you to be here. I don't need you to do this.

MEL. Right.

FAYE. And I'm going to want to take my time – I'm going to want to look through things, and if you're just going to pace about and complain about the smell –

MEL. I'm sorry.

FAYE. I'm not saying be sorry, just… We don't actually have to spend every minute of every day together. (*Beat.*) It's been lovely – having you around more has been… genuinely it's… You could go down to the canal – it's nice now.

MEL. Yeah.

FAYE. You shouldn't have to do this. It's not your job. It's my family shit.

MEL. Right.

FAYE. I just mean –

MEL. It's okay. You're right.

FAYE. You're not meant to be working. You're meant to be taking it easy –

MEL. This isn't –

FAYE. That is actually a very clear instruction you've been
    given, isn't it? You are actively meant to be avoiding –

MEL. I'm fine.

FAYE. The whole point of –

MEL. Okay!

FAYE. I'm not having a go.

MEL. No. No, you're right. I'll go. I can go for some me time.
    I'll potter. I'll get a mani-pedi. A deep tissue massage. That
    thing with the cups.

FAYE. The what?

MEL. You know. The cups – the hot… What are they? Like
    glass bowls, and they blow in them? No. They put the cups
    in the fire, and then there's suction, and…

FAYE. What are you talking about?

MEL. Olympic athletes do it – that swimmer you fancy. And
    they leave those big red welts.

FAYE. Right.

MEL. Cupping!

FAYE. Really?

MEL. Uh-huh. I'll buy myself some nice new pants first, then
    I'll go for a walk-in cupping. Or the thing with the rocks –
    when they just pile hot rocks up on top of you.

FAYE. Sounds like fun.

MEL. I think it does. Can you imagine just being buried up to
    your neck in hot rocks?

FAYE. I think they used to do that to witches.

MEL. No, I'm into it. I'm going to go find a seven-foot
    Norwegian lady to just absolutely bury me under a pile of
    stones, and leave you to crack on with everything in here. Is
    that okay?

FAYE (*distracted by something in the office*). Yeah. Absolutely.

MEL. And you know what you're looking for?

FAYE. Yeah.

MEL. Okay, good. That's good then. (*Beat*.) Right.

MEL *dithers for a second then starts to leave.*

FAYE. You're actually going?

MEL. Isn't that what – ?

FAYE. Yeah, yeah.

MEL. If you don't want me to –

FAYE. Whatever you'd rather.

MEL. I don't mind.

FAYE. Because I *can* do this – it's not beyond me.

MEL. No.

FAYE. It's fine. I've just got to be systematic. I've got to develop a system. And once I get going it'll be easy.

MEL. I'll bring you back a pastry.

MEL *starts to leave again.*

FAYE. Wait!

MEL. What?

FAYE. Are you really going? Are you just going to leave me with all this?

MEL. You said –

FAYE. In my dead father's office? Without a system in place?

MEL. Would you like me to stay?

FAYE. If you want to – not because I need you to –

MEL. Just for the company?

FAYE. Yeah. (*Beat*.) And where do you think you'd start, just so we can compare?

MEL. Okay. (*Thinks for a second, then claps her hands together.*) Okay. So, first things first, we're dividing the space into quadrants, bisecting along the door line and the rug line, yeah? I'll take left of door, you take the right. We're going to clear the desk to make some sorting space, then we're both going to make a stacking area in our first quadrants, and we can use that for all the things we know we're definitely *not* looking for.

FAYE. Like what?

MEL *glances around. She picks up a cardboard box with 'light bulbs' written on the side.*

MEL. Like… Okay, so light bulbs – we know we're not looking for light bulbs, so this can go… (*Something makes her stop. She opens the box.*) Okay, why is this full of Hobnobs and mousetraps?

FAYE *shrugs.*

Okay, so we've just learnt something. We've got to open the boxes to check what's actually in them, and if they're obviously not helpful you can put them neatly in your stacking area. Big boxes at the bottom, small on top, no playing Jenga…

FAYE. I'm forty-two years old.

MEL. I'm just saying –

FAYE. Are the Hobnobs unopened, or – ?

MEL. We're only looking for papers, so anything that obviously isn't paper we can dismiss. Orders and invoices and that sort of thing don't matter for now. They're important documents, so hopefully they've been put somewhere sensible. The goal is fast, efficient and methodical.

FAYE. Has anyone ever told you you're really hot when you're organising?

MEL. Yes.

FAYE *kisses* MEL.

FAYE. Thank you. I love you.

MEL. I love you too.

Beat.

FAYE. Right. Okay. I'm going to my quadrant.

FAYE moves slightly away.

I miss you already.

A few moments of sorting. Not very long.

Do you think we're codependent?

MEL. What?

FAYE. Nothing. Georgie sent me a quiz.

MEL. Why is Georgie sending you quizzes on codependency?

FAYE. Because Carmen's in therapy again, and she's not very happy.

MEL. Right.

FAYE. I think she wanted us to be her control group.

MEL. So what did it say?

FAYE. What?

MEL. The quiz?

FAYE. Oh. We're not. It didn't think we were. Not conclusively, anyway. I suppose it's all a spectrum.

MEL. Uh-huh.

FAYE. I'm glad you're here though. I don't *need* you here, but I'm glad that you are.

MEL. Got it.

FAYE. I do like having you around more. It's nice having you around at home. It's good for the kids too. I think Joni's going to be really devastated when you go back.

MEL. She'll get used to it.

FAYE. Maybe you could still do a couple of days from home if they'd let you, at least over the holidays? A lot of people are doing that sort of thing now, aren't they?

MEL. Yeah.

FAYE. We've still got the offer of the farmhouse in Keswick if we want it. Alice is going to be in Sardinia all summer.

MEL. God, I hate her.

FAYE. Well she's going to be in Sardinia.

MEL. Yeah, that sounds nice. I don't know.

FAYE. Okay, well think about it. (*Beat.*) I think these are all purchase orders – that's not important?

MEL. Not for now. Check it's the same all the way down.

FAYE. Okay. (*Beat.*) I don't really know what anything here is.

MEL. I can do the first sift by myself if you'd like?

FAYE. No –

MEL. I don't mind. I can just blast through it.

FAYE. No, I'm here, I didn't mean that. It's just a lot.

MEL. Okay.

FAYE. Anyway, I have to be here, don't I? I've got to talk to the man when he shows up.

MEL. I can deal with him.

FAYE. No, he's got to speak to family.

Beat.

MEL. Right.

FAYE. I mean next-of-kin – I mean legally, on paper, when they start asking about –

MEL. Yeah, you're right. You're the one they'll want.

FAYE. It's fine. It's all fine. We'll find what we need, we'll have the conversation…

MEL. And then we'll know where you stand.

FAYE. Yeah.

MEL. You'll be set. Whatever number they put on it, it's going to be massive.

FAYE. But if we can't prove – if we can't find anything –

MEL. It'll turn up.

FAYE. Yeah.

MEL. And if it doesn't – even if it doesn't – then you're next-of-kin, like you say. There are protocols for that. There'll be an automatic…

FAYE. Right.

MEL. So this is a formality. It'll move things along, it'll help us out, but it's not… And when the man comes, he's not going to want to see proof of anything, he's just going to lay some ideas out.

FAYE. Okay.

MEL. They'll be used to situations like this. (*Beat*.) Anyway, we're early. You could still go to that coffee shop – get us a little treat? We've got time. I could do this forever. I won't get bored of it. I don't mind if –

FAYE. It's alright. I'll feel better once it's sorted.

MEL. And you're sure you don't want me to open something – get a bit of air circulating?

FAYE. I'd rather not draw attention to us.

MEL. Okay.

FAYE. Just for now.

MEL. Okay.

FAYE. Just because –

MEL. But you spoke to what's-his-name at the memorial, didn't you? You told him you'd be coming by?

FAYE. Yeah, but I didn't tell him what we were doing. (*Beat*.) I keep thinking about what Dad would say. How livid he'd be. How disappointed.

MEL. That's not –

FAYE. He spent fifty years trying to keep us afloat –

MEL. And that was enough.

FAYE. But we don't have to go through with it, do we? If it's not the right thing.

MEL. It is.

FAYE. But it's not the only option.

MEL. It's the best –

FAYE. How can you know? Why is this so important all of a sudden? We were fine before.

MEL. Maybe they'll be relieved. I think maybe actually everyone will be relieved, to have that decision taken out of their hands. Better than just delaying the inevitable.

FAYE. Maybe.

MEL. It's the sunk-cost fallacy, isn't it? People keep going because they think they have to, because they've poured so much of themselves into something and now they're just stuck in this death spiral. They need someone else to pull the trigger. They could never do it themselves, but if someone else did, it'd be an act of kindness.

FAYE. Do you believe that?

MEL. Look around.

Beat.

FAYE. We, um, we can prop a door open, if you like. I don't mind.

MEL. It's fine.

FAYE. If the smell's getting to you.

MEL. I'm getting used to it. Reminds me of the old records office in Northampton.

FAYE. Ah – back in your secretarial days?

MEL. Behave.

FAYE. What?

MEL. How do you always manage to make 'secretarial' sound so filthy?

FAYE. I just wish I knew what the right thing to do was. I want to be upfront with everyone. I don't like sneaking around.

MEL. What if sneaking around was sexy?

FAYE. I'm serious.

MEL. We're not sneaking. You can't sneak in a building you own.

FAYE. Yeah.

MEL. It's going to be okay, I promise. We're getting everything sorted.

FAYE. Yeah.

Clearly they're both still on edge. MEL *tries to cheer up* FAYE *with a ridiculous accent and spy persona.*

MEL. But first, ve must find ze files. Ze future of ze resistance depends on it.

FAYE. Alright.

MEL. Ze mission is of ze utmost importance, fräulein mademoiselle.

FAYE. Is it now?

MEL. Si señorita.

FAYE. Where are you from, exactly?

MEL. Dat ist highly classified. Capiche?

FAYE. Right. I'm just going to see what's in the cupboard.

MEL. Um – get back to your quadrant!

FAYE sticks her tongue out at MEL and goes into a little walk-in storage cupboard. MEL *sits down at the desk, putting her feet up and examining a file she's found. She keeps talking, getting on a roll. She now seems to settle on a sort of butch Dick Tracy character.*

Now listen here, kid – you've got the moxie, but you've gotta come through with the goods. This isn't a game for schoolgirls, see? You find the blueprints and it's gonna blow this case sky high – I said sky high, ya hear me!

On this, LIV *and* TRENT, *two apprentices in work overalls, burst in, having been listening to a little of this outside the door. To be more accurate,* LIV *bursts in,* TRENT *lurks behind her slightly apologetically.* MEL *jumps,* FAYE *remains in the cupboard, out of their view.*

LIV. Oh my God, he was right!

MEL. Uh. Hi.

LIV. Industrial espionage! Actual industrial espionage!

MEL. Now one moment –

LIV. I didn't believe him. Mason heard you talking and we were all like no way, there's no way, he's just crying out for attention – classic Aries – but actually… We're never going to hear the end of this now.

MEL. This isn't what it looks like.

LIV. It is! Caught you red-handed.

MEL (*getting up*). Okay, just calm down.

LIV. Hold it right there! Espionage! Espionage! You're under citizen's arrest.

MEL. Just –

LIV. Freeze!

LIV glances around, sees a fire alarm on the wall, and instinctively pulls the handle. However, instead of going off, the whole thing just falls off the wall and clatters to the ground. A beat.

Okay, well that's really dangerous. You're still under arrest anyway.

MEL. Can everyone just take a breath, and… Faye, baby, can you come out please? (*Beat.*) Honey? You can't just hide in the closet. You tried that for twenty years.

Reluctantly, FAYE *emerges.*

LIV. How many more of you are there?

FAYE. Hi. Sorry. Hi. Just me.

TRENT. Alright?

LIV. Don't engage with them. Check everywhere – we're conducting a full search.

MEL. Absolutely. Go ahead.

LIV. Well that's clearly a trap.

FAYE. Do you both work here? Oh, are you on the apprentice scheme?

TRENT. That's right.

LIV. Stop talking to them! You're giving away trade secrets.

TRENT. I don't think I am.

LIV (*to* MEL *and* FAYE). Who are you?

FAYE. I'm Faye. This is Mel. I'm Eddie's daughter.

LIV. Prove it.

FAYE. Seriously? (*Beat.*) Um. Okay. I've got my driver's licence?

LIV. Show me then – but slowly.

TRENT. Jesus Christ.

FAYE. Sure. (*Rummages, brings out a purse and finds her driver's licence.*) Faye Spenser. There you go.

LIV. Doesn't mean anything. Could be a fake.

TRENT. No, it is her – she was at the memorial service – they both were. I saw them.

LIV. You went to that?

TRENT. Course I did.

LIV (*referring to* MEL). Who's she then?

FAYE. This is Mel. She's my wife.

LIV. Oh. Alright.

MEL. Do you have a problem with that?

LIV. Why would we have a problem with that?

MEL. I wasn't –

LIV. I've got a problem with randos breaking into our workplace – the bonds of holy matrimony don't really come into it.

MEL. Right. Well… good.

FAYE. We didn't break in.

LIV. Trespassing then.

MEL. No, we're not trespassing either.

TRENT. So why are you here? (*Beat.*) Sorry. Hi, I'm Trent. I'm sorry for your loss.

FAYE. Oh. Thank you.

LIV. But also why are you here?

FAYE. It's a little complicated.

LIV. Was it a sex game? Did we just walk in on a sex game?

FAYE (*together*). No!

MEL (*together*). Not really.

FAYE. Not really?

LIV. Because honestly, I'd rather you were spies.

MEL. You didn't. Honestly.

LIV. Is that why you were doing a voice?

FAYE. Really that's not what was happening.

LIV. Because this is a place of business. Your father's business. And so walking in on… she's got her feet up on the desk – sitting in the chair he actually died in –

MEL. What?

TRENT. Yeah, um, that's where we found him.

MEL. Jesus. (*To* FAYE.) Did you know that?

FAYE. No! I mean they said 'at work', but –

TRENT. We wiped it down.

MEL. Fucking hell!

TRENT. Okay, so everyone's processing some new information. That's okay.

LIV. What are you doing?

TRENT. I'm de-escalating. I watched a tutorial.

LIV. You are the worst back-up ever.

TRENT. I actually feel like I'm really good back-up.

LIV (*to* MEL *and* FAYE). Why are you actually here though?

FAYE. Right. Um. Yeah, fair question. So, Eddie was my dad. We didn't always have the best of… That's not relevant. But we think there are some of his papers in here – some personal bits and pieces we'd like to get hold of. Does that make sense?

TRENT. Uh-huh.

LIV. What sort of papers?

MEL. None of your business.

LIV. See – that's why I don't trust them. (*To* FAYE.) Actually, I trust you, just not her.

FAYE. Just some stuff that belonged to my dad.

LIV. Yeah, but what though?

MEL. Could you just leave us alone please?

LIV. Oh, you'd love that, wouldn't you?

MEL. Yes.

LIV (*to* TRENT). They're definitely hiding something. She – (*Re: Faye.*) was literally hiding. Actually I don't trust either of them.

FAYE. Okay. It's okay. We're looking for his will. Um. It hasn't turned up yet. And there's some stuff with his estate that we're trying to clear up. We're going through everything at his house too, but we think it's more likely to be here.

LIV. Oh.

FAYE. And we didn't want to disturb anyone – I wasn't even sure whether anyone would be here – I thought things were winding down, maybe. But I found a set of keys at his place and thought we'd come check it out. Does that make sense?

TRENT. Yeah.

LIV. So why didn't you just say that?

MEL. Mostly because you started screaming.

FAYE. Is there anything else you'd like to ask us? Anything at all, and I'll do my best to answer.

A moment's thought.

TRENT. Why don't you have a wedding ring?

FAYE. Sorry?

TRENT. You said she was your wife, and she's got a wedding ring but you don't. Just wondered why.

LIV. Trent!

TRENT. What? She said anything.

LIV. What's that got to do with – ?

TRENT. It hasn't. I just noticed.

LIV. Jesus.

TRENT. Sorry. I notice things like that. And I know sometimes in straight couples the man doesn't, but I didn't know if there was like a standard lesbian way of doing things, or… Sorry.
I don't know if that's how you identify. I shouldn't have asked.

FAYE. Yeah, I really meant more questions about my dad, or –

TRENT. Yeah, I appreciate that.

MEL (*to* FAYE). But you did say about anything.

FAYE. Can you not?

MEL. What? I think it's a good question.

LIV. Okay, I'm also curious now.

FAYE. Yeah, I don't have a ring. It's not important.

MEL. Isn't it?

FAYE. Do we really have to do this now?

MEL. I didn't bring it up.

FAYE. Okay. Okay, so… Jesus Christ. So technically we're not actually married. Or civilly partnered. We're just… Just us. Um. But we tell people we're married, because it's simpler. People take you more seriously. But it's not only that. We like the solidity of it. The reassurance. We both agree it's a really nice thing.

LIV. So why not actually get married then?

MEL. That's another great question. I'm warming to you two.

FAYE. We will. We are going to, eventually, only weddings are expensive, and –

LIV. They don't have to be.

FAYE. And they take time to plan –

LIV. My mum and dad just did it at the registry office. Two mates as witnesses, went to the pub afterwards.

FAYE. Okay, yes – yes, we could've absolutely done that already, but… and no offence to anyone, but I don't see the point in that – of doing it *just* for the paperwork. I'm not going to get all Bridezilla, but I do think it should be an occasion – it should be significant. I don't think that's too much to ask. It's not… clerical. It's not like renewing a passport. I would like a proper wedding. And I thought that was understood –

MEL. It's understood.

FAYE. And yes, yes, maybe it's pre-emptory, seeing as we're not yet… but we did start using… We'd put Mrs and Mrs when we booked things, because it's nice, y'know? It made us both feel good. But then one day she just comes home with this ring – not for me, for her – she's wearing this wedding ring she bought for herself –

MEL. Because –

FAYE. And I say 'okay – okay, so should I be getting myself a ring now? Is that just what we're doing? Or are you going to get me one as well? Am I meant to be replacing yours?' because I was – of course I was going to get her a wedding ring, once there was an actual wedding, but now she's just gone and got one, and –

MEL. Because people ask – when you tell everyone you're married, people ask why you don't have a ring.

FAYE. No they don't!

MEL. They do! (*Gesturing to* TRENT.) He did! Case in point!

FAYE. Not on a daily basis.

MEL. And now we don't even talk about weddings any more. She just keeps telling everyone we're married. She introduces me as 'her wife'.

FAYE. That's because –

MEL. She's going to say it's my fault.

FAYE. You always say –

MEL. Because I say – I have been known to comment – that 'her wife' are the two most romantic words in the English language – which they are – they categorically are – she knows I think that. But as much as I do believe that, I also know that I'm not – I'm not actually, technically her wife, because we're not married, so it's a, uh, a bit of a double-edged sword, you know?

FAYE. So you just buy yourself a ring?

MEL. Because if you were ever going to ask me to marry you, you would've done it by now.

Beat.

FAYE. That's not fair.

TRENT. I'm really sorry I asked.

LIV. I'm not.

FAYE (*to* MEL). It takes two people not to propose. Two people not to plan a wedding.

MEL. Right.

FAYE. I have asked you to find time – to sit down with me and… Funny how it was never a priority when you had the big important job and I was the stay-at-home mum, but now, now I might be a sound investment –

MEL. That isn't fair.

FAYE. Isn't it?

MEL. You're right. It's stupid. I don't know why I wear it. It's stupid.

FAYE. Fine. (*To* TRENT *and* LIV.) Listen, do either of you know – is there anywhere else where my dad might have kept important papers? I'm his only real family – I should look into it. Do you know if there's a safe or anything?

TRENT. Got a few bits and pieces up in our workshop. Don't think it's anything important.

FAYE. Okay. Well maybe I could come and have a look. Would that be okay?

TRENT. Don't see why not.

LIV. We should get Omar. (*To* FAYE.) You should talk to Omar.

FAYE. Is he the person running things now?

LIV. He likes to think he is.

FAYE. That's fine. I need to have a conversation with him as well. (*To* MEL.) And you can… You can just keep going in here by yourself, can't you?

MEL. Seriously?

FAYE. That's what you said you wanted.

MEL. Right. Sure.

FAYE. Okay. (*To* TRENT.) Great. Lead on.

TRENT. Yeah. We're over in the main building.

> TRENT *spots the Hobnobs in the open box. He picks them out.*

> Ah – there they are. (*Beat – off their reactions*) What? It keeps the mice out. (*To* LIV.) You coming?

LIV. Yeah, right behind you.

FAYE (*to* MEL). I… It's just sensible, isn't it – to cover more ground?

MEL. You know what you're looking for?

FAYE. I think so, yeah.

MEL. Great. You know where to find me.

TRENT *shows* FAYE *out.* LIV *hangs back. A beat.*

LIV. Wow.

MEL. I'm fine.

LIV. You sure?

MEL. Yeah. You go ahead. Lots to do here.

LIV. I still don't know if I like you, but that was out of order.

MEL. It's fine. I'm sorry you got dragged into… whatever that was. I'm not really sure what just happened.

LIV. It's Trent. He's like that.

MEL. Right.

LIV. He's got bizarre powers of observation and very little filter. Like a really punchable Sherlock Holmes.

MEL. Got it.

LIV. Do you think he's cute?

MEL. Hmm?

LIV. Trent – do you think he's sexy?

MEL. Uh. No. No, I don't.

LIV. And is that because you objectively don't think he's sexy, or because he's nineteen and you're a lesbian?

MEL. The second one?

LIV. Right. (*Beat.*) It's very subjective, isn't it – attraction? It doesn't mean anything.

MEL. Do you like him?

LIV. Is it obvious?

MEL. It wasn't until just now.

LIV. I don't even know if I do fancy him. Mostly I just want to punch him a lot. Do you think that's the same thing?

MEL. Do you mind if I keep looking?

LIV. I don't have many female friends.

MEL. Right.

LIV. Sometimes I wish I was a lesbian.

MEL. Well there's nothing to stop you.

LIV. Yeah. (*Beat.*) Even if I was a lesbian I still wouldn't let my girlfriend talk to me like that. I wouldn't let anyone talk to me like that. Not a girlfriend, or a boyfriend, or a non-binary life partner –

MEL. She's going through a lot.

LIV. You bought your own wedding ring.

MEL. It wasn't expensive.

LIV. I don't think that makes it better.

MEL. It's not important.

LIV. I think it might be the saddest thing I've ever heard.

MEL. You probably have work to do, don't you?

LIV *shrugs*.

LIV. It's alright. Not even seen Omar yet.

MEL. So you're apprentices?

LIV. Yeah.

MEL. What does that mean?

LIV. That they don't have to pay us properly.

MEL. Oh.

LIV. So it's not actually that I'm being lazy, it's that I've got ideological objections to being paid four pounds an hour, and this is an exercise in passive resistance. I'm basically Gandhi.

MEL. Four pounds?

LIV. Shit, isn't it?

MEL. It's illegal.

LIV. Nah, it's because it's training. Technically we're being
trained, so...

*She changes the subject. She's settling herself in – clearly in
no rush to go anywhere.*

How long have you been not-married for?

MEL. Oh, um. Forever. Seventeen, almost eighteen years.

LIV. Wow. That's as old as I am.

MEL. Right.

LIV. Have you got kids?

MEL. Two, yeah. Boy and a girl.

LIV. I think you deserve a wedding. And a ring you didn't buy
yourself.

MEL. It's not important.

LIV. Her dad was a cheapskate too.

MEL. Hmm?

LIV. Eddie – not to speak ill of the dead, or anything.

MEL. You didn't like him?

LIV. He was an old straight white man, so...

MEL. Got it.

LIV. Everyone else will make out like he was a saint. I reckon
he was more of a cult leader.

MEL. Really?

LIV. I knew he had a wife who'd died. Didn't know he had kids
though.

MEL. Just Faye.

LIV. Right.

MEL. She's not his actual daughter – not biologically. She was about four or five, I think, when Eddie got together with her mum, but he adopted her – took the time to woo her back then, but it didn't take long for him to lose interest.

LIV. Because she wasn't an inanimate steel object?

MEL. Something like that.

LIV. Honestly, these fucking scissors. Omar's the same – worse, if anything. You know he doesn't even use computers.

MEL. What – not at all?

LIV. Yeah – (*Gesturing to the desk.*) this is all Eddie's old stuff – Omar won't touch it. Like he's genuinely allergic to them. We don't even have Wi-Fi. And he's in here like sixteen hours a day, driving himself crazy, and the way they'd both talk – in this mystical, this almost spiritual... And it's just bollocks. Like craftsmanship is one thing, then he starts wanging on about Einstein –

MEL. Oh, this is, um, don't tell me – Faye's tried to explain it – thermodynamics.

LIV. Fucking thermodynamics. Fuck-all to do with anything. RIP and everything, but he was a dickhead. Did my head in. (*Beat – a totally new thought.*) You know what, I'm properly gutted you're not industrial espionage.

MEL. Yeah?

LIV. Yeah. Would've been the most excitement I've had all year. You're not even from the paper.

MEL. What paper?

LIV. Omar keeps saying that *The Star* are going to come and do a feature on us. My nan asks about it every time I see her. But no, you're not even that. Just two dysfunctional boomer lesbians. No offence.

MEL. Full offence.

LIV. Have you done couple's therapy?

MEL. We don't need therapy.

LIV. Okay.

MEL. We're not boomers.

LIV. Okay.

MEL. My *parents* are boomers.

LIV. Sorry, anyone over twenty-five looks the same to me.

MEL (*moving things on*). So this boy – what was his name?

LIV. Trent?

MEL. Are you going to ask him out? Is he single?

LIV. I don't know. I think so.

MEL. Because your generation – you're not hung up about that kind of stuff, are you? You can just make a move. You're all just into TikTok and polyamory.

LIV. Yeah, maybe.

Beat.

MEL. She was wearing a wedding ring when I met her – Faye. She wasn't really out – she was sort-of out, a little bit, but she used to wear a wedding ring to stop men hitting on her, because she didn't want to have to say 'leave me alone, I'm gay', she'd rather say 'leave me alone, I'm married'.

LIV. Right.

MEL. Which never actually stopped them anyway. But then we got together, and of course we couldn't get married back then even if we wanted to, civil partnerships had only just become a thing, and what does it matter? It's only a piece of paper. And now we've got two kids, and a mortgage, and a diabetic hamster, and we're as good as married, we are, it makes no real difference, but she was wearing a wedding ring when we met and she doesn't wear one now and that's a bit fucked, isn't it?

LIV. Yeah.

MEL. That's not just me? And she's right, I could've made it happen. I could've proposed, and organised, and arranged,

because that's generally the way round... But I shouldn't
always have to, should I? But no – she has to wear a wedding
ring because she's so irresistible – she has to beat her suitors
off with a stick – not me. I don't wear this because men hit
on me – men have never hit on me, and thank fuck for that –
I wear it because I love her. I love her. It doesn't matter. None
of this matters. It's not important. Sorry.

LIV. What did she mean, when she said 'sound investment'?

MEL. What?

LIV. She said she was a sound investment.

MEL. Oh. Um. It's nothing. It's... We're used to me being the
breadwinner, but things are shifting. I'm not working at the
moment. It's fine. It's temporary.

LIV. And now she's inheriting this place? (*Beat*.) I'm not stupid.
You're looking for a will and she's talking about next-of-kin.

MEL. That's –

LIV. That is what's happening?

MEL. She's coming to realise that she doesn't need me. Which
is good – that's actually really good. It's healthy.

LIV. Right.

MEL. Because couples that need each other too much – that's
codependence.

LIV (*seemingly out of nowhere*). We are making money.

MEL. What?

LIV. We are – or at least we will be. Maybe not right this
second, but soon. Because I know you look around here and
it seems like a shithole, but things are changing.

MEL. Yeah?

LIV. We're making this big order for some company in China –
they want a full batch of everything we do, and if they like it,
they'll order thousands more – tens of thousands.

MEL. Really?

LIV. It's going to turn everything around. She should know about that – before anyone makes any big decisions.

MEL. Right.

LIV. Only it's taking forever, cos now Eddie's gone there's only really Omar who knows what he's doing. The rest of us are just apprentices, and they boot us all out in the summer.

MEL. Boot you out?

LIV. It's only a year-long training scheme.

MEL. And then what happens to you?

LIV shrugs.

Are there other places for you to go?

LIV. To make scissors?

MEL. Yeah.

LIV. What do you think?

MEL. So that doesn't work then, does it? It's not training if there's nowhere for you to go afterwards. It's just an excuse not to pay you properly.

LIV shrugs again.

Good. That's good to know.

LIV. But that's all going to change. It could all change, because we're stretched as it is, and when the new China order comes through it's going to get mental. They're going to need new people.

MEL. Right.

LIV. It doesn't make it okay for you to shut us down.

Beat.

MEL. I –

LIV. Because that's what you're planning, isn't it? I thought for a minute maybe you were just wanting to take over, like 'under new management', but actually –

MEL. It's a big conversation.

LIV. Right.

MEL. It's not –

LIV. Right. Okay, right. So I think I am actually going to go and call the police now. Because I don't know who you are. You could be anyone. But you're not staff, and you shouldn't have a key, and I do feel sorry for you because your life seems very sad to me, but that doesn't mean I like you. You're an intruder. You're intruding.

MEL. But you'll be gone in the summer.

LIV. Not the point.

MEL. Do you like working here?

LIV. Fuck you, actually.

MEL. Maybe you should make a proper plan for what you're going to do next. Set yourself some goals, think about how you're going to achieve them.

LIV. Maybe you should try to fix your failing not-marriage before you start fucking around in other people's business.

MEL. What is it that you'd really like to do – in the long term?

LIV. You're not my mate.

MEL (*with little energy left to argue*). Okay.

LIV. I can see why she doesn't want to marry you.

MEL. Right.

LIV. And whatever it is you're planning, it's not going to work. Let me tell you what's going to happen. You'll come in here, and you'll shut us down, kick us all out, fine – we'll thrive – we'll be off thriving – and you two… it's going to be like *Grand Designs* times a million. It's going to tear the two of you apart, and you'll go bankrupt, and you'll split up, and your children will get taken into care, and you'll die alone on the street as some haggard unemployed alcoholic, and it'll serve you right. I thought lesbians were cool. You bring shame on lesbians. (*She mimes ringing a bell at* MEL.) Shame.

LIV *goes*.

MEL *takes a moment. She checks her phone. She fiddles with her ring. Maybe she takes it off and puts it back on again. She takes a deep breath and turns her attention to the room again. She tries to calm herself by approaching things methodically. She moves a few boxes, checking their contents, and then finds an old, battered briefcase. She's about to open it when she hears other voices approaching. She freezes, she considers hiding in the cupboard, then draws herself up, projecting supreme confidence.*

OMAR (*off stage*). Just through here.

OMAR, *the operations manager of the factory, leads in* SUSIE.

I'm afraid it's not very – (*Spotting* MEL.) Oh.

MEL (*big smile, slightly manic energy*). Hi.

OMAR. Uh –

MEL. Hi. How do you do? Good morning. Let me guess – you must be Mr Sarbani. Omar, is it?

OMAR. Yes, that's right.

MEL. Isn't this place extraordinary?

OMAR. Uh… (*To* SUSIE.) Is she with you?

SUSIE. I don't believe so.

MEL (*shaking* OMAR*'s hand*). I'm Mel. It's a pleasure. (*Turning to* SUSIE.) Oh – and you're… Wait, I do know you! You're Susan – no, Susie, sorry.

SUSIE (*still to* OMAR). Or maybe she is.

MEL. You're Eddie's sister.

SUSIE. That's right.

MEL. We have met, but it was a very long time ago. Really wonderful to see you.

OMAR. Did you say Mel?

MEL. That's right. Would I be correct in thinking I'm in your office?

OMAR. Yes.

MEL. What a pleasure. What an honour. Genuinely.

OMAR. Have we met before?

MEL. No, I don't believe so. Not properly, anyway.

OMAR. Can I ask what – ?

MEL. Yes, yes, of course, yes! I'm Mel –

SUSIE. Yes, we have established that.

MEL. I'm Faye's wife.

SUSIE *and* OMAR *exchange looks*.

Faye Spenser – Eddie's daughter? (*To* SUSIE.) Your niece?
She's just stepped out.

OMAR. Oh!

MEL. I'm sure she'll be back soon.

SUSIE. You mean stepdaughter?

MEL. I'm sorry?

SUSIE. Eddie's stepdaughter.

MEL. Daughter. Eddie's daughter – his… (*Changing focus, to*
OMAR.) Can I just say you've been working miracles here –
genuinely.

OMAR. Thank you.

MEL. You must be exhausted. It can't be easy, trying to keep
your head above water.

OMAR. We don't do it because it's easy.

MEL. Even so –

SUSIE. You can drop the act.

MEL. Excuse me?

SUSIE. We all know what you're up to. I've already met your
fancy man.

MEL. My what?

SUSIE. The one in the cheap suit.

MEL. I'm not with you.

OMAR. There's a gentleman looking for you – well, for your wife, I believe. A Mr MacIntyre.

MEL. Oh.

OMAR. From some estate agents, or something like that? He didn't seem to want to say.

SUSIE. Spineless little snot.

MEL. Oh. Right. Yes. Good. I can handle all that.

OMAR. Handle what, exactly?

MEL. It's nothing to worry about.

SUSIE. Vultures. While his body's barely cold.

MEL. Excuse me?

OMAR. You've arranged some sort of site visit, some inspection, is that right?

MEL (*her smile beginning to waver*). Yes.

OMAR. For redevelopment?

> MEL *changes tack. Less smiley, steelier now.*

MEL. For preliminary assessment.

> SUSIE *laughs/scoffs.*

Just to get a sense of our options.

SUSIE. And what gives you the right?

MEL. This is a family-owned business, yes? It always has been – ever since the Spensers bought it, anyway. No board, no shareholders.

SUSIE. And what family are you?

MEL. And Faye stands to inherit her father's estate – why wouldn't she? It's only responsible that we look into his assets. (*To* OMAR.) And I am sorry, Mr Sarbani, for just arriving unannounced. We do need to have a proper, grown-up conversation, and I don't want you to think we've been going behind your back, but first we wanted to know exactly where we stood. I'm sure you understand.

OMAR. I had no idea she wanted to involve herself.

MEL. I don't think she was ever given the opportunity.

SUSIE. He wasn't her father.

MEL. I'm sorry?

SUSIE. She isn't *real* family – she's not a blood relation.

MEL. That's irrelevant.

SUSIE. When was the last time she came here? What right does she have?

MEL. Of course we want to honour your brother's legacy in any way we can. (*To* OMAR.) And the legacy of all the work you've done here.

OMAR. And what exactly – ?

SUSIE. I'm not prejudiced. I don't mean to speak unkindly. But hasn't he given the girl enough already? He took her in – put a roof over her head. And this is the thanks he gets.

MEL. She is his daughter – his legally adopted daughter – she is next in line to –

SUSIE. And you know that for a fact? You've seen the proof – the paperwork?

OMAR. Ladies, if I may? Of course any Spenser is always very welcome, but I would like to try and understand why either of you are here.

SUSIE (*mostly ignoring this*). Besides, Eddie didn't buy this factory, our father did – he bought it fifty years ago, and for fifty years my brother did as he pleased. Maybe it's time for some new management.

MEL. Yes, I agree.

SUSIE. Well you can get in line.

OMAR. I had no idea you were both so keen to get involved. That's wonderful. This is a very exciting time for us – challenging, but exciting.

SUSIE (*to* MEL). He thinks it's being left to him as well.

MEL. Oh?

SUSIE. We've got ourselves a good old-fashioned Mexican standoff.

MEL (*to* OMAR). You think Eddie was leaving the factory to you?

SUSIE. Sounds almost plausible, doesn't it? 'Bring me a man to carry on my legacy.'

OMAR. That isn't –

SUSIE. Forget about blood, forget lineage, just pluck any man off the street –

MEL (*to* OMAR). Is that true?

OMAR. The important thing is that the work keeps going. That was his only wish. I don't know what arrangements have been put in place, but Eddie was very clear that we should continue to do what we're doing – what we've always done.

SUSIE (*scathingly*). Oh, well so long as it was his dying wish.

MEL (*to* OMAR). But the business isn't viable, is it? Not as things stand?

OMAR. We're making headway.

SUSIE. It hasn't made money for fifty years, why would it change now?

OMAR. We're exploring new markets. We're processing a huge order for a Chinese buyer at the moment – the single largest order we've had in decades. There is demand.

SUSIE. I don't believe it.

OMAR. All the paperwork is here somewhere.

MEL. And who's going to make that order?

OMAR. We're working on it. And lineage is important – heritage was very important to him, I know. It wouldn't be the same without a Spenser at the helm. It's your name on the walls, after all. I think the three of us – (*To* MEL.) the four, with your wife, of course – I think if we could all work together –

SUSIE. Spenser and Son.

OMAR. I'm sorry?

SUSIE. That's what the signage says. 'Spenser and Son', not 'Spenser and Daughter'.

OMAR. I'm sure that –

SUSIE. Or 'Spenser and Stepdaughter', that's for certain.

MEL. She's not –

SUSIE. Daughters don't count – that's what seven decades have taught me.

OMAR. I believe –

SUSIE. I'm not especially interested in what you believe, Mr Sarbani, nor in what my brother would've wanted – God rest his soul – that is not my priority. I've spent long enough making space for him. But I am my father's daughter. I am the only Spenser-by-blood left standing, and I will take what's mine.

MEL. So what do you want to do with it?

SUSIE. I'm going to make something living. I'm going to bring it alive again.

OMAR. Mrs Spenser –

At this point LEO, *an old friend of Susie's, enters.*

LEO. Sorry to interrupt. (*To* SUSIE.) There you are.

SUSIE. Everything alright?

LEO. Yes, yes. Just seeing where you'd got to.

SUSIE. Melanie, this is Leo – Leo, Melanie. He's my escort for the day. (*Beat.*) Strictly business. Nobody get excited.

LEO (*to* MEL). Oh yes – we've met before. Years before. You're Faye's girl? Not *girl*, woman – you're Faye's –

SUSIE. Wife, Leo. You can say wife.

LEO. Oh – congratulations.

MEL. Thank you.

SUSIE. We're leaving. I don't think we have much left to talk about, do you? It's nothing personal, but it is my turn now. I've got big plans. You can let me know when my band arrives. Come on, Leo.

SUSIE *sweeps out and* LEO *follows*.

MEL. Did she say band?

OMAR. I believe so.

MEL. Is she still in a band? Wasn't she a rockstar or something, back in the day?

OMAR. I couldn't tell you.

MEL. Do you know what she's planning?

OMAR. No idea. (*Beat*.) So I take it you've no interest in making scissors?

MEL. Not especially.

OMAR. That's a pity. Perhaps I could show you what we do here?

MEL. That won't be necessary.

OMAR. And what is it that you do?

MEL. Does it matter? (*Beat*.) I'm a senior payroll manager.

OMAR. That sounds impressive.

MEL. I'm not working at the moment.

OMAR. Oh.

MEL. Just at the moment. Right now neither of us are working.

OMAR. I see.

MEL. Only recently. It's a new development. And we're not the sort of people... I've worked ever since I was sixteen. Faye only stopped when we had the kids. We've got two children now, and bills to pay, and Faye's mum didn't leave her anything.

OMAR. I understand.

MEL. And I know this is a building that at one point or another has meant a lot of things to a lot of people. I understand the emotional attachment. But I need to provide for my family. I need to make sure they're looked after. (*Beat.*) Are you married?

OMAR. Divorced.

MEL. Do you have children?

OMAR. One – a daughter. Zara.

MEL. How old?

OMAR. Twenty-four.

MEL. A grown-up then?

OMAR. I suppose. She's here today, actually. She helps out sometimes.

MEL. And she'll take over from you one day – is that the plan?

OMAR. No. No, I could never persuade her. Far too clever. She's going to do great things.

MEL. So you're not doing this to provide for her?

OMAR. I'm not motivated by money.

MEL. That must be very nice for you.

OMAR. I used to be. I was working in Canary Wharf before I came here – a metals analyst.

MEL. Really?

OMAR. But I needed to make some changes in my life. For myself – for my family. Tell me – do you enjoy being a senior payroll manager?

MEL. It's fine.

OMAR. Are you happy, Mrs Spenser?

MEL. I'm fine.

OMAR. What do you know about Heidegger?

MEL. Who?

OMAR. Martin Heidegger. German philosopher. He talks about living authentically. Existence is not a state of being, it is a series of actions and possibilities. To exist is to contain potential. And all of us – all of us are defined by what we do and what we could still do. Are you with me?

MEL. I'm going to keep going, if that's okay?

MEL *is half-listening while looking through some more papers.*

OMAR. We exist for the sake of ourselves. We're shaped by the world we're born into, we must live by rules we had no hand in creating, but within those systems we must always strive to remain true to ourselves – to live authentically. And the workman – the craftsman... To live authentically is to live as the craftsman does, wielding his hammer – the master craftsman, who doesn't think about where to place each blow, but knows it, deep within him. Instinct. Muscle memory. The hammer is an extension of his arm. He doesn't decide where it will fall, it just falls where it must. The craftsman lives a totally authentic existence.

MEL. I see.

OMAR. Everything we do here is done by hand. It cannot be replicated by machinery. It's instinctual. It's human. It's authentic.

MEL. Is it at all possible you've dedicated a large portion of your adult life to what was almost definitely only intended as a metaphor?

OMAR. It's a tricky concept to grasp.

MEL. I understand, I just don't *agree*.

OMAR. What we do here goes far beyond anything we make. It's the product and the gesture of the product. Did you ever meet Eddie?

MEL. Yeah, a handful of times.

OMAR. Did he talk to you about thermodynamics?

MEL. He tried to.

OMAR. The first law of thermodynamics is conservation. Conservation – to conserve – from the Latin *con*, meaning together, and *servare*, meaning to keep. To keep together. So conservation is heritage, it's stewardship. To *conserve*. To protect something, especially something of environmental or cultural importance, from harm or destruction. To preserve something authentic.

MEL. I thought it was a type of jam.

OMAR (*ignoring this*). But Einstein – Einsteinian conservation is about energy – energy transfer – that's your thermodynamics. Nothing created, nothing destroyed, only transformed. This is a transformative space, yes? We are in the business of transformation, and we embrace that contradiction – to preserve the past while adapting to the challenges ahead.

MEL. Transformation – like tearing the whole place down and starting again?

OMAR. Nothing destroyed.

MEL. No, only transformed.

OMAR. Conserved – kept together.

MEL. What if some things are better taken apart?

OMAR. I'm not sure I follow.

MEL. Do you pay a living wage?

OMAR. We run a training scheme.

MEL. So no?

OMAR. We offer something far more valuable – something transformative. If you met some of our apprentices here –

MEL. I have.

OMAR. You have?

MEL. A couple of them earlier.

OMAR. Okay.

MEL. You pay them four pounds an hour?

OMAR. It's a little over four pounds.

MEL. And your scissors sell for more than ninety. That's certainly transformative.

OMAR. Of course we'd like to pay them more. The goal is to have a fully funded workforce, absolutely, but the issue has been –

MEL. Victorian techniques, Victorian values, Victorian salaries?

OMAR. No –

MEL. It's not viable, is it? For all the romance of it. I might not know much about thermodynamics or German philosophy, but as someone who works in payroll –

OMAR. The government set the apprentice rate.

MEL. Right.

OMAR. They're training roles, we're very clear about that. And with the new relationships we're developing, I fully expect we'll be able to start offering salaried positions again soon. But the work is what matters. (*Beat.*) Can I ask what your plans are?

MEL. My plans?

OMAR. For the site – if you got your way?

MEL (*thinks*). Why not? It's very early days, but we think residential units offer the best yield.

OMAR. Housing?

MEL. Yes. Destination housing.

OMAR. I see.

MEL. It's a practical use. You have far more space here than you need. You can't maintain it. You could always set up somewhere else – after the summer, maybe, once this batch of apprentices have gone.

OMAR. You can't just force us out.

MEL. What 'us'? Won't it be only you then?

OMAR. We'll find a way to keep going.

MEL. We'll do it properly – keep as much of the spirit of the
building as we can – preserve – *conserve* it. Spenser House.
The Spenser Building, maybe. Spenser Works. A new legacy.

OMAR. Bulldoze it all and make the Spenser Memorial Car
Park?

MEL. No, I don't think that would be a good return on
investment.

OMAR. No.

MEL. People need housing. That's not frivolous, that's a basic
need. There's a housing crisis in this country, actually. A crisis
of affordable... And people will be employed to renovate, to
refurbish, to market the properties, draw up contracts, dozens
and dozens if not hundreds of people, all getting paid a real
wage. And new people will come and live here and get jobs
and start families and support the local economy with
artisanal coffees and furniture made from reclaimed industrial
equipment, and maybe, maybe each flat could get a pair of
scissors as a moving-in present. Maybe we could commission
that, as a parting gift. A lovely little presentation box, a silk
ribbon, a link to your website, and they'd feel like they were
a part of something, that they were living somewhere special,
somewhere with history, but it *is* history. It is past. People
don't need scissors. They don't need beautiful, hand-crafted,
ninety-pound scissors, however impressive they might be.
But they do need somewhere to live.

OMAR. So this is altruism?

MEL. It's a more sensible use of the space.

OMAR. And they'd be affordable, would they?

MEL. I would hope so. Within reason.

OMAR. I see.

MEL. I won't pretend it's charity. I'm not particularly interested
in your opinion. I don't require you to like me. I have a
family. I'm going to secure something for them.

OMAR. I think if you had a chance to properly connect with what we're doing –

MEL. But it's making scissors.

OMAR. Yes, but –

MEL. I haven't misunderstood that?

OMAR. It's so much more than –

MEL. No, it isn't. You make scissors – very nice, very good scissors. But… I'm going to say something now and it's going to sound ruder than I want it to, but the problem with men like you is that ultimately you're neither as special or as interesting as you think you are. I see it all the time, and it's great that you think you've found your calling, but it doesn't make it significant. If you made candles, you'd talk about Prometheus, and cavemen discovering fire, if you were a carpenter, you'd talk about… Jesus, probably. And I am all for passion, I am, believe me, but this isn't alchemy, it's manufacturing. It's only rare because there are better ways to do it now. Find something else.

FAYE *comes in. We're not sure how long she's been outside for.*

FAYE. Is that what you think?

MEL. Hey. (*To* OMAR.) I'm sorry. I did say it was going to sound rude.

OMAR. And you were right.

MEL (*to* FAYE). How did you get on?

FAYE. Yeah, fine. (*To* OMAR.) I'm Faye – Faye Spenser – we have met before. Can I apologise for my wife?

MEL. I'd rather you didn't.

OMAR. I'm very sorry for your loss, Mrs Spenser.

FAYE. Thank you.

OMAR. I've just been getting up to date on all your plans.

FAYE. Well, nothing's set in stone yet.

OMAR. I don't think you've visited us here for quite some time. Perhaps this is a moment to reconnect.

FAYE. Yeah, that's what I've been doing actually.

OMAR. I'm glad to hear it.

MEL (*to* FAYE). Do you want to go outside? Get a coffee and talk?

FAYE. No thanks. (*Looking around*.) You know this used to be a really nice office. It wasn't always like this.

MEL. Did you find anything?

FAYE. Not really, but I did have some good chats. I'd love an office like this. Your office is horrible. Your old office, I mean. But this could be lovely. (*To* OMAR.) I used to have a lovely office back in the day, back before the kids. Much nicer than hers. (*Beat*.) He died in here?

OMAR. Yes, I'm afraid so.

FAYE. Probably what he would've wanted. I suppose you knew him much better than I did?

OMAR. We certainly spent a lot of time together.

FAYE. Do you know he only wrote to me twice in his life? I mean who writes letters these days anyway, but still… He wrote me two of them, not including birthday cards. The first one was when he adopted me, and it was beautiful, and it was illustrated – he was actually a pretty good artist – and it talked about Mum, and how much he loved her, and how he was going to provide for us, and he explained what this place did – lots of scissors doodled in the margins, and – and I know this came from a good place – and he wrote about how one day once I was married, my husband would take over from him. And there's a little sketch of us – me and my hypothetical future husband – sat probably at this very desk, but he's the one in charge, I'm just sort of hovering behind him. And I can't be mad about it, not really. He was a product of his time, and he was trying his best. And the second letter – the second one was after the second or third time he'd met you – (*Re: Mel*.) and we were already living together by then, we'd been together for years, and he wrote me this actually in some ways very sweet letter that was sort of an apology, and he said 'I'm sorry – I always thought this was a phase you were going to grow out of, but I see now I was wrong, and I see that she makes you happy, and I don't...' and he was very precise with language, so I have memorised this – 'I don't entirely understand it, but I accept the reality of the situation.' And I thought okay – okay, that's good enough for me. And anyway, would you believe it, but it's actually only a week or so later that I first hear about you, Mr Sarbani, this dazzling young man who just arrived on his doorstep, who talks about physics and philosophy and knows all about metal and is the answer to all his prayers. And I realise then that these two things are connected – he's not giving me his blessing so much as he's letting me go, he's writing me off, because he's found his son and heir now. Because he's finally accepted I'm never going to snag a husband, and of course no husband means no grandchildren, so that's the end of the road, really. And I'm only adopted family anyway, so why not cast the net a little further? And here you are.

OMAR. I'm sorry if I ever came between you. Perhaps there's an opportunity now – ?

FAYE. No, I think we're past all that. (*To* MEL.) Yeah, we should talk.

A knock at the door. OMAR *sighs.*

OMAR. What now?

MEL. Don't look at me.

OMAR (*calling off*). Come in!

XANDER *enters. He wears a slightly shiny suit.*

XANDER. Hello. (*To* OMAR.) Sorry. Hello again. I'm looking for Mrs Spenser?

MEL. You'll have to be more specific. (*To* FAYE.) Did you know your aunt's here too?

FAYE. Is she? Why?

MEL. Hard to say.

XANDER. Sorry. Faye Spenser?

FAYE. That's me.

XANDER. Xander MacIntyre, Claybourne-Harris.

FAYE. Oh, right, yes.

MEL (*shaking* XANDER'*s hand*). I'm Melanie – I think we spoke on the phone.

XANDER. Excellent. I'm sorry we're late getting started.

MEL. Not at all – I'm glad you could come.

OMAR. Right. Right, this is what I'm going to allow. I have work to do. I have staff to check in on. You can stay in here – discuss whatever it is you need to discuss. You won't find me to be unreasonable, but there is nothing more important than the work we do here. The work has to continue. Well then.

OMAR *goes*.

XANDER. I didn't realise the site would be so active.

MEL. No, neither did we. Thanks for bearing with us.

XANDER. Of course.

FAYE (*to* MEL). Why were you being so horrible to him?

MEL. I wasn't.

FAYE. You were – I heard you.

XANDER. Did you still want to have a walkaround?

MEL. Yes, absolutely.

FAYE. Actually, we need to have a conversation first.

MEL. I think we've wasted enough of everyone's time already.

FAYE. No, it's important. (*To* XANDER.) Do you mind?

XANDER. I'm sorry?

FAYE. Xander – was it Xander?

XANDER. Yes.

FAYE. Do you think you could just wait outside for us for
a minute – it isn't raining or anything, is it?

XANDER. No.

FAYE. Great.

MEL. Can we just – ?

FAYE (*still to* XANDER). Thank you – I really appreciate it –
we won't be long.

XANDER *smiles a little awkwardly and goes*.

MEL. What's going on?

FAYE. I don't like fighting with you.

MEL. Okay.

FAYE. I didn't mean anything before.

MEL. Which specific thing didn't you mean?

FAYE. I…

MEL. It's okay. We can talk about it later.

FAYE. No, this is important.

MEL. No, the inspection is important. It's fine. It can wait. We
should get on.

FAYE. I met another of the apprentices – got to know them all
a bit better. They're good kids. They've been totally screwed
over.

MEL. Yeah.

FAYE. It made me really sad.

MEL. We'll be doing them a favour.

FAYE. Hmm?

MEL. It's like I said. Shutting it down will be doing everyone
here a favour.

FAYE. Do you think?

MEL. It's slave labour. It's criminal. You know they're on four
pounds an hour?

FAYE. Yeah, they said – something like that.

MEL. It's exploitation. He got to me – that's why I was having a go.

FAYE. Right.

MEL. He's not a good guy.

FAYE. I kept on thinking about Max and Joni, and how we'd feel if –

MEL. Max and Joni aren't going to end up somewhere like this.

FAYE. How do you know?

MEL. Because they won't.

FAYE. They could!

MEL. Because we're going to provide for them. That's what we're doing here. We're going to make sure they're provided for.

FAYE. What if we changed our plans?

MEL. How do you mean?

FAYE. What if we did take things over? They were talking about this big new deal with China, this huge… What if we could turn it around? We don't have to just sell it off. We could get involved. Hear me out –

MEL. No.

FAYE. Just no?

MEL. We made a plan.

FAYE. They train them for a year and then they just get kicked out onto the street again.

MEL. I know, but –

FAYE. We could offer them something real.

MEL. We need something real. We decided for our family –

FAYE. This is my family!

MEL. Excuse me?

FAYE. My family. My history, my heritage, my… We could create a new… Spenser and Daughter. Wouldn't that be better?

MEL. No, I don't think that would be better.

FAYE. I think I can make you change your mind. Wait there.

FAYE *gets down on one knee. She digs into her pocket and pulls out what looks like two somewhat misshapen rings.*

MEL. No. Stop it.

FAYE. Melanie Spenser – Melanie Larchwood –

MEL. What are you doing? Where did you get these?

FAYE. Will you do me the honour –

MEL. No, just stop for a second. What actually are these?

FAYE. Scissor handles.

MEL. Right.

FAYE. Off the little embroidery scissors. I just found them – offcuts – they were going spare.

MEL. Uh-huh.

FAYE. So actually they might still be a bit sharp in places.

MEL. Great.

FAYE. Think of it as a prototype – work-in-progress.

MEL. Can you get up?

FAYE. But two lesbian wedding rings made out of scissor handles – come on –

MEL. Faye –

FAYE. No, but seriously – I'm serious – because here's the thing about scissors. The scissors they make here are matched pairs, right? You do all the sharpening, the buffing, the whatever, and then the very last bit is making sure they fit together perfectly – that's the hardest step – because it's all just done by feel. No two pairs are the same.

MEL. She's right, it is an actual cult.

FAYE. You're my other half.

MEL. Can you just stand up please?

FAYE. It's not codependency, we're just a perfectly matched
    pair.

MEL. Please.

FAYE. You wanted this!

MEL. No, not like –

FAYE. I'm trying my best. What more do you want?

On this, MASON, *another apprentice, walks in.*

MASON. Omar? You in here? There's these two women and –
    (*Sees them.*) Nope. Not interested. Don't need to know.
    Didn't see it.

MASON *walks straight out again.*

MEL (*to* FAYE). Stand up. Just stand up. Let's do what we
    came for.

FAYE. What's the matter?

MEL. Please.

FAYE. I know they look shit right now. I'll get them finished
    properly. We can have stones put in them if you like. I just
    got excited by the… Two rings from the one perfect pair!
    Isn't that romantic?

MEL (*unenthusiastically*). Yeah.

FAYE. So, Spenser and Wife. What do you say?

MEL. That wasn't the deal.

FAYE. I know, but –

MEL. We're not going to take over a scissor factory.

FAYE. Why not?

MEL. I shouldn't have to explain why not.

FAYE. This is –

MEL. No. No. We need security. We need stability. We need –

FAYE. But it's not your choice, is it?

MEL. What?

FAYE. I mean technically you don't get to decide. It isn't yours. It isn't your family.

MEL. Oh. Right.

FAYE. Is it? So maybe for once you don't get to tell me what to do.

MEL. That isn't fair.

FAYE. No, it isn't.

MEL. We agreed.

FAYE. I don't actually remember agreeing. I remember coming back from town one day and you showing me a spreadsheet.

MEL. I wanted to look at the numbers before –

FAYE. About what *we* should do. What you had calculated was best for *us*. Because you were feeling guilty. Because you went postal at work and got put on enforced leave and now you don't know what to do with yourself. But this isn't a *you* thing, or even an *us* thing, it's a *me* thing, a my-family thing – you don't have any claim over it. And I'm asking you to do this with me, I'm inviting you, but I don't have to. And you can't just keep deciding things unilaterally. You can't just come home one day wearing a wedding ring and act like I'm the crazy one. You can't just decide you have a wife, you need to be a wife too. You need to participate, you need to talk to me, you need to get on board with… Forget it.

MEL. Okay.

FAYE. But this was me trying. This was me trying to bring you in.

MEL. We came here today with a plan.

FAYE. I know you did.

MEL. And it's a good plan. It sets us up.

FAYE. I don't care about that.

MEL. I do. I'm going to go and talk to Xander. He's come out to meet us and it'd be rude not to. I want his opinion on the space. Do you want to come with us?

FAYE. No.

MEL. Okay, that's fine. I'll make notes.

FAYE. I'm serious about this.

MEL. Then we can compare notes.

FAYE. You're saying no then? Just to be clear?

MEL. I don't mind being the bad guy. That's fine. I'm going to take care of our family. (*Beat.*) I'll be just outside.

MEL *goes.* FAYE *doesn't move.*

End of Act One.

ACT TWO

About fifteen minutes later. The space is empty. COCO *and*
MOLLY, *both early twenties, enter. They're an art-pop duo
dressed in their civilian clothes, carrying bags with them. They
look very much like they could be Faye and Mel, around fifteen
years ago.*

MOLLY. You sure?

COCO. It's fine. (*Calling out.*) Hello? (*Back to* MOLLY.) See,
    it's fine.

MOLLY. But are we allowed to be in here?

COCO. We're allowed to be anywhere.

MOLLY. But genuinely? As in you've actually cleared it with
    someone?

COCO. No one's around, are they?

MOLLY. What's that smell?

COCO. Don't be rude.

MOLLY (*looking around*). What's going on with all this?

COCO. Leave things alone. It's fine. We're out of the way.

MOLLY. So we're not allowed in here?

COCO. I just mean no one's going to disturb us. I heard voices
    from the big building across the yard.

MOLLY. Right.

COCO. But I'll keep a lookout.

MOLLY. Is it weird that I want to do some filing?

COCO. Yes.

MOLLY (*picking through some papers*). Look at the state
    though. Who can work like this?

COCO. Stop it! Just stop it and pay attention to me.

MOLLY. Okay! (*Spotting something*.) Ooh, nice lamp.

COCO. You're ridiculous.

MOLLY. Am I?

COCO. Now get your clothes off, we haven't got all day.

MOLLY. Wow.

COCO. I mean it.

MOLLY. What is it that they make here?

COCO. Scissors.

MOLLY. Really?

COCO. Yeah. They're like really famous scissors.

MOLLY. I was just imagining something a bit more glamorous – from how you'd described it.

COCO. Well that's our job.

MOLLY. What is?

COCO. To bring the glamour. (*Beat*.) We didn't have to come. I thought you were into it.

MOLLY. No, I am.

COCO. Yeah?

MOLLY. Course.

COCO. So you're not pissed off at me?

MOLLY. Why would I be pissed off?

COCO. I don't know, that's why I'm asking.

MOLLY. I'm not.

COCO. Okay, good. (*Beat*.) Look, I know it's not... I'm not saying it's ideal, but any time you want to find us something better –

MOLLY. I wasn't complaining.

COCO. Okay.

MOLLY. It's good. It's great. It's...

>MOLLY *opens the walk-in cupboard door. She screams.*

Jesus shitting Christ!

COCO. What?

>FAYE *emerges from the cupboard. She's been crying.*

FAYE. Sorry – I'm sorry.

COCO. What the fuck?

FAYE. I'm really sorry.

MOLLY. What's going on?

COCO. Mace her! Mace her in the face.

FAYE. Please don't.

MOLLY. Who are you?

FAYE. I'm sorry. I wasn't expecting... I thought if I was quiet you might just leave, but –

COCO. Who are you though?

FAYE. I'm Faye. I'm not... Everything's okay.

COCO. No it isn't.

FAYE. It is. It's fine. I'm fine. Do you, um, do you both work here too?

MOLLY. What?

FAYE. Are you the other apprentices?

COCO. No.

FAYE. Who are you then?

MOLLY. Um – we'll ask the questions.

FAYE. I... I'm the owner, actually.

COCO. Really?

FAYE. Yes. Why wouldn't I be? I'm a very good owner, as it happens. I'm a natural. It's in my blood. Not my actual blood, but... This is all mine, anyway.

COCO. So you're Susie?

FAYE. Excuse me?

COCO. You're Susie Spenser?

FAYE. No.

COCO. Because that's who we're meant to be meeting.

FAYE. Really?

COCO. That's what it says in my email. Hang on, I'll check.

FAYE. Why are you...? Susie doesn't own anything.

MOLLY. Why were you hiding in the cupboard?

FAYE. It's been a long day.

MOLLY. It just doesn't seem like something someone in a position of power or authority would do.

FAYE. You'd be surprised.

COCO (*finding her email*). Yeah, here it is. Susie Spenser. Is she here?

FAYE. I think maybe somewhere, but –

COCO. Great. Well she hired us, and she's in charge, so... (*Beat.*) Do you think you could go away then please? We need to get changed.

FAYE. Hired you for what?

COCO. For the photoshoot.

FAYE. Right...

MOLLY. We're Co-Codamol. (*Beat.*) We're the band? (*To* COCO.) Are you sure we're in the right place?

COCO. Yes!

FAYE. Did Susie tell you she owned this building?

COCO. Doesn't she?

FAYE. No!

MOLLY. Then why is her name above the door?

FAYE. It isn't! That's not her name – well it is, but she's not *the* Spenser, she's *a* Spenser. I'm the Spenser in charge.

MOLLY. So why were you in the cupboard?

FAYE. Why has she hired a band? No. You know what? It doesn't even matter. I think she's already left, actually. I don't think there's any reason for you to be here.

COCO. I don't believe you.

MOLLY. Maybe we should go though, because this feels really dodgy.

COCO. She's dodgy, this is fine.

MOLLY. You said we weren't even getting paid.

FAYE. Well then –

COCO. *Yet* – I said we weren't getting paid *yet*.

MOLLY. But –

COCO. No buts! We're not going anywhere.

FAYE. You're on private property, actually.

COCO. Call the police then. (*To* MOLLY.) She won't. She's dodgy as fuck. But we're professionals. We made a commitment. And we've played weirder gigs than this, let's be honest.

FAYE. No. No, I'm sorry but I really think you should leave.

MOLLY (*to* COCO). Can we?

COCO *sits down in Eddie's old chair.*

COCO. I'm not going anywhere.

FAYE. You might not want to sit there though.

COCO. I'll sit where I want. I don't get pushed around by mad women in closets.

MOLLY. What if she's about to murder us though?

COCO. Then we'll murder her first.

FAYE. Uh –

COCO (*to* MOLLY). Fine – go. You can go if you want to go. This wasn't your thing. I'm the one who's set it up, who's been replying to a million emails –

MOLLY. That's not –

COCO. Do you know the way old women write emails? They're insane. And yeah, I know this all seems a bit shit, I get it, but we're hardly being inundated with offers. And what have you been doing, Mol? What are you finding for us?

MOLLY. I –

COCO. You know what, I'd actually like you to go. It's about time I went solo.

MOLLY. That's not what I'm saying.

COCO. I am. Piss off, both of you.

MOLLY. Fine. Enjoy being murdered.

MOLLY *picks up a bag, starts to leave.*

FAYE (*firmly*). Wait!

MOLLY *stops.*

Wait, just wait a moment. (*To* MOLLY.) Now you – you come back here, young lady. Put that down. (*To* COCO.) And you, just cool down for a moment. Is this how the two of you communicate?

COCO. What?

FAYE. Is this how you talk to each other?

MOLLY. What's happening?

FAYE. You're a band, yeah? You said you were a band. Are there any more of you? Is it just you two?

MOLLY. Um, yeah, actually it's us and Svetlana, and she's six-foot-six and she knows how to karate so if you try anything –

FAYE. Okay.

COCO. It's just us two.

FAYE. Right.

COCO (*to* MOLLY). Svetlana?

MOLLY *shrugs*.

FAYE. And how long have you been together? (*Beat*.) Please.

MOLLY. Four or five years.

COCO. More than five now.

MOLLY. Yeah?

COCO (*to* FAYE). We met at uni.

FAYE. Five years. And do you always fight like this?

COCO. It's normal to –

FAYE. Yeah. No, you're right, it is. It's normal to fight. It's healthy. But you're a band, yeah? You've been a band for five years – you can't just walk out on that. You've built something between you. You have a history. You share… Do you, uh, do you write songs together?

MOLLY. Yeah?

COCO. We're a real band.

FAYE. Okay. So what happens to your songs, if you break up? Who owns them? What happens to you? Are you just going to start another band with someone else?

COCO. Are you okay?

FAYE. You can't talk to her like that.

MOLLY. It's not –

FAYE. You can't just say 'I've made a decision, and if you don't like it you can leave', because maybe one day she will.

COCO. I wasn't –

FAYE. No. Don't give ultimatums. Don't call her bluff. Because you don't know. You don't. You don't…

COCO *gets up*.

COCO. Here, why don't you sit down?

FAYE. I'm fine.

COCO. Go on.

FAYE. No, honestly. That chair's not…

COCO. What?

FAYE. Nothing. Doesn't matter. It was my father's, that's all. (*Beat*.) He, um, he used to run this place. He's the Spenser on the sign. Well, he's the son, technically. (*Moving away, looking around at the mess*.) We really didn't get very far, did we? Still so much to do.

> FAYE *picks up an archive box. As she does, its bottom immediately collapses, and papers spill all over the floor. FAYE lets out a whimper and sinks to the floor.*

COCO. Hey – hey – it's okay.

FAYE (*fighting back tears*). This isn't even my quadrant.

> MOLLY *mouths 'what the fuck?' to* COCO *over* FAYE'*s head.*

COCO. That's okay. Don't worry about that. So your dad was… Does that make Susie your aunt?

> FAYE *nods.*

That's cool. I'd love it if she was my aunt. Although that'd make me what – fifty?

> FAYE *sighs. She's recovering.*

No, because she's a legend, isn't she? Old-school rock and roll. The real deal.

FAYE. She'd certainly like to think so.

COCO. I actually didn't believe it was her when she emailed me – thought it was spam or phishing or something – but we chatted, and she said she'd found us online, and she'd inherited this old scissor works from her brother and it's going to be epic, like the new Factory.

FAYE. The what?

COCO. You know – Factory Records in Manchester?

MOLLY. Or The Factory in New York.

COCO. Yes! Like Andy Warhol.

MOLLY. Yes! Legend.

COCO. She talked a lot about Andy Warhol, and art, and industry, and the next generation. And she needs images to sell it, because she won't actually get any gigs on for a while, so we're coming down for a photoshoot and it's going to be this massive thing, it's going to be... (*Now more to* MOLLY.) People would kill for this. Bands would literally kill for... You can't buy that publicity.

FAYE. A music venue?

COCO. And a studio – like a whole complex. (*To* MOLLY.) And we'd be the face of it! (*Back to* FAYE.) Look, clearly this is the right place, so do you know where she is?

FAYE. I don't, sorry.

MOLLY (*to* COCO). Should we go and try to find someone a bit less... Sorry, I'm trying not to say 'insane'.

FAYE. No – no. You stay here. I'm going to go. I've got to talk to... A music venue, really? Doesn't matter. You stay here. If I bump into her I'll send her your way. Just... Open communication, and... (*Spots something.*) Great shoes. I used to have shoes a bit like that. Okay. Sorry for... I'm going to leave now.

COCO. Great.

FAYE *goes. A beat.*

MOLLY. I'm not being dramatic, but I think we're going to die here.

COCO. It's fine – let's just get changed.

MOLLY. We're not even getting paid. If this Susie woman is such a big deal –

COCO. It's good – it's good for...

MOLLY *starts tidying/moving boxes through this.*

MOLLY. People die of exposure, Coco.

COCO. It's not –

MOLLY. I'm just saying. Mountaineers, Sherpas.

COCO. Okay.

MOLLY. Starving artists.

COCO. I know.

MOLLY. You go into M&S and try to pay with exposure –

COCO. I know, Molly! I know! I saw when you tweeted it! What are you doing?

MOLLY. It calms me down.

COCO. Leave it alone.

MOLLY. Maybe there's something in here we can use – for the pictures.

COCO. Anyway, it isn't just about exposure, it's about getting in on the ground floor.

MOLLY. Ground-floor flats are the most dangerous places to live.

COCO. Oh for fuck's sake!

MOLLY. What? They are. That's just a true fact.

COCO. Susie Spenser is important. She's got her own Wikipedia page.

MOLLY. Really?

COCO. I sent you a link. (*Beat.*) Let's just get through it.

MOLLY. Fine.

They start to get their costumes out of their bags. They're basically highly customised boiler suits – not a million miles away from the uniforms the apprentices wear, but heavily blinged up. The more ridiculous accessories the better. Think Lady Gaga with a hot-glue gun and too much spare time at the Moor Market.

I still feel weird that we don't have instruments.

COCO. We don't need them for pictures.

MOLLY. But they make us look legit.

COCO. She said not to. (*Beat.*) Have you got the LED strips?

MOLLY. We don't use them in photoshoots.

COCO. Okay.

MOLLY. They look cheap.

COCO. Okay.

   Beat.

MOLLY. Before – that was a her-problem, wasn't it?

COCO. What?

MOLLY. That woman – she clearly had something else going on? We're okay.

COCO. Yeah.

MOLLY. Good. (*Beat.*) And this Susie woman – she's good vibes?

COCO. A hundred per cent.

MOLLY. Do you think she was really mates with Andy Warhol?

COCO. Probably. We could be the next Velvet Underground.

MOLLY. Right.

COCO. Or Rolling Stones.

MOLLY. Or Salvador Dalí.

COCO. Okay.

MOLLY. Salvador Dalí used to hang out with Andy Warhol. (*Beat.*) He did.

COCO. Picasso came here.

MOLLY. What?

COCO. She was telling me, in one of her emails – Picasso came to Sheffield in the fifties and he got shown round here. Even sketched it. Because what they do here is art.

MOLLY. Did she know Picasso?

COCO. Maybe? I don't know. (*Beat*.) It's just raw, isn't it? But raw is good. Didn't you get shivers when you walked in?

MOLLY. I get shivers from haunted houses.

COCO. All the best gig venues look like somewhere you might get murdered.

MOLLY. Yeah, fair.

COCO. Is that really true about ground-floor flats?

MOLLY. What?

COCO. That they're more dangerous?

MOLLY. Yeah.

COCO. Why?

MOLLY. Cos they're easier to break into. You know my parents bought that flat for Jamie in Manchester?

COCO. Uh-huh.

MOLLY. The ground-floor ones were going for way less, cos people didn't want them.

COCO. Right.

MOLLY. There's probably a tweet in that.

COCO. What?

MOLLY. 'Getting in on the ground floor means you're more likely to get robbed.'

COCO. Right.

MOLLY. Do you think that's something?

COCO. Maybe.

MOLLY. Twitter stresses me out.

COCO. Houses have ground floors.

MOLLY. What?

COCO. All houses have ground floors, don't they? And they cost more than flats.

MOLLY *shrugs. Around this point they start to change into their performance costumes.* MOLLY *is now changing her shoes for platform boots.*

You didn't say you were doing platforms. (*Beat.*) I've not got heels.

MOLLY. That's fine.

COCO. Were you actually serious about walking out before?

MOLLY. Were you serious about going solo? (*Beat.*) We don't have to talk about it.

COCO. Okay.

MOLLY. You wouldn't get anywhere.

COCO. I know. I didn't mean it, I just… I'm trying to make something happen. We do actually have to make something happen, don't we? If we're serious about this –

MOLLY. You can't force it.

COCO. Yeah, but –

MOLLY. It's an organic process.

COCO. That's an excuse.

MOLLY. No, it's… We don't have to do the shit stuff. We don't have to jump at every little… Why would we want to be the face of anything before we even know what our sound is? We should be getting back in the studio, making demos –

COCO. We can't afford to get back in the studio.

MOLLY. It's about priorities.

COCO. We need to book gigs – get ourselves out there.

MOLLY. Only when we're ready.

COCO. But –

MOLLY. I'm in no rush.

COCO. Yeah, Mol, but you're minted.

Beat.

MOLLY. That isn't fair.

COCO. It's not an attack.

MOLLY. That has nothing to do with –

COCO. It does. It kind of does. Because I'm really skint. I'm skint and my mum won't bail me out any more, and I need to make something happen. Because if I can't show her… I'm sorry you think this is shit. I'm sorry it smells in here. I'm sorry no one takes us seriously, or likes your tweets, or books us for Brixton Academy, but I'm working with what we've got. I'm twenty-four and I've got like fifty grand of debt and –

MOLLY. That doesn't matter!

COCO. It does!

MOLLY. Student loans don't matter – you don't have to pay them back.

COCO. You do.

MOLLY. Not if you never earn enough.

COCO. So just be skint forever?

MOLLY. I'm in this for the music – I don't care about the money.

COCO. That's because you already have the money though.

MOLLY. How much do you need?

COCO. That's not –

MOLLY. Go on.

COCO. I'm not –

MOLLY. It's not like you've never asked me for money before.

COCO. I know.

MOLLY. So don't just fucking ambushing me with –

COCO. I'm sorry.

MOLLY. You're not poor.

COCO. What?

MOLLY. I know your parents. I've seen their place.

COCO. Yeah, but –

As MOLLY *gets angrier she starts to take off her boiler suit again, which proves quite tricky. She's hopping around.*

MOLLY. But nothing. Don't make excuses. If you want to go solo, fine. If you think you can do this without me, then fine. Or actually if you're just trying to pick a fight – great, you can have one. I don't need you either. She was right – that mad crying woman. You don't get to give me orders. It's not photoshoot at the murder factory or nothing. That's a really shitty ultimatum.

COCO (*as* MOLLY *struggles with a zip*). Stop it – you're going to tear it.

MOLLY. So I'll buy another one, right? I'll just throw money at the problem.

COCO. Molly –

MOLLY. It's cheap, anyway. It's cheap and it's shit and I'm tired of it too.

COCO. You're caught on something.

MOLLY. You're not better than me.

COCO. I know. Come here –

MOLLY. Get off me.

COCO. Don't just pull it.

MOLLY. Let go!

MOLLY *pushes* COCO *away, stumbles, and they both end up on the floor,* MOLLY *in a state of undress. At the same moment,* AVA, *another apprentice, walks in. She sees them.*

AVA (*gasps*). Lesbians!

MOLLY *and* COCO *pull themselves back up to their feet.*

MOLLY. Excuse me?

AVA. Sorry. That just came out.

MOLLY. Fucking hell!

COCO (*to* AVA). Who are you? Don't you knock?

AVA. Sorry. Liv did say that two dysfunctional lesbians had broken into the offices, but she made it sound like you were much older.

MOLLY. No, no, I am done with this –

COCO. Mol –

MOLLY. I'm finished. (*To* AVA.) Actually, who the fuck are you though?

AVA. I'm Ava. I work here.

MOLLY. So there are people still working here?

AVA. Oh yeah. You've made up then?

COCO. What?

AVA. They said you were fighting earlier. So was it make-up sex or break-up sex? Or just general sex? Doesn't bother me. I'd have put the lock on though.

MOLLY. It locks?

AVA. Yeah, there's a latch.

MOLLY. Fuck's sake!

AVA. I'll leave you to it.

AVA *starts to leave*.

MOLLY. Hold up – who called us dysfunctional lesbians?

AVA. Oh, no one. Liv. Don't worry about it.

COCO. We're not –

AVA. She's a bit gobby, but she's actually a lot more capable than she likes to let on. Although look, if you are taking over, and I know you've got this plan to like bulldoze the whole site and put up a tower block or something, but… First off, don't do that. You should keep us open, keep us working,

give us all proper jobs, but if you absolutely did have to
make some changes, I'd say Liv was probably more
expendable than say, me, for example. Not being harsh.

MOLLY. Who are you?

AVA. Ava? I feel like I've said that. I'm basically a supervisor.
Unofficially.

COCO. Okay.

AVA. Counter-offer – if you are going to blow this place up, can
I plunge the detonator?

COCO. What?

AVA. It's a bit of a life goal.

MOLLY. Who do you think we are?

AVA. Aren't you the lesbians who're buying the factory?

COCO. No.

AVA. Oh, okay.

MOLLY. We're Co-Codamol.

AVA. Right?

COCO. We're the band.

AVA. Oh. Oh! You're the band!

COCO. Yeah.

AVA. Everyone's looking for you.

MOLLY. Really?

AVA. Paracetamol?

COCO. Co-Codamol.

AVA. Right.

COCO. I'm Coco, she's Molly.

AVA. Oh.

MOLLY. It's –

AVA. Cute. Yeah, that's really cute.

COCO. Thanks.

AVA. Is that why you started a band – because of your names?

MOLLY. No.

AVA. Anyway, there's a photographer waiting for you.

MOLLY. Really?

AVA. Yeah. Just across the yard.

COCO. We should go. (*To* MOLLY.) If they're already set up? If you're okay to?

MOLLY. Yeah, it's just a bit of stitching.

AVA. Why are you getting your pictures taken here?

COCO. It's really good exposure.

AVA. Oh. Okay.

MOLLY. Where are we going?

AVA. Main building – big double doors straight ahead of you.

MOLLY. Thanks.

COCO. You're sure you're okay?

MOLLY. I'm sure. What would The Rolling Stones do?

COCO. Or Salvador Dalí?

MOLLY. Or Pablo Picasso?

COCO. Exactly. (*To* AVA.) Can we leave our stuff in here?

AVA. I'd have thought so.

COCO *picks up the old, battered briefcase Mel moved earlier.*

COCO. I'm borrowing this.

MOLLY. Why?

COCO. I don't have heels – we should be on the same eyeline. (*Before* MOLLY *can comment further.*) Come on.

COCO *and* MOLLY *start to leave. As they're leaving they pass* LEO *coming in.*

LEO. After you, ladies.

LEO *holds the door for them as they go. He has a paper bag with pastries/buns in it.*

(*To* AVA.) Sorry, I didn't know if I'd be disturbing anyone in here.

AVA. That's okay.

LEO. I'm Leo. I'm a friend of Susie's. She's –

AVA. Eddie's sister?

LEO. That's right. You've met her?

AVA. Yeah, just now.

LEO. I won't stay long. She thinks she left a bag behind earlier. Do you mind if I – ?

AVA. No, go ahead. I came in for sanding belts.

LEO. Right.

AVA. It's a bit of a free-for-all in here.

They both start to rummage. What little was sorted in Act One is getting progressively more jumbled.

LEO. You're one of the apprentices?

AVA. That's right.

LEO. You make beautiful things.

AVA. Thanks.

LEO. And what about the two who just left?

AVA. Oh, they're Calpol.

LEO. I beg your pardon?

AVA. They're a band.

LEO. Oh! So they showed up after all. Good for her.

AVA. So this Susie – is she your lady friend?

LEO. Just a friend.

AVA. Yeah?

LEO. A very old friend.

AVA (*pulling a chocolate bar out of a box*). Do you want a Time Out?

LEO. I didn't think they made those any more.

AVA (*examining the label*). I don't think they do.

LEO. I think I can do better. (*He offers her the paper bag.*) Cardamom knot?

AVA. Are they from that place on the corner?

LEO. That's right. I thought Susie might enjoy one, but I'm happy to share.

AVA. You must really love her then.

LEO. Why do you say that?

AVA. I know what they charge in there. You should save them.

LEO. Please, I insist.

AVA *shrugs and takes a pastry.*

Not the kind of place I'd expect to find around here.

AVA. We're on the up, didn't you know?

LEO. Right.

AVA. Are they famous, that band?

LEO. I couldn't tell you.

AVA. Maybe it'll be the hot new thing – celebrity scissor making. Like that smug guy who makes his own cheese – he was in a band, wasn't he?

LEO. Who was?

AVA. I don't know – someone. Is she famous – your Susie?

LEO. Oh, infamous.

AVA. And did you use to date, or…?

LEO. Can't a man and a woman just be friends?

AVA. Depends. Are you both straight?

LEO. More or less. With all the reasonable caveats.

AVA. Respect.

LEO. Susie dates rockstars.

AVA. So nothing's ever happened between you?

LEO. It wasn't meant to be.

AVA. Right.

LEO. There was a moment. A thousand years ago, before she left for California, there was a moment. Anyway.

Beat. LEO *turns back to looking.*

AVA. You can't stop there!

LEO. There's nothing more to say.

AVA. No, I'm fully invested now.

LEO. I'm sure I've taken up enough of your time already.

AVA. No, go on – please.

LEO (*stops, thinks*). Ava, was it?

AVA. Yeah.

LEO. Do you think we're likely to meet again?

AVA *shrugs*.

Perhaps we shan't – and if that is the case, I suppose it doesn't matter much, does it?

AVA. What doesn't?

LEO. Could I share something with you?

AVA. Sure.

LEO. How to put it? If you're lucky, you will encounter in your lifetime people who always shine a little brighter than anyone else around them. If you're *very* lucky, they will, on occasion, direct that light towards you. Not carelessly or indiscriminately, but with great and deliberate attention shine that light on you, in such a way that you would swear no one else has ever experienced it before. It will not expose your weaknesses or highlight your flaws, it won't blind or dazzle you, but it will very gently and very completely fill you from within, warm you to your bones, and you shall feel content, and replete, and just so long as you remain in their presence you shall want for nothing. But these people are rare, and their light is in great demand. You can't compete with it. You can't generate it yourself. You know within your heart of hearts that your own light can never quite match up, so you don't blame them when they choose to focus it elsewhere. You're grateful for whatever part might fall on you. That has to be enough.

AVA. Wow.

LEO. I'm sorry.

AVA. I mean fucking hell. I wasn't prepared for that.

LEO. I'm not suggesting – I'm sure your own light is –

AVA. Right. Yeah, right.

LEO. Forgive me, if –

AVA. Does she know how you feel?

LEO. She's not a fool.

AVA. But have you ever actually told her?

LEO. I know what she'd say.

AVA. Do you though?

LEO. I know her very well.

AVA (*distracted*). Right. I need to go. Sorry. I need to go and… Yeah.

LEO. Are you okay? Have I – ?

AVA. His name's Trent.

LEO. Oh?

AVA. My shiny man. My man with a lamp. However you said it. He works here too, um, and we've never… I need to go find him.

LEO. Right.

AVA. Cos all our apprenticeships finish in a couple of months, and then who knows – I am absolutely petrified of what happens after that – but if he wanted me to go to California with him, I wouldn't say no. I don't think I would. So probably, probably I shouldn't overthink it too much and I should just go and talk to him, yeah?

LEO. Why not?

AVA. And you should too. Not to Trent. To her. To your light lady.

LEO. Good luck.

AVA. I mean it. You've got sticky buns and poetry and –

LEO (*going to take something out of his jacket*). I did find a poem for her, actually.

AVA. You found her a poem? Fucking hell. You have to tell her.

LEO. You have the advantage of youth. I hope age might at least afford me a little dignity. (*He spots a box.*) Ah – sanding belts!

LEO *picks up a box from a high shelf/cabinet/position that does indeed say 'SANDING BELTS' on it. As he lifts it down for* AVA *it splits/spills open, and he is covered in glue or oil or ink or something similar. It splashes all over his coat/jacket. A beat.*

Not sanding belts.

AVA. No.

LEO. Never mind.

AVA. Sorry. The labelling in here isn't very…

LEO. Yes.

AVA. Maybe you just go talk to her shirtless. Maybe that's your in.

LEO. Don't worry – you get on.

AVA. Here.

AVA *takes a worker's coat/jacket off a peg and gives it to* LEO.

LEO. Thank you.

AVA. Okay. I'm going to go now.

LEO. Of course. Good luck.

AVA. Ta.

LEO. Ava?

AVA. Yeah?

LEO. I'm sure your light shines just as brightly as anybody else's.

AVA *smiles and goes.* LEO *looks around at the carnage. Maybe he takes a few moments to try and futilely clear up some of the mess. He puts the worker's jacket on the back of the chair and sits at the desk, turning his attention to his own coat. He checks the piece of paper in his pocket – still intact. He sees what he can do to clean his coat. He's hunched over, his back to the door.*

After a few moments, FAYE *enters on her mobile.*

FAYE (*on phone*).... Yeah. No, I already sent that form. Okay, I'll double check. Thank you.

She hangs up. She sees LEO. *She drops her phone.*

Dad?

LEO *spins around.*

LEO. Oh Christ – Faye!

FAYE. Leo?

LEO. Sorry, sorry!

FAYE. No, that's –

LEO. I am so sorry.

FAYE. No, it's just... Today's been... And his coat – his chair.

LEO (*getting up*). Of course. Forgive me. I had a little mishap.

FAYE. I didn't know you were here. I knew Auntie Sue was, but –

LEO. Yes, still tagging along.

FAYE. Good. That's great.

LEO. It is?

FAYE. She's always much nicer when she's with you – you balance her out.

LEO. I dull her down, you mean?

FAYE. No! So have you made an honest woman of her yet?

LEO. I think we both know that's beyond me. (*Beat.*) I'm very sorry about your father.

FAYE. Thank you. (*Beat.*) What's she playing at? Auntie Sue – what's she trying to do here?

LEO. Leave a legacy. (*Off* FAYE*'s look.*) What's so wrong with that?

FAYE. She's interfering.

LEO. And you're not?

FAYE. I... No, I am. We are. I thought I knew what I was doing coming in, but... I was always so dismissive of what Dad was doing here – now I'm not so sure.

LEO. I meant to reach out, after he passed. I should've done.

FAYE. That's okay.

LEO. I saw Melanie too, earlier. Congratulations. I didn't know you got married.

FAYE. Oh, uh...

LEO. Susie never mentioned. Not that I'd necessarily expect her to mention. (*Beat.*) Not that she'd necessarily even know, I'm now coming to realise.

FAYE. It's, um, it's complicated.

LEO. I remember your father had some rather misguided feelings about –

FAYE. Yeah, that's not –

LEO. Wonderful, anyway. I'm delighted for you.

FAYE. Thank you.

LEO. When was the big day? Was it recent?

FAYE. It hasn't actually happened yet.

LEO. Oh.

FAYE. It's just we tell people – we introduce each other as…
It doesn't matter.

LEO. I see.

FAYE. But it will. Soon. We're working on it, and it will be
soon.

LEO. Wonderful.

FAYE. If I haven't ruined anything too much. And you'll be
invited. If we were already married, you would've been
invited.

LEO. Then I'll look forward to it.

Beat.

Is everything – ?

FAYE. We need to tie down our women, before they slip
through our fingers.

LEO. I'm sure there's no chance of that.

FAYE. I didn't use to think so, but now… You don't want to
hear about this.

LEO. Please.

FAYE. I'm getting a lot wrong.

LEO. Don't we all?

FAYE. It's hard at the moment. She's going through something
– I don't really understand it. I've been taking her for
granted. I need to give her a reason to stick around. You'd
think two children would be enough, but… I thought more

time together might help. It hasn't. Maybe she just needs a project. Something to stop her going solo, or running off with a Norwegian physiotherapist.

LEO. Right.

FAYE. Spenser and Wife. Because this… This is a serious undertaking – it's a commitment. This is how I can keep hold of her.

She's interrupted by the return of ZARA.

ZARA. Dad? Are you in here? (*She sees the others.*) Oh, hello.

FAYE. Hello again. Zara, wasn't it?

ZARA. That's right.

FAYE (*to* LEO). Omar's daughter. Omar who –

LEO. Yes, we met earlier.

FAYE. Right.

LEO. I should be leaving.

ZARA. You don't have to.

LEO. No, I should – see what trouble Susie's getting herself into now.

ZARA. Okay.

FAYE (*to* LEO). Will you tell Mel I'm in here if you see her?

LEO. Of course.

FAYE. Will you come to our wedding?

LEO. I wouldn't miss it for the world. Zara – a pleasure.

LEO *goes*.

ZARA. I'm just trying to find somewhere quiet to get on.

FAYE. Right. Of course.

ZARA. My dad wanted me to look at the website – they've had some issues.

FAYE. Uh-huh.

ZARA. What are you hoping to find in here?

FAYE. I don't know. Answers. Don't really know where to start. (*Beat.*) Could you get me into his computer?

ZARA. No.

FAYE. Just to –

ZARA. That's all Eddie's – I don't know how to use it.

FAYE. But didn't your dad share the space with him?

ZARA. Not the computer.

FAYE. No?

ZARA. Dad's very analogue. Doesn't do screens if he can help it.

FAYE. What, any kind of screen? (*Beat.*) Really? And you couldn't – ?

ZARA. I really only do the website. I don't even do that particularly well.

FAYE. Right.

ZARA. It's all just templates and stuff – nothing complicated.

FAYE. It's nice that you're so involved.

ZARA. I don't do much.

FAYE. But you're a part of it. Do you know how to make them – the scissors? Has he ever taught you?

ZARA. No.

FAYE. My dad didn't either.

ZARA. He would, if I asked him to – if I was around more.

FAYE. Right.

ZARA. The apprentices shout at me when I touch things.

FAYE. Oh.

ZARA. They don't like me very much.

FAYE. It can be tough, being the boss's daughter.

ZARA. Yeah.

FAYE. You're still a student, is that right?

ZARA. Finishing my PhD.

FAYE. That's impressive.

ZARA. I've not finished it yet.

FAYE. Where are you studying?

ZARA. UCL – London.

FAYE. And that's where you grew up, isn't it? Must be nice to be back.

ZARA. All Dad's family is in Manchester. Seems like we're outsiders wherever we end up, so…

FAYE. Right.

ZARA. You could help him. (*Beat*.) I don't really know what's going on today – I don't know what your plans are, but I'm starting to get a picture. I met your wife too, and I'm getting the impression you're the more reasonable one. You know what it meant to your dad – you know why it matters. You could join forces. You could find a way to keep it going.

FAYE. And you'd inherit it one day?

ZARA (*laughs*). No! God no. I don't want it. I've got my own thing. But you've got kids, haven't you?

FAYE. Yeah.

ZARA. So leave it to them. He can't do it alone, but it is worth doing. What do you think?

Before FAYE *can answer,* COCO *and* MOLLY *strop back in, both in a foul mood.*

MOLLY. Fucking ridiculous.

COCO. I'm sorry.

MOLLY. Fucking humiliating. (*Spotting* FAYE.) Oh great. She's back. The mad woman's back.

FAYE. Hi. How was – ?

MOLLY (*referring to* ZARA). And who's she?

ZARA. Who are you?

MOLLY. Actually you're really pretty – do you want to be in a band?

ZARA. What?

MOLLY. I might be starting a new band. Might need a replacement.

COCO. I've said I'm sorry! Come on, we can just go.

MOLLY *slumps into a chair.*

MOLLY. No. I'm done. I'm not moving.

COCO. Mol –

MOLLY. Go away! Can everyone please just leave my dressing room?

ZARA. Who are you though?

FAYE. They're the band. There's a –

ZARA. Oh! Don't tell me! Co-Codamol!

COCO. You've heard of us?

MOLLY. Does anyone have any chocolate?

FAYE. Oh – hang on –

FAYE *starts rummages in a couple of open boxes.* FAYE *pulls out a packet of biscuits.*

Bingo!

She passes them to MOLLY.

MOLLY. Thank you.

FAYE. Are you okay?

COCO. She's fine. We're fine.

MOLLY. Don't speak over my feelings, please.

FAYE. What happened?

MOLLY. She wants to break up.

COCO. I didn't say that.

MOLLY (*still to* FAYE). And it's all your fault.

COCO. Can we not do this here?

ZARA. Great idea.

MOLLY. She doesn't think she needs me.

FAYE. Have I really…? I haven't really done something, have I, to make you – ?

COCO. No.

MOLLY. Yes.

FAYE. Because I don't know if –

COCO. I'm just asking how long we're going to give it. Realistically. Because if you're not a popstar by the time you're twenty-five… It's like boys, isn't it? Every teenage boy reckons he could play for England, but –

MOLLY. Um, girls play football too.

COCO. You know what I mean. They all think they could – everyone thinks they're good enough, but actually it's a tiny percentage of a percentage and you have to start *so young*. If we haven't made it yet – if we're fucked by the time we're twenty-five –

MOLLY. Debbie Harry was thirty-one when Blondie put out their first album.

COCO. And what if we're not Blondie?

FAYE. I am so happy you're communicating. Now I think you need to find practical ways to support each other's goals.

MOLLY (*ignoring this, to* COCO). But isn't it about…? Yes, money, yes, luck, yes, talent, but it's *wanting it*, isn't it? That's what really makes the difference – if you want something enough… (*To* ZARA.) What do you want?

ZARA. Me?

MOLLY. Actually really want? Like right now, what are you doing here and what do you want?

ZARA. I... I want to help my dad. I want him to be happy.

MOLLY. For *you*.

ZARA. I want to improve people's lives.

MOLLY. Ugh! *You!*

ZARA. I don't know! I want... I want to learn things. I want to figure that out.

MOLLY (*to* FAYE). How about you?

FAYE (*with conviction*). I want to marry my wife.

MOLLY. Yes! Good! Weird but I love it. (*To* COCO.) What do you want, Coco?

COCO. I want to be in our band.

MOLLY. Yeah?

COCO. Yes, but –

MOLLY. No buts.

COCO. But if nothing changes –

FAYE. Would this make a difference? If they turned this place into a music venue and you were the face of it – how much of a difference do you think that would make?

ZARA. That's not –

FAYE. I'm only asking.

COCO. I don't know. It's really good exposure –

FAYE. But it wouldn't be *the* difference?

COCO. I don't know!

MOLLY. But you never know. Maybe. (*To* COCO.) It might've gone better than we thought.

COCO. Yeah.

MOLLY. And we always look great, don't we?

COCO. Yeah.

MOLLY. So we should wait and see. And we should give it a little longer. Just a little. Cos we're good, aren't we?

COCO. Yeah, we're good. Come on.

COCO pulls MOLLY up. MOLLY shoves the biscuits into her bag.

MOLLY. Fine. But I'm taking these as payment.

MOLLY kisses COCO. We can't quite tell whether it's platonic or romantic.

COCO. Thanks for having us. They know how to get hold of us, right? Get your people to call our people.

FAYE. Right.

COCO and MOLLY go, passing MEL and OMAR coming back in.

MOLLY. Don't worry, we're leaving!

They're gone, taking all their bags with them.

MEL (*to* FAYE). There you are!

FAYE. Everything okay?

MEL. Yeah.

OMAR. Why were they back here?

ZARA. Doesn't matter, they're gone now. (*To* FAYE.) So were they a couple, or…?

FAYE. Honestly? No idea. Hope so.

OMAR (*looking around*). Did they make this mess?

FAYE. Uh-huh. Yeah. Looks like it.

MEL. Omar agreed we could take a look through everything together – see if we can't get a bit of clarity on where we all stand.

OMAR (*to* MEL *and* FAYE). I started trying to tackle all the paperwork a while back. I didn't get very far.

MEL. Nor did we.

FAYE. Do you think there might be something on the computer – like an email chain or something? She says she can't get in.

MEL. Let me have a look.

MEL *sits at the desk.*

FAYE (*to* OMAR). She says you avoid screens altogether – how does that work?

OMAR. We have a… a way of doing things without – a system designed to –

FAYE. Seriously?

ZARA. Why does it matter?

OMAR. We have a fully automated system – web orders print out as soon as they come through – there's no need.

FAYE. But why?

MEL. The password's stuck to the bottom of the keyboard. You're all hopeless.

FAYE. Do you want me to – ?

MEL. No, it's fine.

MEL *gets into the computer, starts looking through emails/files.*

OMAR. Right now it's all just China anyway – we don't have to worry about anything else.

MEL. Just how big is this China contract?

OMAR. Huge. That's what I was trying to explain before. We were months, maybe weeks even, from having to shut up shop for good, but this will turn everything around.

MEL. So you're making a profit now?

OMAR. We will be, as soon as this first shipment goes out.

FAYE. But –

OMAR. Eddie always swore he'd find us something.

FAYE. But… No, I can't get my head around this.

ZARA. It's all true.

FAYE. Not China – I followed all that. I'm saying your father can't manage international operations without a computer.

MEL (*quietly*). Leave it.

FAYE. No, I'm serious.

OMAR. This set-up allows me to focus solely on the making. Other people can –

FAYE. But you're in charge! You were his chosen one!

OMAR. I am a craftsman.

FAYE. Does no one else think this is crazy?

ZARA. Don't worry about it.

FAYE. How on earth are you still operating?

OMAR. People made scissors long before the internet.

FAYE. Yes, but –

MEL. Honey, leave it, please.

FAYE. I'm still missing something. No one just doesn't 'do' computers. Not in 2022. Not when you're in charge. (*To* OMAR.) And you were a city boy! Canary Wharf, right? So that's impossible – just impossible.

ZARA. Stop it.

FAYE. What's going on?

OMAR. Nothing.

FAYE. What are you hiding from us?

MEL (*suddenly*). Please! Jesus Christ, Faye, just leave him alone!

A beat.

FAYE. Excuse me?

MEL. I love you, but just *think*.

FAYE. What?

MEL (*to* OMAR). You were an analyst?

OMAR (*quietly*). Yes.

ZARA. You don't have to.

MEL (*still to* OMAR). And you've been here well over a decade now. Which means you left when? 2008?

OMAR. 2009.

MEL. Rough time for people like you. People in the city.

OMAR. Yes.

MEL. How hard did you fall?

ZARA (*to* OMAR). You don't have to talk to them.

MEL. No, you don't. And I'm sorry, I thought it was just an affectation – all of this, it was basically just historical re-enactment – but it's not, is it?

OMAR. No.

MEL (*to* FAYE). He doesn't do computers. Not because he doesn't like them, because he just can't. (*Back to* OMAR.) It's why you came here in the first place, isn't it? To get away from them – to do something with your hands?

OMAR. We have family up this way.

MEL. And you had a wife too, and a big flash job in the city.

ZARA. Leave him alone.

MEL. And it's the only way something like this could've happened. It's one hell of a blind spot. (*To* OMAR *and* ZARA.) I'm sorry, but I think one of you needs to have a look at this. (*To* OMAR.) I understand if you can't, but maybe your daughter can.

ZARA. Look at what?

MEL gets up and moves away from the computer.

MEL. Your China order. It's not difficult to see. You just have to follow the money.

ZARA *takes her spot.*

FAYE. What is it?

MEL (*to* OMAR). When did you first hear about it? When did Eddie tell you?

OMAR. About six months ago. A little earlier. It was just before Christmas.

MEL. And you were running out of options?

OMAR. That's right.

FAYE. What's going on?

MEL. It isn't real. Of course it isn't.

FAYE. What?

ZARA (*studying the screen*). No, this isn't… You did this somehow.

MEL. No.

ZARA. This is impossible.

FAYE. What are you saying?

MEL. I think Eddie invented it. He placed the order himself – bounced it around a bit –

FAYE. No –

MEL. It's not particularly well hidden – not once you get in his emails, if you know what you're looking for. But I suppose he knew no one else would be looking.

ZARA. But… but the money was real, wasn't it? It came in, it paid for materials, wages –

MEL. There are some bank statements there too. Loans. Mortgage statements. It paints a picture.

FAYE. This place never had a mortgage.

MEL. No, it never used to. It certainly does now. I don't think finding a will is important any more. I think he went all-in with this. He remortgaged, and borrowed, and offset, and overdrew. I don't think there's anything left but debt. You

might be able to fight it – I don't have a grasp of it all yet –
but this says the bank are foreclosing. I don't know what
options are left.

ZARA. But why? Why would he – ?

MEL. I don't know. Mr Sarbani?

OMAR. I…

FAYE. It was almost Christmas. They were going bust.

ZARA. But that's insane. How does that help anyone?

FAYE *goes over to the computer with* ZARA.

OMAR. It was never real?

MEL. Weren't you even a little bit suspicious, when it all just
appeared out of nowhere?

OMAR. He told us he'd been working on it for months.

MEL. And you didn't question it.

OMAR. I believed. I had faith.

MEL. You didn't want to know.

OMAR. I… I just wanted to keep making.

MEL. Right.

ZARA. But why would anybody do that?!

OMAR. Because he loved them.

ZARA. You don't believe her?

OMAR. He loved them, and this place, and… He always
believed things would turn around – we just had to keep
things going until they did.

ZARA. Dad –

OMAR. Perhaps things could still turn around.

MEL. I don't think so.

OMAR. The product is good. He always said if the product is
good, there'll be someone to buy it.

ZARA. We can... You can... This isn't... This can't be legal. It can't be –

OMAR. Stop looking. It's okay.

ZARA. It's not okay!

OMAR. I should talk to the apprentices. I don't know what I'll tell them, but they should know something. (*To* FAYE.) And someone should tell your aunt, I suppose. Send her home. (*To* ZARA.) Perhaps you could?

FAYE. I don't mind if –

ZARA. No, that's okay. We had a good chat earlier. (*To* OMAR.) I'll find you after.

FAYE. Thank you.

ZARA *goes*.

He wouldn't have wanted it to get this far. He would've just been running out the clock, waiting for things to turn around.

OMAR. Yes.

FAYE. We can turn everything off in here. Lock it all up.

OMAR. Thank you.

OMAR *starts to leave*.

MEL. Were you good at what you did before?

OMAR. Yes. Very good.

MEL. And this – you're good at what you've been doing here?

OMAR. Yes.

MEL. That's something, isn't it? (*Beat*.) I do get it – doing something with your hands. We've got these friends up in County Durham and they bought this... It's not even a farmhouse, it's more of a shack. The actual farm is about a mile and a half away down the hill, and then it's another five miles beyond that before you see another building. They had to put their own pylons up across the valley just to get power to it. Bleak out there – incredible, but bleak. Hard. Anyway, we all went up, a group of us, a couple of months ago, to help them do some work on it. Shift rubble, clear everything out. I was already off work by then. I didn't *choose* to stop working either, but that's another story. Anyway, the stone and the brickwork inside had been plastered over decades ago, but it all needed to come off again, so I got handed this sledgehammer and I just went to town. No finesse required, not like what you do here, only brute force. Wouldn't take a break. Didn't need one. Bash, bash, bash. I felt the most alive I had in years. And yes, there was an element of queer joy to it I'm not expecting you to relate to, but... Incredible. Like this is what we're built for, y'know? Not office work, not cubicles. But... Authentic. I think you're lucky, to have found that.

OMAR. I'm sorry we didn't get the chance to work together.

MEL. Yeah. Good luck.

OMAR *goes*.

FAYE. Okay. Let's just... just... Put things back into piles, maybe. Tidy things up a little.

MEL. We can leave it.

FAYE. You don't like leaving a mess.

MEL. It doesn't matter.

FAYE. I'm sorry about –

MEL. It doesn't matter.

FAYE. We'll be fine.

MEL. Can we go home?

FAYE. Are you okay?

MEL. I'd like to go home please.

FAYE. What's the matter?

MEL. I'm sorry too.

FAYE. What for?

MEL. Nothing.

FAYE. What's going on?

MEL. Nothing.

FAYE. What have I done?

MEL. You're perfect. Can we go?

FAYE. Not until you tell me what's wrong.

MEL (*softly*). I had a plan.

FAYE. I know. Is there anything you think we should be printing out before we go? Or we could email things to ourselves?

MEL. No.

FAYE. It wasn't a bad plan. I'm sorry if I derailed things.

MEL. It's okay.

FAYE. I just wanted to help them. I wanted to help the kids – they're all only kids – the apprentices, and then the girls in the band – even Zara, not that I think she'll need it. But it's never easy – being the boss's daughter is never easy.

MEL. But kids are resilient, aren't they? They can bounce back from just about anything.

FAYE. Maybe.

MEL. They'll be fine.

FAYE. I know you think I'm ridiculous.

MEL. No –

FAYE. You do. And I know they're not our responsibility, and you're just being sensible and practical and responsible but I just wanted to do *something* for them. Something that contributes one drop of good.

MEL. Yeah.

FAYE. I'm sorry.

MEL. Don't be.

FAYE. What's going on?

MEL. Nothing.

FAYE. Talk to me.

MEL. Let's go.

> *Frustrated,* FAYE *sweeps a stack of papers off the desk and onto the floor.*

> Fuck's sake.

FAYE. Talk to me.

MEL. What are you – ?

> FAYE *sweeps another stack of papers.*

FAYE. Talk to me.

MEL. I'm fine.

FAYE. You can either talk to me or I'm going to find you a sledgehammer.

MEL. Not now.

> FAYE *sweeps more papers.*

FAYE. Now.

MEL. Fine.

> MEL *does the same.*

FAYE. Fine. Bring it.

> *Goading each other on, they proceed to trash the office – first deliberately, taking turns to knock things over, daring the other to break first. Then they get caught up in the moment, continuing with increasing abandon. This can go on for some time until everything is carnage. Important to note: they're making a mess, not breaking/destroying things. Everything they're doing can be undone. They're getting breathless. They come to a natural rest.*

> Are you ready to talk?

MEL. There's nothing to talk about.

FAYE. Clearly there is!

MEL. I've just been trying to put things in place. To make arrangements.

FAYE. For what?

MEL. The future.

FAYE. Okay.

MEL. To make sure you were set – you and Joni and Max.

FAYE. If you don't go back to work? (*Beat.*) Can you go back to work?

MEL. I don't think so.

FAYE. Okay.

MEL. I haven't told you everything that happened.

FAYE. Oh?

MEL. I'm sorry.

FAYE. That's okay.

MEL. I just need to know you're taken care of. If I'm not around.

FAYE. Why wouldn't you be around?

Pause.

Why wouldn't you be around?

MEL. It doesn't matter. I'll figure something else out.

FAYE. Right.

MEL. I promise. I will find something for you, before –

FAYE. You don't need to do that job. It was a terrible job. It made you miserable.

MEL. Yeah.

FAYE. It made both of us miserable. It made you someone you're not. It's good that you're not going back to it.

MEL. Yeah.

FAYE. You can do anything. You can start over. Find a new purpose. You can take your time – no rush.

MEL. Right.

FAYE. Maybe something with your hands.

MEL. Uh-huh.

FAYE. Something outdoors if you wanted. Something totally different. And then things will be better, won't they?

MEL. I thought I'd found a way out.

FAYE. What do you mean?

MEL. I thought with this… It would be an easy sell, we'd push it through quickly and you'd be set for life – all three of you. You'd never have to work another day. It would pay off the mortgage, cover any extras, tuition fees, anything else you needed.

FAYE. And then you'd leave?

MEL. It's not –

FAYE. Then you'd leave us?

MEL. Not like that.

FAYE. Then what? Then we'd retire together, travel the world – ?

MEL. Don't.

FAYE. Don't what?

MEL. Don't make me say it.

FAYE. Say what?

MEL. I wouldn't do it until you were all set. I wouldn't go before –

FAYE. Go where? (*Beat*.) Where are you going, honey?

MEL (*quietly*). I had a plan.

FAYE (*she realises*). Oh.

MEL. I'm sorry.

FAYE. I know. It's okay. You can tell me.

MEL. I thought I'd go out to Stanage Edge. Very early. Watch the sunrise. I'd take a flask of coffee and I'd leave the three of you sleeping and I'd sit very quietly hoping to find a moment of calm at the last, and I would – I think I would – because I'd know that you were all sorted. I'd been responsible. I'd done everything I could. So I could stop. I could stop worrying. I could let go.

FAYE. Right.

MEL. I'm sorry.

FAYE. Is this because of the wedding?

MEL. What?

FAYE. Because I never proposed?

MEL. No!

FAYE. Because we're going to –

MEL. No! It's nothing to do with that. It isn't about you. it isn't –

FAYE. Okay.

MEL. I love you so much. More than anything. And the kids – of course I do. But I just can't… I don't know if I can…

FAYE. Okay.

MEL. I'm sorry.

FAYE. I know. But that's all ruined now, isn't it? You can't do any of that. Because this place isn't worth anything, so nothing's set, nothing's certain, nothing's taken care of. And so that means we have to carry on. You have to carry on.

MEL (*very quietly*). Yeah.

FAYE. You promise me? You have to carry on.

MEL. Okay.

FAYE. We have a wedding to plan.

MEL. Yeah.

FAYE. We have so much living to do.

MEL. Yeah.

A knock at the door.

FAYE. We can sneak out the back?

MEL. No, it's okay. (*Calling off.*) Come in!

BILLY *enters. He holds the old battered briefcase that* COCO *took earlier.*

BILLY. Hi. Hello. Sorry ladies, sorry to interrupt.

MEL. That's okay.

BILLY. I'm Billy – I've been doing photos? Doesn't matter. (*Holding up the briefcase.*) This got picked up with the rest of my gear. They said it came from in here. I'll leave you to it.

BILLY *sets down the briefcase and goes.* FAYE *seems a little stunned.*

MEL. What is it?

FAYE. Does it matter?

MEL. But do you know what it is?

FAYE. It's his briefcase.

MEL. Whose?

FAYE. Dad's. Actually, my granddad's. Actually, not even his, originally – it came with the factory when we took things over. It was the old foreman's.

MEL. And...?

FAYE. And what?

MEL. And open it! What's in it?

FAYE. It doesn't matter.

MEL. I know you want to open it.

FAYE. Alright! (*She puts it on the desk and opens it.*) Okay, so... So we have some business cards, we have... a Valentine's Day card from my mum. I hope it's from my mum. Uh... (*She laughs in spite of herself.*) Yes! Would you believe it? We have extremely old legal deeds of transference for a property which is now almost certainly worthless. We have… (*Something stops her.*)

MEL. What? What is it?

FAYE. Another letter.

MEL. To who?

FAYE. To me. To us.

MEL. From your dad?

FAYE. Yeah.

> FAYE *takes out a letter and opens it. She smiles. She wipes away a tear. She passes it to* MEL *to look at.* MEL *starts to read.*

Sentimental old bastard. (*Beat.*) Hold on – there's something else.

MEL. What?

FAYE. There's a false bottom to the case.

MEL. What's behind it?

> FAYE *takes out an old ink sketch.*

FAYE. Nothing. It's a picture.

MEL. A picture?

FAYE. A drawing. (*She laughs.*) It's me and you.

MEL. What?

FAYE. It's me and you making scissors.

MEL. Let me see.

> FAYE *is still laughing.*

FAYE. The two of us bent over the grindstone! Look!

MEL. Why would – ?

FAYE. Don't you remember? That first letter he wrote me when I was tiny – where he drew me and my husband?

MEL. You think he drew this?

FAYE. Of course he did. Look at it!

MEL. Why have I got a nose where my ear should be?

FAYE. He was old – he had cataracts and arthritis – give him a break!

MEL. I'm a bit… sturdy, aren't I?

FAYE. He drew us! In action! He drew us making scissors.

MEL. Don't say it's a sign.

FAYE. It's… What is that if it's not a sign?!

MEL. Okay.

FAYE. Not that we should be taking things over, just a sign that… It means he changed. It's why he wrote the letter. Too chicken to send it, but… It means he was capable of transformation – *everyone* is capable of… You have to carry on. You have to carry on because you never know what change you're capable of.

MEL. Yeah.

FAYE. Promise. Promise me you'll carry on.

MEL. I promise you I'll try.

Beat.

FAYE. We've made a mess.

MEL. It doesn't look that different to me.

FAYE. We can't just leave it.

MEL. We could.

FAYE. Only if we were going to come back.

MEL. Okay.

FAYE. Tomorrow.

MEL. Sure.

FAYE. We'd have to promise. You'd have to promise you were coming back.

MEL. Yeah.

FAYE. I mean it. For however long it takes to sort everything out. Even if it takes a lifetime.

MEL. Okay.

>FAYE *picks up a pen from the desk, and one of the legal documents. She goes to write on it.*

What are you doing?

FAYE. Leaving a note. A promise. All done.

MEL. All good?

FAYE. All good. Let's go home.

>FAYE *takes* MEL*'s hand. They flick the lights off as they leave.*

>*End.*

SCISSORS

ACT ONE

A small workshop space in a much larger factory. This is the only space still used for making on a day-to-day basis, because it's relatively poky and cheaper to heat. It might not have always been a making space, perhaps just a storeroom or break room that's now been repurposed. Four workstations are set up, one for each MASON, AVA, LIV and TRENT, in their workers' overalls. They're busy at work – sharpening blades, polishing handles, fixing the scissors together, whatever is practically achievable onstage. This goes on in silence for a few moments, until gradually they fall into a collective percussive rhythm. They exchange the odd look, enjoying getting into a groove. Then, one of them starts to hum a simple familiar riff over the top – something catchy and well known. Could be 'Seven Nation Army', 'We Will Rock You', something relatively simple and iconic – something they can build and play with. They let it build and grow. They're having a giggle.

Then ZARA bursts in, casually dressed, singing the melody to whatever the song is altogether too loudly and too well. Immediately the others stop.

MASON. No, stop it, you've spoiled it. She's spoiled it.

ZARA. What? Why?

MASON. You know why.

AVA (*to* ZARA). Alright?

MASON. She knows why.

ZARA. I was only –

AVA. Ignore him.

ZARA. What's the problem?

LIV. Ugh!

TRENT. Leave it.

ZARA. What did I do?

MASON. I'm not being the dickhead.

LIV. You are though.

MASON. I'm not!

LIV (*to* ZARA). You are too.

ZARA. What have I done?

MASON. This is what you do. It's what she does. Spoils everything. Can't just let us have a nice thing. Has to come in all Ariana.

ZARA. Right. Sorry.

MASON. When we're all happy and –

ZARA. I'm sorry.

AVA. He's being a dickhead.

ZARA. You keep going then. I'll just sit here.

MASON. What do you mean, 'keep going'?

ZARA. Whatever – I won't join in – don't let me stop you.

MASON. We can't just... It was fucking spontaneous, weren't it? It's gotta be organic. That was an *organic*, spontaneous –

ZARA. Okay –

MASON. No, it's not – it's not okay.

TRENT. It's alright –

MASON (*pulling out his phone*). See what it says on my Co–Star? 'Leave yourself open to spontaneous outbursts of joy.'

LIV. Fucking hell.

MASON. She's stolen my spontaneous outburst of joy and I'm not having it.

ZARA. What's that?

AVA. It's an astrology app.

TRENT. Can I see it?

ZARA (to MASON). Sorry, I really can't tell if you're being serious.

MASON. I am. Deadly serious. I was in a bad mood already, and then I start to enjoy myself for one second –

ZARA. I'm sorry.

AVA. Don't apologise to him.

ZARA. Oh, I didn't mean it.

MASON. Fuck it, I'm going for a smoke.

TRENT. Mason –

MASON. I'm not gonna hang around here and get picked on. I'll be back in five, yeah?

MASON *huffs out*.

ZARA. Is he going to be okay?

TRENT. He'll be fine.

ZARA. Is everything – ?

AVA. It's fine. Didn't know you were in today.

ZARA. Yeah, for the morning at least. Dad wants me to do some work on the website. Someone's told him they can't see all the products.

LIV. So why're you here?

ZARA. I just said.

LIV. Yeah, but that's computers, isn't it?

ZARA. Yeah?

LIV. So you can do computers from anywhere.

ZARA. It's easier if I'm in the same room as him.

LIV. He's not here though.

ZARA. I won't be staying here long. I just thought... Doesn't matter.

LIV. Okay.

ZARA. What is it?

LIV. Nothing.

ZARA. What's Mason upset about really?

TRENT. He'll be okay.

LIV. He's got Mercury in his anus. (*Beat.*) Is that not a thing?

TRENT. He's fine.

ZARA. Should I go talk to him?

LIV. No!

ZARA. Ava?

AVA. No.

ZARA. Trent?

TRENT. I'd leave it.

ZARA. I think I'll just go talk to him.

LIV. Fuck's sake.

ZARA. Just to –

LIV. He's not going to jump off the roof, he's having a fag.

ZARA. Okay.

TRENT. I don't think your dad's in yet. The lights weren't on in the office.

LIV. And there's no Wi-Fi in here.

ZARA. Sorry?

LIV. So you won't be able to get any work done in here, will you? Not on the website.

ZARA. Right.

LIV. And you can't even tether properly cos the signal's shit.

ZARA. Uh-huh.

LIV. Just because he likes to live in the Dark Ages it doesn't mean we should all get screwed. It's barbaric.

AVA (*to* ZARA). She has got a point actually. Wi-Fi would be good.

TRENT. It is annoying, to be fair.

ZARA. Yeah, I'll ask him.

TRENT. Thanks.

LIV. But anyway – anyway, the point is there's not really much you can be doing from here, is there? For all the aforementioned reasons?

ZARA. Yeah.

LIV. So…

ZARA. If you want me to piss off you can just tell me to piss off.

LIV. Great. Piss off then.

ZARA. Got it.

    ZARA *starts to leave.*

TRENT. Wait –

AVA. Don't. Zara. Come on.

ZARA. It's fine. One sec.

    ZARA *goes.* AVA *throws* LIV *a 'what the fuck?' look.* LIV
    shrugs. A moment later ZARA *returns with four takeaway*
    coffees in a cardboard holder.

    I just put them down outside so I could do my big entrance.
    Anyway.

    She starts handing them out.

    (*To* AVA.) Just black for you, yeah? Hot chocolate for
    Trent –

TRENT. Ta.

ZARA. And a hazelnut latte for Liv – extra hot, extra shot.

LIV. Right. So I suppose I say 'thank you', do I?

ZARA. That would be a normal human response, yeah. (*Beat.*)
    That one's Mason's. I could go and –

AVA. It's fine – you can leave it on his station.

ZARA. And is it safe to…?

LIV. The scissors get tempered at over a thousand degrees centigrade.

ZARA. Right.

LIV. Is that coffee hotter than one thousand degrees centigrade?

TRENT (*to* ZARA). Anywhere's fine.

ZARA. Okay. Cool. Well I'll be… around somewhere, if anyone… I'll see you later.

ZARA *goes*.

TRENT (*after her*). Thanks Zee!

LIV (*muttering in a silly voice*). 'Thanks Zee!'

AVA. Why are you always such a dick to her?

LIV. Boss's daughter. She's the enemy.

TRENT. She's nice.

LIV. Only little bitches drink hot chocolate.

TRENT. I don't feel pressured to use caffeine as a substitute for personality.

Beat.

LIV. Wow.

TRENT. Sorry. Was that – ?

AVA. Brutal.

LIV. Bit early for that, isn't it?

AVA. Fucking slayed you.

TRENT. Sorry.

LIV. I mean, Jesus Christ, Trent, we're all just having a laugh, but –

TRENT. Sorry, I just…

LIV. I should hope so.

TRENT. You did call me a little bitch though.

LIV. Um, women are allowed to say 'bitch' – we reclaimed it.

AVA (*to* TRENT). You wanna be careful though – all that
    lactose –

TRENT. Nah, she gets it me with oat milk.

LIV. Fucking hell.

AVA. Yeah, I'm not defending that.

TRENT. What? It's delicious. You can't shame me. I cannot be
    shamed.

LIV (*moving the conversation on*). Anyone else think these new
    blanks are a bit wank?

AVA. In what way?

LIV. Dunno. They just feel different.

AVA. Is it a different grade?

TRENT. No.

AVA. Because it does feel –

TRENT. It's offcuts.

LIV. What?

TRENT. It's the same steel, it's just reforged from the offcuts.

AVA. Does that work?

TRENT. It's good. It's efficient.

LIV. Is it Omar being a cheap bastard?

TRENT. No, it's eco.

LIV. Okay, is it Omar being an environmentally friendly cheap
    bastard?

TRENT. It's molecularly identical.

LIV (*mocking*). Oooh.

TRENT. It is.

LIV. Says the motherfucker who drinks oat milk. Don't trust you on anything now.

MASON *comes back in.*

MASON. There's someone in the offices.

LIV. What?

AVA (*to* MASON). Were you just hiding until Zara left?

MASON. No.

LIV. Really?

MASON. No! I was having a fag in the yard, and there's someone in the office.

AVA. Yeah, it'll be Omar.

MASON. Nah, it sounded like a woman.

LIV. Omar can sound a bit like a woman, to be fair.

MASON. Two women.

TRENT. Omar's got two women in his office?

LIV. Didn't know he had it in him.

MASON. So what should we do?

AVA. What, you want to go ask for a foursome?

MASON. No! And I'm not... It didn't sound sexy, it just sounded like there were two women in his office and I don't know why.

AVA. Right.

LIV. Does anyone else think it sounds like Mason's saying women don't belong in the workplace?

MASON. No –

AVA. Wow that's actually really misogynist, Mason.

LIV. Yeah I would've expected better.

MASON. I wasn't!

AVA. Um, are you gaslighting us now?

LIV. Are you invalidating our lived experience?

AVA. Deeply sus.

MASON. Fuck's sake.

TRENT. Was Omar with them?

MASON. No – I don't think so – I just heard women.

LIV. I doubt Omar even knows two women. I bet he just locks himself away in there and wanks off over a pair of gardening shears.

AVA. Liv!

LIV. What?

AVA. It's too early.

MASON. Can we fucking focus? Two women have broken into the office, and –

AVA. Broken in?

MASON. Why else would they be there?

LIV. When they should be in the kitchen making you a sandwich?

MASON. I wasn't – !

TRENT *laughs*.

Who are they then? Cos it's just us, right? It's us four, and Omar, and Zara sometimes, and it was Eddie but now he's dead, so who are they? Cos we're the only people who have any business here.

LIV. So did you come back for back-up? You need me and Ava to go sort them out?

MASON. Fine. Whatever. Forget it.

AVA. Mason –

MASON. Let them rob us – see if I care.

LIV. What're they gonna rob?

MASON, *in a bit of a strop, tosses his jacket over the chair/stool at his workstation. This accidentally knocks over the cup of coffee that he hasn't noticed yet.*

MASON. Fuck! What the fuck?

AVA. Oh yeah, Zara brought you a coffee.

MASON. Fuck's sake.

He starts trying to clean up the mess.

AVA. She's very thoughtful like that.

MASON. I'm not in the mood, alright?

TRENT. Here – I'll sort it.

MASON. Try to be a good fucking Samaritan.

TRENT *helps* MASON *clean up.*

AVA. What if they're from the paper?

MASON. What?

AVA. You know – Omar's been saying for ages that someone from *The Star* is coming in, gonna do a big story on us. Like a local – a heritage – a sort of…

TRENT. Today?

AVA. I dunno.

LIV. Yes! So that's why she's in.

TRENT. Who?

LIV. Zara!

AVA. Why would – ?

LIV. Could've done all her stuff from home, couldn't she? Could still be in bed. But she wants to get herself in front of the camera – wants all the credit.

AVA. She's alright.

LIV. I don't trust her.

MASON. Me neither.

LIV. This isn't even nice coffee.

TRENT. You should've gone for hot chocolate.

AVA (*to* LIV). Why are you being like this?

LIV. What's she doing buying us coffee anyway? Buying us *nice* coffee? Like this round's got to be what – fifteen quid?

TRENT. Because she's a nice person?

LIV. Grow up, Trent. Nobody's just a nice person.

AVA. Okay.

LIV. No, genuinely though. Name me one actually nice person. You're not – Mason's definitely not.

MASON. Thanks.

LIV. No offence.

MASON. None taken.

AVA. What about Trent? Trent's nice.

LIV. Yeah, but Trent's not really a person, is he? He's like a sexy Labrador with a haircut.

TRENT. Er…

LIV. It's a compliment. Jesus.

TRENT. Right.

LIV. Point is, what's she doing spending fifteen quid on coffee for us, when she knows we don't even like her? What's her angle?

AVA. So you're just having a full-on meltdown this morning then?

TRENT. Should've gone decaf.

LIV. Don't you start. I've just been nice about you.

TRENT. Have you?

MASON. Have we just decided we're ignoring the two women robbing us then?

LIV. Oh my God.

TRENT. Do we know for sure there's a reporter in today?

LIV. I'm telling you, that's why she's here. Y'know, she's just gonna… (*She flaps her arms, a bit like a giant bird*.)

MASON. Um. What?

LIV. Swoop. Swoop in – Zara – she's here to swoop in, distracting us with fancy coffee – probably counting on you spilling it, actually, as an act of sabotage – so we all look a state and she can get her face in the papers – her and her dad, all family-family, and we don't get a look in.

TRENT. Omar's on our side.

LIV. Is he though? Cos the China order, right – this massive new order – that wasn't anything to do with him, was it? That was all Eddie from day one. Only now Eddie's dead, so they can spin it like it was their masterplan the whole time. That's why he's got this journo in. That's why she's here. That's what it's all about.

AVA. Reckon you need to cut down on the true-crime podcasts.

LIV. She's a snake.

TRENT. She's really not.

LIV. She is! And it'll still be us doing the work and her getting the glory.

AVA. You would actually have to do some work for that to be true though, wouldn't you?

TRENT. She doesn't even want to be here. She's just helping her dad.

LIV. And how do you know?

TRENT. I listen. People tell me things.

LIV. Okay, fine. (*She gets up*.) Mason, your two criminal masterminds?

MASON. Yeah?

LIV. You reckon I could take them in a fight?

AVA. Jesus.

MASON. Didn't get a look at them, so…

AVA (*to* LIV). What are you doing?

LIV. One of two things – either I'm going to go and foil an act of industrial espionage like an absolute baller, or I'm going to have a nice chat with a couple of journalists and get my picture in the paper. I reckon it's win-win.

AVA. Well take Trent then, just in case they're serial killers.

TRENT. Shouldn't we be getting on?

LIV. Exactly. Sooner we go, sooner we'll be back. (*Beat.*) You know Omar's got a stash of Hobnobs in his office?

TRENT. Really? (*Beat.*) Fuck it. Why not?

MASON. No he hasn't.

LIV. He has, I swear.

MASON (*still to* TRENT). She's manipulating you.

TRENT. I'm willing to take the risk. Open heart. Say yes to the universe.

MASON. Whatever.

AVA. We do actually have to have this batch finished soon though.

TRENT. Won't be long, I promise.

LIV. Come on then. Last one to get their photo taken by a murderer is a rotten egg.

LIV *goes.* TRENT *shrugs and follows. A beat.*

AVA (*to* MASON). That's your fault, is that.

MASON *shrugs.*

MASON. You gonna share your coffee then?

AVA. Piss off.

MASON. What? (*Beat.*) It was a stupid place to leave it.

AVA. And?

MASON. Go on. Just pour a little bit in my cup.

AVA. You didn't even want one.

MASON. I never said that.

AVA. You hate her. You're horrible to her.

MASON. Don't hate the coffee though.

AVA. Why is that?

MASON. Why's what?

AVA. Why're you such a dick? Do you fancy her?

MASON (*dismissive*). Sure.

AVA. Do you though? Is it like pulling her pigtails in the playground?

MASON. She's not my type.

AVA. Okay.

Pause. They get back to work throughout this exchange.

MASON. Not everything's sexual chemistry. Sometimes I just don't like people.

AVA. Okay.

MASON. If that's allowed?

AVA. Okay.

MASON. I'm not negging her, I just don't like her. If I wanted to fuck everyone I didn't like, that'd be...

AVA. Okay!

MASON. Not enough hours in the day, mate. Don't have that kind of stamina.

AVA. Fine, I believe you.

Beat.

MASON. Do all girls think that?

AVA. What?

MASON. That if someone doesn't like them it's because they actually fancy them? Cos that might explain a lot.

AVA *shrugs*.

Do you think that?

AVA. I don't know.

MASON. Bit egotistical, isn't it?

AVA. I wasn't –

MASON. To just decide –

AVA. It was a casual… You're making it a big thing now – not me.

MASON. You know what that is – what I reckon that is?

AVA. What?

MASON (*proud of himself*). Toxic femininity.

AVA *sighs*.

Isn't it? No, it is, because you are… are perpetuating a culture of… like incels and shit, complaining about being nice guys, cos you lot are teaching boys 'treat 'em mean, keep 'em keen – pull their hair, right – kick a football at their head – '

AVA. Definitely didn't say that.

MASON. No, but –

AVA. Do you go around kicking footballs at girls' heads?

MASON. I wasn't –

AVA. Because please don't tell me that's something you do.

MASON. Be a dickhead, though. Be a dickhead if you want them to like you.

AVA. Right.

MASON. See what I'm saying?

AVA. 'What if men never have to take responsibility for their actions and it's actually always someone else's fault?'

MASON. No –

AVA. Does sound like that's what you're saying.

MASON. Yeah, well… well… (*Running out of clever things*.) get your ears cleaned then.

AVA. Okay.

Pause. They carry on for a few seconds.

It's not like I'd be judging you if you did fancy her.

MASON. Oh my God.

AVA. I see it. She's a very attractive… older woman.

MASON. Wow.

AVA. What?

MASON. Can I just concentrate on this actually?

AVA. Fine. (*Beat.*) Maybe you don't even know that you do fancy her. Maybe it's subconscious.

MASON *puts down his work and gets up again.*

MASON. Right. I'm going to go bring up some more blanks.

AVA. No – don't.

MASON. Cos I'm almost done with these, and if you're going to –

AVA. Sit down!

MASON. Why is everyone bullying me this morning? Cos honestly, I've had enough of it.

AVA. I'm sorry! Sit down – I'll drop it – I promise.

MASON. I know when I fancy people.

AVA. Okay.

MASON. I would know if… I don't even *have* a subconscious.

AVA *laughs.*

I don't! I just think something and then that's what I think. End of.

AVA. Actually I believe you. If that were going to be true of anyone, it'd be you.

MASON. Well then.

AVA. I just meant that sometimes – because sometimes, for me – and as someone definitely more emotionally intelligent than you –

MASON. Are you fuck?

AVA. Uh, yeah, I am – I'm a girl, so of course I am.

MASON. Right.

AVA. Sometimes I could know someone for years before realising I liked them. Like years and years and then be like 'oh shit, I've actually been like properly in love with this person forever and I didn't even know about it.'

MASON. I don't fancy you either.

AVA. What?

MASON. In case you were –

AVA. What? No!

MASON. Okay.

AVA. That is… No!

MASON. Good.

AVA. Good.

MASON. Good.

AVA. I wasn't –

MASON. And I'm even nice to you. Comparatively. So I definitely can't fancy you, according to your theory.

AVA. That isn't what I was saying.

MASON. Alright then.

AVA. And I don't have to tell you who it is, because that's my business.

MASON. Okay.

AVA. Not saying there even is anyone.

MASON. Right.

AVA. So don't ask me.

MASON. Okay.

Beat.

AVA. Do you honestly think you're nice to me?

MASON. I said 'comparatively'.

AVA. You're genuinely the weirdest person I've ever met, you know that?

MASON. See – this is what I mean.

AVA. What?

MASON. I do get bullied.

AVA. Come on –

MASON. I do. Workplace harassment. There's always one of you having a go.

AVA. We have a go because you're a mardy twat.

MASON (*getting up again*). Well thanks for proving my point.

AVA. Oh sit down.

MASON. I won't.

AVA. Don't be a baby.

MASON. Don't be such a bully then.

AVA. Seriously?

MASON. I'm going to register a formal complaint. I have rights.

AVA. Okay.

MASON. I mean it.

AVA. Okay.

MASON. Okay.

MASON *heads for the door, but before he gets there* OMAR, *the site manager, enters.*

OMAR. Good morning.

AVA. Morning, Omar.

MASON (*to* OMAR). Good. I'd like to register a complaint.

OMAR. Morning, Mason.

MASON. Officially. About her.

OMAR. Where are the others?

MASON. I'm serious.

OMAR. Has Zara been through?

AVA. I think she went to find you.

OMAR. Okay.

MASON. Right – two complaints, actually. I don't think she should be here. She's a liability. She hasn't had the health and safety training.

OMAR. So she was here?

MASON. It's a hazardous environment. She doesn't know what she's doing.

OMAR. Noted.

AVA. Omar?

OMAR. Yes?

AVA. When are you going to get us Wi-Fi?

OMAR. You don't need Wi-Fi.

AVA. Everywhere has Wi-Fi. *Buses* have Wi-Fi now.

OMAR. Then check your Facebook on the bus, and come here to do your job.

AVA. Yeah, but actually –

MASON. I have a workplace grievance.

OMAR. Your phones should be in your lockers anyway.

MASON. It's not about that. Although also I agree.

AVA. I don't even have Facebook.

MASON. So actually it's three complaints. Three workplace grievances.

OMAR. Just the three?

MASON. Actually the third one's definitely a multi-part grievance.

AVA (*still to* OMAR). I just think proper internet would make me a more productive team member.

OMAR *spots the mess.*

OMAR. What's all this? Is that coffee?

MASON. Yes – so this is it – this is a part of it –

OMAR. Why have you got hot drinks at your workstations?

MASON. Yes – good question – valid.

AVA. Zara bought them for us, actually.

MASON. Exactly. She's not –

OMAR. And she threw them on the floor, did she?

AVA. No, but –

OMAR. And where's Liv? Where's Trent?

MASON. They've gone to deal with the industrial espionage.

OMAR. What?

MASON. We've got intruders onsite.

OMAR. Intruders?

AVA. It's nothing. We think they might be from the paper.

OMAR. The paper? Oh – *The Star* – they came?

AVA. Maybe. Are they meant to be coming today?

MASON. Or they might be robbing us. Either way, Liv's on it.

OMAR. Is anybody getting any work done?

AVA. Yes – look – we're all over it!

OMAR. Okay, good.

AVA. Can we talk about next year, actually? Because I wondered
    if –

OMAR. Not today.

AVA. Okay, but maybe we could pencil –

MASON. When can I talk to you about my grievances?

OMAR. When this batch is finished.

MASON. Yeah, but –

OMAR. And when you've cleaned this up properly.

MASON. That wasn't my fault.

OMAR. Is that your station?

MASON. Yeah, but –

OMAR. So it's your responsibility.

    OMAR *picks up half a pair of scissors.*

    Whose are these?

AVA. Liv's.

OMAR. She's not putting enough pressure on the blade. Still
    scared of it. I'll come back later on.

    He picks up a pair of completed scissors from MASON*'s
    station.*

    These are yours?

MASON. Yeah.

    OMAR *tests them, snipping a piece of cloth. He's impressed.*

OMAR. Good. Wipe everything down properly – thoroughly –
    don't start up again until it's spotless. Understood?

MASON. Yeah, but –

OMAR. I'm going to track down the others. Keep this up.

    OMAR *goes.*

MASON. Dickhead.

AVA. Why?

MASON (*handling the scissors*). These aren't good.

AVA. Are they not?

MASON. Look at them.

AVA. What's wrong with them?

MASON. Nothing. They're fine. They're not *good*. Eddie
would've never said these were good.

AVA. And that makes Omar a dickhead?

MASON. Eddie would've shown us how to make them better.

AVA. At least he likes you.

MASON *shrugs*.

He does. I mean not as a person – I'm not saying anyone
likes you as a person, but he respects you. (*Beat*.) I keep on
trying to talk to him about what happens once the
apprenticeships are over. Has he said anything to you?

MASON. No.

AVA. Nothing at all?

MASON. It just ends, doesn't it? It's fixed. Twelve months and
done.

AVA. They got Trent to stay on last year.

MASON. That was a one-off.

AVA. Yeah. (*Beat*.) So he's not staying either?

MASON. Hmm?

AVA. Trent? They haven't asked him to stay on?

MASON. I don't think so.

AVA. He's not said anything?

MASON. No.

AVA. But do you think he'd want to?

MASON. I don't know.

AVA. Cos I suppose if he didn't, that might open something up.
And I'd rather he stayed, that we could all stay, but…
Actually I don't think they can afford to lose all of us.
Because we've got the China order now – they didn't have
that last year. They need us. Omar can't do everything by
himself, and they can't just start up again with a fresh bunch
of randoms in September, cos there's too much to do now –
it'd be carnage.

MASON. Right.

AVA. What they need is consistency. And with the money we're
gonna be making… The China order is massive. It's got to
cover some proper salaries – like actual salaries – permanent
roles – none of this training bullshit. (*Beat.*) You'd stay,
wouldn't you – if they asked you to?

MASON. Maybe.

AVA. Have you got anything else lined up?

MASON. Reckon someone can get me in at Ikea.

AVA. Yeah?

MASON. In the warehouse.

AVA. Oh. Nice. (*Beat.*) But if it really takes off – if this deal
does everything Eddie told us it would – then they'll be
begging us all to stay. They'll have to get in new apprentices
too, and make us all supervisors. Not master craftsmen, not
straight away, but we'd have to train up the newbies as well,
because Omar can't do everything.

MASON. You can't train anyone.

AVA. Yeah I can.

MASON (*clearly doesn't believe her*). Okay.

AVA. Course I can.

MASON. There's still stuff Omar can't do yet – not properly –
and he had Eddie to teach him.

AVA. Yeah, but –

MASON. And Eddie was here forever.

AVA. So what?

MASON. Takes decades.

AVA. Yeah, but we don't have decades, do we? The reality is we don't have decades, and we don't have Eddie any more, so we've just got to make the best of it. What else can we do? So... so... so we finish off the China order – this first part of it – we get that in, and they're like 'cracking – you've proven yourselves – now keep going, we'll take another thousand – another five thousand, ten thousand of everything.' We're not gonna say no, are we? Omar's gonna get in a bunch of new recruits, he's gonna keep all of us on so we can get them up to scratch, and I'm gonna ask – no, I'm gonna tell him – I'm gonna be like 'yeah, I'll stay, but I wanna be a supervisor. I want a bit of respect from you, actually. I want to be treated with respect. I want an hourly wage in double digits – no, I want a guaranteed, salaried position' – and he's got to say yes, cos who else is he gonna get?

MASON. Okay.

AVA. What else are we gonna do?

MASON. You reckon if you work at Ikea they give you free meatballs?

AVA. I'm serious.

MASON. They'll get shit.

AVA. What?

MASON. The scissors are gonna get shit. You think these are as good as what was going out three months ago, back when we had Eddie to check them?

AVA. I don't know. I reckon.

MASON. They're not.

AVA. Close enough.

MASON. They're not! 'Close enough' isn't... The whole point of... The scissors you get in TK Maxx are close enough. Wilkos are close enough. That's not why we do it.

AVA. We'll get better.

MASON. How?

AVA. With practice, with –

MASON. You can't just practise, you have to be taught.

AVA. We're getting good. Even Omar said –

MASON. Omar's a dickhead and you can't make scissors for shit. (*Beat*.) I'm not having a go, I'm just…

AVA. Whatever.

MASON. I wasn't.

AVA. And who died and made you fucking Scissor Jesus?

MASON. No one.

AVA. Fine. I don't even have to make the scissors at all. Fuck that. I'll run the office. Cos Omar does need someone. Who doesn't even have Wi-Fi? It's a state.

MASON. Right.

AVA. I could do that.

MASON. Okay.

AVA. Zara's not the only one who can do computers. So I'll sort all of that out, Liv and Trent will stay on, Omar can go back to pretending it's still the Industrial Revolution, and you can fuck off to Ikea.

MASON. Okay.

AVA. You're gonna hate it there.

MASON. Why?

AVA. Cos you hate everything, cos you're a dickhead, but also you're an obsessive dickhead. You're as bad as Omar – as bad as Eddie – you need everything to be just so. You're telling me you've got a lot of faith in Ikea's craftsmanship?

MASON. That's different.

AVA. Why?

MASON. I won't be making the stuff there. It doesn't matter.

Beat.

AVA. I think we're better than you think we are. I think you're
just in a mood. (*Beat.*) I think we're gonna smash this lot, get
another massive order in, and they're gonna have to beg to
keep us. Fifteen pound an hour. Fuck it – twenty. Why not?

MASON. Okay.

AVA. So it'll be me, and Liv, and Trent, and a bunch of cool new
people who all look up to us, and we'll have the best time.

MASON. Okay.

AVA. But you enjoy your meatballs.

MASON. Okay.

AVA. Flat-pack wanker.

Beat. MASON *stands up again.*

Sit down. You're not going to go anywhere so sit down.
We've got to get this done. We're in control here. Our
destinies are actually in our control right now, because yeah,
we were only meant to be here for a year, but these are
exceptional circumstances, aren't they? They're uncharted
waters. We didn't know Eddie was going to die, we didn't
know we'd have ten thousand pieces still to make, and what
that's done is it's given us value – it's increased our value –
so now we're in the driving seat. And we can piss that away,
and sulk, and run around playing spies, or we can get on with
the order – which is boring, I get it – but if it means I still
have a job in September, I'll suck it up.

MASON. I didn't think you liked it.

AVA. Who said I did?

MASON. Right.

AVA. I don't like it, it's a job. It's not even really a job, is it? It
was just something to keep me busy for a year, keep me out
of trouble, but now it might be more than that, it might be a
real opportunity, and that's worth something.

MASON. Yeah.

AVA. You're good at it.

MASON. I'm okay.

AVA. No, you're good. You're annoyingly good, and you don't deserve to be, because you don't work any harder than I do – I don't think you work anything like as hard as I do, actually, but it comes naturally to you.

MASON. No.

AVA. It does.

MASON. I just do what Eddie showed me.

AVA. And he always took his time with you, didn't he? (*Beat.*) It's fine. I don't care. I'm getting there. I'm getting better. But you don't even have to try, and you still bitch about it all day.

MASON. I don't.

AVA. You do. Why wouldn't you want to stay here? And you know what'd happen if I took over the office?

MASON. What?

AVA. No more reason for Zara to come up here. She'll fuck off back to London, finishing her degree, taking over the world or whatever. You'd see her a couple of times a year, max.

MASON. Okay.

AVA. You'd miss us if you weren't here.

MASON. No I wouldn't.

AVA. You would.

MASON. Nope.

AVA. You wouldn't miss me?

MASON. It's not personal.

AVA. Or Liv? Or Trent?

MASON. I'd still see Trent.

AVA. Why?

MASON. Because I'd miss him otherwise.

AVA. Why do you want to go work in Ikea?

MASON. Because I wouldn't be having this conversation.

AVA. Fine.

MASON. Fine.

AVA. Fine.

Beat.

MASON. I never said I wanted to work in Ikea. I said they might have jobs there. You said 'what'll you do when the apprenticeships are over?' and I said I might go to Ikea, cos Antoine reckons they're gonna need people in the warehouse, and you know the thing about warehouses?

AVA. No – what?

MASON. They're big and noisy and you get on by yourself without talking all day.

AVA. Right.

Beat.

MASON. And Ikea would have an HR department. So all this workplace harassment I'm experiencing – I wouldn't have to put up with it.

AVA. Right.

MASON. I'm just saying. They'd have policies in place.

AVA. Yeah.

Beat.

MASON. You have got better.

AVA. Don't.

MASON. What?

AVA. Fuck off. Don't try to be nice to me now.

MASON. Let me finish then. You have got better. You used to be even shitter than you are now. Happy?

AVA. Thanks, Mason.

MASON. You're welcome.

AVA. Right, fuck it.

   AVA *gets up, starts to put a jacket on.*

MASON. Where are you going?

AVA. Taking a break. Clearly no one's working today. Why fight it?

MASON. Very mixed signals from you today.

AVA. If Omar comes back, just tell him something.

MASON. Like what?

AVA. I don't know. Use your imagination.

MASON. Like you were eaten by bears?

   Beat.

AVA. What?

MASON. Too much imagination?

AVA. Fuck it. Whatever you like.

   AVA *starts to go.*

MASON. Rumbler needs unloading.

AVA. What, still?

MASON. Liv was meant to do it.

AVA. Fine.

MASON (*gesturing to a tray/rack of scissor parts*). And that lot can go in.

AVA. Can't you take them?

MASON. It's Liv's turn.

AVA. I'll do it later.

MASON. Just saying, if someone wanted to show some initiative – if they were trying to demonstrate they were supervisor material –

AVA. Whatever. Fine.

AVA picks up a tray/line of scissors.

MASON. Not my fault she's lazy.

AVA. She's not lazy, she just doesn't like getting sliced to pieces.

MASON. Yeah, cos we all love it.

AVA. It's fine. I'm doing it.

MASON. She still is proper lazy though.

AVA. And you're still a prick.

AVA starts to leave.

MASON. Get me another coffee while you're gone then?

AVA sticks a finger up at MASON as she walks out.

MASON starts clearing up angrily. It takes as long as it takes. After a few moments, TRENT returns with FAYE, Eddie's adopted daughter.

TRENT (*to FAYE, while entering*). It's this way. I don't think there's much in here, but you're welcome to look.

FAYE. Thanks.

TRENT. This is Mason – he's another one of us.

FAYE. Nice to meet you. I'm Faye. I didn't realise there'd be so many of you – or that you'd all be so young.

MASON (*to TRENT*). Who's this?

TRENT. She's Eddie's daughter.

MASON. Oh.

TRENT. She was the one in the office. It wasn't espionage, she was just looking for some of his things.

MASON. Well she would say that, wouldn't she?

TRENT. Where's Ava?

MASON. Doing the rumbler. Where's Liv?

TRENT. Thought she was right behind me. (*To* FAYE.) This is more of a work space really – I think there are some archive boxes out in the corridor.

FAYE. Great.

MASON. Who was she with? (*To* FAYE.) I heard two voices – who were you with?

FAYE. Oh, that was Mel, my, uh, my partner.

MASON. What, business partner?

FAYE. No. No, she's… Uh…

TRENT. Her wife.

MASON (*uninterested*). Oh, alright. (*Beat.*) You're definitely not here to rob us then?

FAYE. Sorry?

MASON. When I heard you earlier I thought you might be here to rob us.

FAYE. No – no, absolutely not. And I want to honour everything that you do here, honestly. I have a lot of respect for it. And thank you – thank you, all of you, for keeping things going for as long as you have.

MASON. Why are you talking like the Queen?

FAYE. I'm sorry?

MASON. She's talking like when the Queen goes to look round somewhere.

FAYE. I didn't mean to.

TRENT. Don't mind him.

MASON. I'm just trying to get on.

FAYE. How many of you are there working here?

TRENT. Just the four of us, and Omar.

FAYE. And you're all trainees, is that right?

MASON. Apprentices.

FAYE. So who trains you?

TRENT. Just Omar now.

MASON. But he knows fuck-all compared to your dad.

FAYE. Right.

TRENT. I've been here a bit longer than the others. It's only meant to be a year-long programme, but they kept me on – re-enrolled me. Cos when Eddie got worse they needed another pair of hands – someone who'd been around a bit.

FAYE. That's good of you.

TRENT. I liked him. We all did.

FAYE. Yeah?

MASON (*still not really giving much attention*). Yeah. It's a shame he's dead.

FAYE. Right. Yes.

MASON. Because he's left us in the shit now.

TRENT *shoves* MASON.

FAYE (*to* MASON). How do you mean?

MASON. Sorry. It's true though.

FAYE. Why?

MASON. Cos he's gone, and none of us are actually good enough. We're not. He needed to plan better – train up Omar better. Cos everyone's banging on about China – this big new deal with China, and it's going to be worth millions – but it doesn't matter. We could have all the orders in the world – doesn't matter if there's no one left who can make it.

FAYE. Right.

TRENT. But we're still learning. We're doing our best.

FAYE. It takes decades to learn, doesn't it?

TRENT. Yeah.

FAYE. But you only train here for a year?

TRENT. Yeah.

FAYE. How does that work then?

MASON. It doesn't.

FAYE. Right.

MASON. But we all get fired at the end of the summer, so it's not our problem.

FAYE. And what do you do afterwards?

MASON *shrugs. A beat.*

TRENT. Do you know how to use all this?

FAYE *laughs.*

FAYE. Me? No.

TRENT. I just thought – as you're his daughter.

FAYE. Yeah, I mean I've watched him, but –

TRENT. He never showed you?

FAYE. No.

MASON. Really?

FAYE. I think it's something he would've loved to teach my husband. (*Beat.*) Doesn't matter. (*Spotting something.*) Are these from the embroidery scissors?

MASON. Yeah, Ava mangled them, snapped the handles right off.

FAYE. Can I have them?

MASON (*with a shrug*). Sure.

TRENT (*to* FAYE). Do you want a go?

MASON. What're you doing?

TRENT. Just asking.

MASON. That's weird.

TRENT. It's not weird. (*Beat – to* FAYE.) Is it?

FAYE. I don't know. Could all get a bit Patrick Swayze. (*Beat.*) *Ghost*? Patrick Swayze?

MASON. Who?

FAYE. Potter's wheel, with the…? Never mind. I'm old.

MASON. It's not pottery.

FAYE. Yeah, I know.

MASON. It's not that kind of wheel.

FAYE. It's from a film.

TRENT. *Flashdance* – that's metal. But she's like a welder.

FAYE. Yep. Yeah, that's right.

TRENT. My mum loves *Flashdance*.

MASON. Is it black and white? Cos I don't do black and white.

FAYE (*trying to change the conversation*). Anyway – thank you, but that's fine. I'd probably just slice my thumb off or something.

TRENT. We've got gloves.

FAYE. You're alright. Thank you though, really. (*Beat.*) But are you happy to be working here? Is it a good thing to be doing?

MASON. Why're you asking?

FAYE. No reason.

MASON. So why did you ask?

FAYE. Just because… I don't know. Because I know how much it meant to him – my dad. He put a lot of himself into it, and not a lot of people appreciated – *I* never really appreciated that, so it's nice to know it means something to other people too.

TRENT. It did. It does.

MASON *shrugs*.

(*Still to* FAYE.) Mason cares more than anyone. He's just always like this.

MASON. Like what?

TRENT. Like you are.

MASON. What does that mean?

TRENT (*still to* FAYE). It's not his fault, he's just part of a generation of young men who've been raised to find sincere passion socially unacceptable.

FAYE. Right.

MASON. I swear to God if you don't stop listening to that podcast –

TRENT. Personal growth is nothing to be ashamed of.

MASON. You're such a dickhead.

TRENT (*still to* FAYE). We're actually very close.

MASON. I've got sincere passions.

TRENT. I know. (*Back to* FAYE.) He's very sincere. Very passionate. (*To* MASON.) You should tell her about Einstein. Tell her about the energy.

MASON. Why?

FAYE. Einstein?

MASON. It's stupid.

FAYE. Did my dad used to talk to you about Einstein?

MASON (*to* TRENT). See, she knows about it already.

TRENT. Yeah, but tell her like how you told me.

MASON. You tell her.

TRENT. It's your thing.

MASON *shrugs*.

(*To* FAYE.) Energy transfer.

FAYE. Energy can never be created or destroyed, only transformed.

TRENT. Right.

FAYE. Conservation.

MASON (*to* TRENT). See?

FAYE. My dad was weirdly into this – so was his dad, actually – that's where he got it from.

MASON (*still to* TRENT). See, she says it's weird.

FAYE. No, I didn't mean it like that. Sorry.

TRENT (*still to* MASON). But your thing is transformation, yeah? (*To* FAYE.) There are two types of transformation. Except there aren't. (*To* MASON.) Will you just explain it?

MASON. Why?

TRENT. Because it's interesting.

MASON. Then will you shut up?

TRENT. If you want.

> MASON *continues to work while explaining angrily, punctuating his speech with hammer blows.*

MASON. Okay. So transformation, yeah? Transformation means making something into something else. GCSE Chemistry. Chemical change versus physical change.

FAYE. Uh-huh.

MASON. And physical change – physical change is like bashing something with a rock. And even though you've bashed it to pieces – you've changed the form, yeah, but not the substance – the chemical composition. It's still the same thing, only now it's in bits. But in a chemical change you're making something new – a chemical reaction rearranges atomic structures to form new chemical bonds. Right?

FAYE. If you say so.

MASON. I do say so, and so does the AQA exam board. So physical change – that's like melting an ice cube. It's still water. You could just freeze it again. But chemical change is like eating a sandwich and then taking a shit. Cos the digestion process has altered the chemical composition of the sandwich. You can't take that shit and turn it back into a sandwich again.

FAYE. Right.

MASON. Wrong. That's what they teach you, but the thing about science at school is that they actually just lie to you about a whole bunch of stuff because they can't be fucked to teach it properly. So they tell you that physical changes are reversible, but chemical changes aren't, because even if you smash something to pieces you can always put it back together again, but mucking around with atoms is different. But it's not true. Any kind of change can be reversed if you put it through the right set of processes. Nothing is ever fixed forever. You can unboil an egg. You can – it's on YouTube. And even if there's stuff we can't do right now, it's only because we don't have the technology yet. One day you'll be able to take your shit and turn it back into a meatball sub, and then turn those meatballs back into a cow. Cos it's all just chemistry. And that's Einstein, right?

FAYE. Is it?

MASON. Conservation. Nothing created, nothing destroyed, only stuff moved about.

FAYE. Right.

MASON. Anything can be remade. (*Beat.*) Can I get back to work now?

FAYE. Right. That's uh, it's just a little different to how Dad used to explain it, but –

MASON. Maybe I'm just thick then.

FAYE. No –

MASON. Because I did fail Chemistry, so…

FAYE. No, I think it's beautiful. Thank you for sharing – it's actually really beautiful.

TRENT. Isn't it?

FAYE. Anything can be remade. And that's what this place is, isn't it? A place for transformation.

MASON. You what?

FAYE. I never really looked at it that way before. I never really knew much about where you all came from, or what he was teaching you, beyond... I didn't imagine it would be Einstein. But why wouldn't it be? That's my fault. And the idea that somebody can come here, and... it doesn't matter who they are, or where they've been – anyone can be transformed. Anything can be remade.

MASON. I didn't say that.

FAYE. It's lovely.

MASON. It wasn't a metaphor. I don't do metaphors.

FAYE. No?

MASON. What's wrong with everyone today?

FAYE. I'm sorry.

MASON. Fuck's sake.

FAYE. What have I – ?

MASON. No metaphors. No subconscious. I'm just talking about the thing I'm talking about.

FAYE. Okay.

MASON. I'm talking about scissors, yeah? And not just any scissors – these scissors.

FAYE. Okay.

MASON. And Einstein.

FAYE. Right.

MASON. And chemistry. And transformation.

FAYE. Uh-huh.

MASON. And the climate crisis.

FAYE. Um. Okay. Why is – ?

MASON. Because everything's about the climate crisis.
Because it's actually legitimately terrifying – like shit-your-pants terrifying, to the point that I don't even want to think

about it, but we have to, because you fuckers aren't. And this is the thing. Cos when I was little, they basically recycled fuck-all. Bottle banks, but that's about it. I remember it was a treat, going to throw our empties in. Go down to the big Tesco's, different bins for all the different colours of glass. Then cardboard. Newspapers. Tin cans. Soak the labels off first, clean them properly. Now it's almost everything. Film. Foil. Tetra Paks. Stuff they couldn't do before. My mum's friend Abi, she's found this special place that just takes toothpaste tubes – that's all they do. Anyone here ever recycled a toothpaste tube? Course we haven't, cos we're all cunts, but we could do if we went to the effort, and that is because science teachers lie to us, and there is no sort of change – physical or chemical – that can't be undone if you put your mind to it. Costs energy – uses energy – but you can always do it. Everything can be remade, if you're prepared to expend the energy. But we don't. We still just chuck all our shit away. Clothes and shoes and phones and laptops and batteries and chargers and non-flushable baby wipes and microplastics that cause fatbergs and garbage islands in the Pacific Ocean that murder turtles, and shitty pairs of scissors with cheap blades and plastic handles that break a month or two after you bought them. And you can't fix them. They weren't built to be fixed, and they weren't built to last, only to be replaced. That's actually their business model – cos if you made it properly, you'd only get to sell it once. And so actually we can keep recycling and recycling, and it's better than landfill, but it's still expending energy, it's still worse – it's actually way worse than it was a few generations back, because things lasted then, so you got through less. And that's not our fault, but it is what it is, so they tell us 'okay, just buy less, consume less,' which means actually just stop owning shit full stop. We're the first generation who've never been allowed to own our stuff. Not just big stuff like houses – everything. We rent everything. So everything we think of as ours – our photos, our TV shows, our music – it isn't actually. We can't hold on to it. It's all just online – in the cloud – and that's just as well, because we don't have anywhere to put anything, but actually what it means is it's only there until someone decides to take it away from us. And they will, because they always take everything away from us in the end

– it's only a matter of time. And it's not even a good system –
it's server farms and databanks and big fucking fizzing stacks
of computers that use more power than the things they're
replacing, so the turtles are still going to get murdered
anyway, and so the thing is – and this isn't a metaphor, this is
just a very literal observation – the bigger thing is wanting to
have something that can't get taken away. And it might not
seem like much, because it isn't really, but a pair of scissors
like this? They could outlive me. And I can't afford to buy
them, which is bullshit, but I do get to make them, and that's
something. I think it's a good thing to make something that
lasts, that's all. No waste. Minimal entropy, yeah? That's
thermodynamics. Preservation of energy. *Conservation*. That's
why your dad told us about Einstein. That's why I think he
did, anyway. And I think he was right.

Beat.

FAYE. Thank you.

LIV *steps in. We're not sure how long she's been listening
for.*

LIV. Shame you're shutting us down then, isn't it?

MASON. What?

FAYE. Oh, hello.

LIV. Hiya. I've just had an illuminating conversation with your
missus.

FAYE. Oh?

LIV. Oh yeah, we really got into it. Have you told them why
you're really here?

TRENT. What do you mean? What's happened?

LIV (*still to* FAYE). Do you want to, or shall I?

TRENT (*to* FAYE). I thought you were just looking for papers.

FAYE. I am.

MASON. What papers?

LIV. Yeah, what papers?

FAYE. Dad's papers. Business documents. That's all.

LIV. So you can sell us off?

FAYE. I...

LIV. The other one's already told me, so you might as well be honest.

MASON. Is that true?

FAYE. No.

LIV. Isn't it?

FAYE. Nothing's decided.

LIV (*to* TRENT). Didn't I tell you we should've called the police the second we saw them?

MASON. How can she do that?

LIV. Cos she thinks she's inheriting it all. (*To* FAYE.) You say 'papers' – you mean what-do-you-call-them – deeds, don't you? Proof of ownership?

FAYE. We thought it would be a good idea to know what our position is.

TRENT. But you won't keep us running?

FAYE. I... I don't know.

TRENT. When do you think you'll know?

FAYE. We did have a plan. An idea. The beginnings of... Nothing set in stone.

LIV. And why are you actually here now? Why are you sneaking around?

FAYE. We weren't.

MASON. You were. I heard you both. Definitely sneaking.

LIV. And we caught you red-handed.

FAYE. We have every right to be here.

MASON. Do we even know for certain she's his daughter?

LIV. Nope.

MASON. Because she doesn't look like him.

TRENT. No, she was at the service, remember?

MASON. That could mean anything. Could be part of the con.

LIV. Right, police? Do we all think police? (*She gets out her phone*.) Why is there never any fucking signal?

FAYE. Eddie was my dad, I promise, and I want to honour –

LIV. Oh, well if you *promise*.

MASON. Definitely dodgy. If this was legit there'd be a… I don't know. A letter. A lawyer. You'd be in a suit.

LIV. All middle-aged lesbians own suits.

FAYE. Excuse me?

MASON. Exactly. Where's your suit, where's your lawyer, where's your proof?

LIV. Who's to say she even is a lesbian? Lesbians are cool. All lesbians are anti-capitalist. That's a fact.

FAYE. Okay, everyone just calm down.

LIV. You calm down. No one asked you here.

TRENT (*to* FAYE, *calmer than the others*). You can't prove it yet, can you? You don't actually know yet whether it's yours. (*Beat*.) No offence, but if you had the proof already you wouldn't be here looking for it. That seems pretty obvious.

FAYE. Actually it's not important.

LIV. It seems pretty important.

FAYE. I'm still his next-of-kin – the only next-of-kin. Yes, we haven't found his will yet, yes, it would be useful for a number of reasons, but ultimately, ultimately –

LIV. So he might've written something different.

FAYE. That isn't –

LIV. He might've left it to us.

MASON (*gasps – to* FAYE). Were you trying to destroy records?!

FAYE. No!

MASON. Espionage! Industrial espionage! I bloody told you.

FAYE. It's not –

MASON. Right, basically can we all agree that I'm always right about everything from now on?

LIV (*to* FAYE). So that's why you were sneaking.

FAYE. We weren't!

MASON. You were. Sneaker. Bang to rights.

FAYE. That really isn't what this is.

MASON. I'm going to find Omar. I know he's in now – I'm going to get to the bottom of this. You're sneaky and I don't like it.

MASON *goes*.

LIV (*to* FAYE). Well I hope you're proud of yourself now.

FAYE. I'm sorry – I didn't mean to upset anyone. Today we're really just trying to get the... the lie of the land –

LIV. What the fuck does that mean?

FAYE. And I wanted to visit – I wanted to see in person – I wanted to get a sense of... Because my father gave his life to this place, and I need to process –

LIV. Oh fuck off.

FAYE. Excuse me?

LIV (*to* TRENT). Did you ever see her in here while he was alive?

FAYE. I'm sorry. Honestly I'm very sorry. I see now we've handled this badly.

TRENT. Do you think maybe you should come back another time?

FAYE. This really wasn't how I imagined it. That's my fault, but for some reason I never thought of young people being here. I did know there were apprentices, but I always just pictured Dad pottering around by himself, maybe a couple of old-timers with him, and so once he was gone, I didn't think it'd really matter. And it doesn't, does it? Ultimately it doesn't matter because in a month or so your apprenticeships will have ended and you'll all be gone too, so actually now is a really good time.

LIV. Yeah, she's his daughter alright.

FAYE. What do you mean?

LIV. Piss off then. Nothing changes, does it?

TRENT. It'll be alright.

LIV. Will it though? (*To* FAYE.) Do you know what we get paid to work here?

FAYE. No. Uh, minimum wage, is it? Eight pounds something?

LIV. Four eighty-one.

FAYE. What?

LIV. Four eighty-one. Apprentice minimum wage is different. That's what me, Ava and Mason are on. Trent gets six eighty-three cos he's been here a year now and he's turned nineteen, so they have to give him more. A hundred and ninety-two pounds and forty pence a week. That's what we get.

FAYE. Right. So okay – so exactly – you're being exploited –

LIV. Yeah, no shit. Used to be a five-year training programme. Five years would get you to a pretty good place, and chances are they'd want to keep you on after. Then it went down to three, then two, now it's just the one, cos after a year they have to start paying you more. Some other places still do five, but not here. So what they do is they pay us four eighty-one an hour for twelve months, get whatever they can out of us, then boot us out and bring another lot in. And they get a fucking government grant for us cos they call it training. Training for what? There's fuck-all else to go.

FAYE. So why do it?

LIV. Oh yeah, it's a good question. Ava's a prima ballerina.
I was gonna be a neurosurgeon. Mason got headhunted by
Man United. Trent was cast as the new James Bond. But the
thing is we just fucking love scissors so much.

FAYE. Okay.

LIV. You know why I'm doing this? It's in the family. You're
not the only one. My great-grandma was a grinder here, back
in the day.

FAYE. Really?

LIV. Yeah. Except it wasn't Spenser and Son back then. But
fifty years ago The Hallamshire Scissor Company gets
bought by Thomas Spenser – your granddad, right? And he
gives it to his son Eddie. And what's the first thing he does?
Lays off half the staff. More like three-quarters. Including
my nana.

FAYE. I'm sorry.

LIV. But fuck them, right? Cos who'd want to work here
anyway? Cos if your workforce is being exploited it's
probably better just to fire everyone.

FAYE. I know things were in a pretty dire state when he took
over.

LIV. Yeah.

FAYE. How can I help you? How can I make this better?

LIV. You can piss off.

FAYE. Would you want to stay working here if you could?

LIV. I mean it. And there aren't any papers in here, so you're
not going to find anything. You can go.

TRENT (*to* FAYE). When she looks at you like that it's best to
just do what she says.

FAYE. Yeah, I'll… Okay. Yeah. Sorry.

FAYE *goes*.

LIV. Bitch.

TRENT. It's alright.

LIV. It's not though, is it? How is that alright?

TRENT. It will be. I swear.

LIV. It should be mine. It should be ours.

>   AVA *comes back. She holds two mugs of tea.*

>   (*Still worked up.*) And where the fuck have you been?

AVA. Nowhere. Sorting the rumbler – getting on with stuff. Where's Mason?

LIV. Huffed off again.

AVA. Fuck's sake. I made him tea and everything.

LIV. I might go and catch him up.

TRENT. Don't you think we should actually do something?

AVA. Yes – exactly.

LIV. We've been doing something – we've been doing plenty.

TRENT. But the thing we're actually getting paid to do?

LIV. What's the point? We're getting shut down anyway.

AVA. What?

TRENT. We don't know that.

AVA. What do you mean shut down?

TRENT. No one's said that.

AVA. What did I miss?

LIV. Basically we're fucked because two evil lesbians broke into Omar's office and they're trying to destroy the evidence which would stop me rightfully inheriting the factory and avenging the spirits of my ancestors.

AVA. Okay. Got it. Trent, what did I miss?

TRENT. No, that's pretty accurate to be fair.

AVA. Really?

TRENT. I mean I wouldn't say 'evil', that seems unconstructive.

AVA. Right.

TRENT. Morally questionable, for sure. But I don't like to judge.

AVA. What's happening? Because I was only gone for five minutes.

LIV. Yeah, well, you snooze, you lose.

TRENT. Eddie's daughter's here with her other half. They were the ones in the office.

AVA. And they're going to shut us down?

TRENT. They're looking for his will. That's all we know.

AVA. Why would his will be here?

LIV. What if he did change it though – for real? Omar always said Eddie wanted us to keep things going – what if he has actually left the whole place to us?

TRENT. I guess.

LIV. It's the least he could do, isn't it? And then the four of us could run everything together, like joint owners.

TRENT. Seizing the means of production?

LIV. Yeah, that sounds good. Let's do that.

AVA. And I could be supervisor? (*Beat.*) I mean we'd all be supervisors then, wouldn't we? If we were the ones in charge?

LIV. I guess.

AVA. And has Omar said something? Is this a thing that's happening?

LIV. We don't know that it's not happening.

AVA. Yeah, but who's said that?

LIV. No one yet, but –

AVA. Right.

TRENT. It's just a hypothetical.

LIV. No it's not! He changed his will. Why else would they be looking for it here?

AVA. Okay.

LIV. And we could keep things going, couldn't we, if we wanted to? Just the four of us.

TRENT. And Omar.

LIV. Nah, screw Omar.

TRENT. We couldn't do it without him.

LIV. Yeah we could! It'd be like… *Charlie and the Chocolate Factory*, right? Charlie's only a little boy, and he takes over the whole thing. Just him and his grandpa, who in real life probably got fired for no good reason when it went under new management.

TRENT. When you say 'in real life'…?

LIV. I'm saying I'm Charlie, the spirit of my great-grandma will guide me, and you're all my Oompa-Loompas.

TRENT. Right. I do think that book probably contains a few inaccuracies.

AVA. No, just stop – just shut up, both of you!

TRENT. Okay.

LIV. What's your problem?

AVA. What are you talking about?

LIV. It's espionage – Mason was right –

AVA. Mason is never right!

TRENT. We're just speculating.

AVA. Well don't.

TRENT. Are you okay?

AVA. I'm fine. I'm not… I'm fine, I'm just trying to get on. I'm the only one who… We just need to keep working. We need to smash this lot out, finish off the China order, and then we'll be set. Doesn't matter who owns it, no one's going to shut us down if we're making money. So we just carry on, and then Omar can keep all of us on, and we don't have to change anything. It'll be okay.

TRENT. Okay.

AVA (*to* LIV). Don't go aggravating things.

LIV. I wasn't!

AVA. Don't go kicking off about... If it makes us look bad – if it makes it look like we're not worth saving... Things are fine as they are.

LIV. Wouldn't go that far.

AVA. Fucking Oompa-Loompas? What are you on?

LIV. I was only –

AVA. No one's going to give us a factory – are you that fucking stupid?

TRENT. Ava –

AVA. We've just got to do the work and stay out of trouble. Did you know Mason wants to go to Ikea?

TRENT. He doesn't.

AVA. He does. He told me.

TRENT. It's just a back-up.

AVA. So you knew already?

TRENT. He just wants to make sure he's got something in place.

AVA. Are you going to talk him out of it?

TRENT. No.

AVA. You should. He'd listen to you.

LIV. Who gives a shit what Mason does?

AVA. I do. Because he's a part of this. He's important.

LIV. Really? Mason?

AVA. We need him.

LIV. He's no better than the rest of us.

TRENT. Nah, he is. No offence.

AVA. Right. So he needs to stay too. If he goes, that jeopardises –

TRENT. It's alright.

AVA. We're less viable without him, and if the orders get bigger –

TRENT. Hey –

AVA. Don't shush me!

TRENT. I wasn't.

AVA (*getting increasingly worked up*). We need to be able to deliver, otherwise this is all over. The whole place gets shut down, or they let us go anyway. And we have a window right now – a window where we have some control. He's right – the product's getting worse. And if the product isn't good enough, China won't order any more of it, and if there aren't any more orders –

TRENT *puts a hand on* AVA's *shoulder.*

TRENT. Ava? Okay. Breathing. With me. In, hold, out. In, hold, out. With me.

AVA *gradually calms.*

Okay?

AVA. Yeah.

TRENT. You're okay.

AVA. Thanks.

LIV. You alright?

AVA. Yeah, yeah.

TRENT. Do you want to go outside for some air?

AVA. Nah, I'm fine.

TRENT. You're sure?

AVA. Yeah. Too much coffee, that's all. You were right.

TRENT. Well you've got your tea now.

AVA. Yeah.

TRENT. You're okay.

AVA. Yeah. I'm good I'm chill. You're really good at that.

TRENT. You're fine.

AVA *sits back down at her station.*

AVA (*to* LIV). Sorry.

LIV *shrugs.*

I mean it. I'm sorry. I'm sorry I called you stupid.

LIV. S'alright.

AVA. I don't need this. I could do something else. Anything else.

TRENT. Yeah.

AVA. It was only ever meant to be a year.

LIV. I bet it's dead clean in Ikea. I bet they have a proper break room with like a fridge just for water, and an actual coffee machine. I bet they don't even have mice.

TRENT. Everywhere has mice.

LIV. I bet they're clean mice then. I bet you get free meatballs.

AVA. Why is everyone obsessed with meatballs?

LIV. They're iconic.

AVA. They, um, they make cars in Derby, don't they?

TRENT. Do they?

AVA. Toyotas. Maybe I'll go do that. Maybe I'll make cars.

LIV. You can't. It's all robots now.

AVA. What?

LIV. Nobody makes cars any more – the robots do.

AVA. Fine – I'll make the robots that make the cars. I could do that. I can learn new things. I didn't know how to do this before, but I learnt.

TRENT. You know the brain keeps developing until you're at least twenty-five. They call it neuroplasticity. Loads of time.

LIV. Weirdo.

TRENT. Knowledge is power.

AVA. I think I'd like to weld something. I bet I'd be good at welding.

TRENT. Like *Flashdance*!

AVA. You what?

TRENT. Right? *Flashdance*! (*Beat.*) You weren't there.

LIV. What if we formed a union?

AVA. Just the four of us?

LIV. What if we staged a protest? What if we chained ourselves to our stations?

TRENT. Who'd see us?

LIV. We could livestream it.

AVA. No Wi-Fi.

LIV. Shit, you're right.

TRENT. We'll think of something.

LIV. What about the paper though? We can talk to them when they come.

AVA. What if we actually just talked to them – Eddie's daughter, and –

LIV. We have been.

AVA. Were you nice to them though?

LIV. They were trying to rob us!

AVA (*to* TRENT). Did you talk to them? You've been here the longest. You should explain – you should tell them why it matters.

TRENT. Mason explained.

LIV. Oh well we're fucking doomed then.

TRENT. Ava's right – we just have to finish this order. That's all we can do.

AVA. You're good at talking to people though. You've got a calming manner.

TRENT. Thanks.

AVA. So you tell them – you explain to them why it's going to be alright. You tell them they should keep things going, because we've got this big new order, and it's not a one-off, it's a start of a relationship, it's the dawn of a new era, and they're lucky – they're actually really lucky – they're coming in at exactly the right time, because even a few months ago we were fucked, and actually it used to be that apprentices would just hang around and sit on their arses and do tea runs, but now – now – now we're actually properly busy for the first time in decades, and they *need us*. You've got to tell them that they need us – all of us – even Mason – especially Mason – save him from the meatballs. Cos we're the only ones who know what we're doing. (*Beat*.) Can you tell them that?

TRENT. It'll be okay.

AVA. But will you tell them?

TRENT. I think Omar's got some ideas.

LIV. Omar isn't on our side! The boss is never on your side.

AVA. But he doesn't want us shut down either.

LIV. He's minted. It doesn't matter to him. He was minted before he came here, and he'll still be minted now.

TRENT. Omar stays behind for hours every night fixing all the stuff we fucked up.

LIV. Yeah. He cares about the scissors, he doesn't give a shit about us.

AVA. But if we could just sit everyone down, and explain… Cos it doesn't make any sense, does it? It makes no sense to pull the plug now, not when we're finally getting somewhere. They'd have to see that.

LIV. It's not even a real job. It's a year of bullshit. That's all.

AVA. Yeah, I know.

TRENT. Maybe we'll start up again somewhere else. Even if they sell the building, that doesn't matter. We don't need to do it here.

AVA. Somewhere warm?

LIV. Somewhere clean?

TRENT. Exactly.

AVA. Somewhere state-of-the-art – with robots.

LIV. Okay. I could live with that.

AVA. And they'd still need keep us on, wouldn't they? They should keep us all on, otherwise they'll never be able to keep going. (*To* TRENT.) Would you stay?

TRENT. Me?

AVA. Has Omar asked you already?

TRENT. Not yet.

AVA. But you'd stay if he asked you?

TRENT. Sure.

AVA. Good. Then that's settled – I would if you would.

TRENT. Right.

AVA. And I'd look after the robots. Scissor-tron 3000.

LIV. Scissor-tron 3000 is going to murder us all.

AVA. Not if you're nice to me. (*Beat.*) I'll talk to them. Because it isn't fair. A year isn't enough. It's nowhere near enough, and it's stupid to pretend… We'll explain, and Omar will back us up, because he's not stupid. He knows he needs us. And we'll have a big feature in the paper, and that's gonna get interest, drive up sales, and it'll be fine. We'll be fine.

LIV. Yeah, I'll believe it when I see it.

BILLY*, a photographer, enters. He carries a camera round his neck and other bits of gear with him.*

BILLY. Knock-knock! So this is where you're all hiding.

LIV. Um, hello?

BILLY. Sorry to keep you – been on a bit of a wild goose chase. I'm Billy.

TRENT. Hi.

BILLY. Here to take your pictures?

AVA. Oh!

LIV. Really?

AVA. Did you hear that, Liv? This is Billy and he's here to take our pictures.

TRENT. Nice to meet you.

BILLY. Is this all of you?

LIV. Um. Yeah, that's right.

AVA. Liv –

LIV. What? I'm not having Zara in on it.

AVA. What about Mason?

LIV. He'd hate it anyway.

TRENT. Yeah, he would.

BILLY. So this is everyone?

LIV. Yep. This is all of us. If you see anyone else – especially any other women – you can just ignore them – we're the only proper ones.

BILLY. Okay. (*Glancing around.*) Well, this is cosy.

TRENT. It's the only bit they can afford to heat.

AVA *elbows* TRENT.

What?

AVA (*to* BILLY). But it's got character, hasn't it?

BILLY. Oh, bags. Looks like it just needs a new lease of life to me.

AVA. That's exactly what we've been saying.

LIV (*still to* BILLY). So you wouldn't tear it down then? You'd keep it as it is?

BILLY. Oh, absolutely.

AVA. And you'll say that, to anyone who asks?

BILLY. They're not talking about demolition, are they? Just remodelling.

TRENT. It feels like there's a lot of uncertainty at the moment.

BILLY. I can appreciate that. Not gonna be cheap, either.

AVA. What isn't?

BILLY. Turning somewhere like this around.

AVA. It just needs investment though, doesn't it? Places like this need investment.

BILLY. Absolutely.

AVA. And looking after by people who actually care about them.

BILLY. Right.

LIV (*building on this*). Yeah – yeah, because actually it's not about the owners, is it? It doesn't matter who owns somewhere like this – it's the people who're here day-in, day-out, who know what it's like on the ground – they're the ones who're the most invested. That's who should get a say. (*Beat.*) Do you need to be writing any of this down?

BILLY. Uh…

LIV. My great-grandma used to work here.

BILLY. Did she really?

LIV. Yeah. Decades ago. Ages. She started working here during the war. That's human interest, isn't it? You can use that.

BILLY. Yeah, cracking. And how long – ?

LIV. She met Picasso.

BILLY. I'm sorry?

LIV. Yeah. She was working here when Pablo Picasso – the painter, right – he visited the city, and he got shown round here, and he drew a sketch of her.

AVA. What are you doing?

LIV. It's true! He drew this little sketch of her and her mate Dylis both at grinding wheels, and it was probably worth millions, but Dylis kept it – she said the foreman took it from her, but then two months later she moved to a semi in Harrogate, so you put two and two together.

BILLY. Right.

AVA (*to* LIV). What the fuck are you talking about?

LIV. What? It's true!

AVA. But why are you telling him?

LIV. It's a good story.

BILLY. And, uh, how long have you all been together for?

TRENT. Just coming up on a year now.

BILLY. Is that all?

AVA. But we're in for the long haul. We're all sticking around.

BILLY. Smashing. So we can head over to the old factory floor whenever you're ready. Just grab any bits and pieces you need from here.

LIV. Not in here?

BILLY. Nah. We need to show off the space to its full potential, that's the brief.

AVA. But there's nothing over there.

BILLY. Don't worry about that. We just need to give a sense of what it was, what it could be. No good if you can't see the scale of it.

AVA. And do you think it'll really make a difference?

BILLY. How do you mean?

AVA. Doing a feature like this – how much do you really think it's going to help?

BILLY. Well, we won't know until we try it, will we? I've seen the space – the light down there, it's something else. It's stunning. And you – beautiful people – are going to look stunning in it. We're gonna tell them a story, yeah? Past, present, future. We're going to transform it – won't recognise it by the time we're done. So come on then – with me. Let's rock and roll.

BILLY *ushers the others out.*

A beat. MASON *enters to find the space deserted. He sighs, sits down, and gets back to work. Lights come down around him.*

End of Act One.

ACT TWO

SUSIE, *sister of recently the deceased Eddie, and her friend*
LEO, *are sitting with cups of tea.* MASON *is trying to work.*
SUSIE *is mid-anecdote.*

SUSIE. No, you see I was on the road with Joe – I had been for
months. (*To* LEO.) Had we met by then? We must've done.
Anyway, long story short, he abandoned me in LA – or I
abandoned him – it's hard to remember. And of course there
are far worse places to be abandoned in. I'm not talking to
my father – I can't recall why – but I have no intention of
coming home. I'm renting this extraordinary little flat in
West Hollywood – I say *renting*, I'd charmed my way into it.
It was owned by this very sweet little Lithuanian man who
would dress in traditional Lithuanian dress – I presume it
was traditional – and I'd sing him folk songs, and he'd weep,
and then excuse himself, and leave a few dollars on the side
table as he left. It was all very innocent. Of course they
weren't Lithuanian folk songs, that was somewhat beyond
my capability – Irish mostly. My maternal grandmother was
Irish, you see, so I learnt them from her. Anyway, one day
Jurgis – his name was Jurgis – brings along a friend – an old
friend from the old country, he says, who wants to hear me
sing, so I do, and they both weep, and applaud, and a few
nights later there are five men, and that weekend around a
dozen, and it's a very beautiful apartment, but it is very
small, but one of these men – his name was Domantas – he
owned a club, and he said 'you must sing there, it would be
such an honour, and you must permit me to buy you a new
gown.' (*To* LEO.) Have I told you this before?

LEO. You carry on.

SUSIE. 'You must permit me!' so I thought of course I must.
And he's a much larger gentleman than sweet little Jurgis, far
more difficult to say no to, so of course I must, and off I go,
and I really am expecting the worst at this point, but on the

evening in question this limousine – this powder-blue
limousine – comes to collect me, and whisks me away to this
ballroom – just stunning, just unbelievable, like something
out of a dream – I'm taken into hair and make-up, then out
onto the stage like a deer in the headlights, and that's how
I ended up dressed as Pippi Longstocking singing 'La Vie en
rose' to Ronald Reagan. (*Beat.*) How did we get on to this?

MASON. I asked if you needed sugar.

SUSIE. No, this is splendid, thank you.

LEO (*to* MASON). Very kind of you to let us sit in. We're just
trying to stay out of people's way.

SUSIE (*looking at her phone*) The signal in here really is
appalling, isn't it? (*To* LEO.) I think this room was all just
storage, back in the day.

LEO. You're not getting anything through?

SUSIE. I'm not sure. (*Beat – she remembers.*) Ronald Reagan!
That was it. So I'm formally introduced – Governor Reagan,
as he was back then – and of all things we end up bonding
over sweet tea, only the funny thing is his idea of –

MASON *very purposefully presses a blade against the
loudest machine in the room, drowning* SUSIE *out. He holds
it there for a few seconds.*

(*Picking back up.*) His idea of sweet tea, which –

MASON *does the same thing again.*

You really know your way around that thing, don't you?

MASON *grunts a response.*

What a charming conversationalist.

MASON. We've got a lot to get through.

SUSIE. Oh, of course.

LEO (*to* MASON). They keeping you busy?

MASON. Yep.

LEO. Good man. Good for you.

Beat.

SUSIE. Of course after LA I went up to San Francisco –

More grinding from MASON. SUSIE *sighs.*

LEO. So that's good, isn't it? Good that you've got so much to get through. (*Beat.*) I was surprised. I thought perhaps there was nothing here at all being made now. (*Beat.*) And China – I guess that's an emerging market, isn't it? A growth market.

SUSIE. Now Shanghai in the nineties – that was something else.

A smaller but deliberate grinding noise from MASON.

But perhaps that's a story for another time.

MEL, *Faye's partner, and* XANDER *enter.*

MEL (*as they enter*). I'm not sure, but I think… Oh, hello. (*To* SUSIE *and* LEO.) Hello again.

LEO. Ah, Melanie.

MEL (*stopping*). Hi.

SUSIE. I think we've taken up enough of everyone's time. Come on, Leo.

SUSIE *drains her mug and stands.*

MEL. Don't feel like you have to leave on my account.

SUSIE. Oh, I don't feel like I have to do anything on your account. (*To* XANDER.) So you've found the one you were looking for? Yes, this is a much better fit for you.

XANDER. Hello, Doctor Spenser.

SUSIE (*to* MASON). You should consider this man a cautionary tale – he's what happens if you allow yourself to become respectable.

MASON. Okay.

SUSIE (*to the others, gesturing to* MASON). And this is what happens when the youth of today are denied all light and life and conversation and culture. Pay close attention. (*Beat.*) Leo, shall we?

LEO. Yes, I think perhaps we should.

SUSIE (*to* MASON). Sweet tea! Never order sweet tea in California, that was the purpose of the story. Never trust Americans with anything as important as tea. Anyway, lots to get on with. Come on, Leo.

SUSIE *pats* MASON *on the back and sweeps out.* LEO *follows slightly sheepishly. A beat.*

MEL (*to* MASON). Hi. Sorry about that. I'm Mel. Sorry, you're trying to work.

MASON. Yep.

MEL. We won't be here long. I'm –

MASON. Don't care.

MEL. Right. Um. This is Xander.

XANDER (*extending a hand*). Xander MacIntyre, Claybourne Harris.

MASON *doesn't take his hand.*

MASON. Don't care.

MEL. We met very briefly before. I think maybe you spoke to my wife already? Eddie's daughter – Faye?

MASON. Yep.

MEL. And I met a couple of your friends – your colleagues earlier.

MASON. Uh-huh.

MEL. Great. I don't know what she said to you – what Faye… We didn't want to upset anyone.

MASON. I'm not upset.

MEL. Good. (*Beat.*) It isn't very nice in here, is it?

MASON. No.

MEL. Can't be a very nice place to work.

MASON. Not today.

MEL. Yeah. We'll get out of your hair in a minute. We're just taking a quick look around. It's... Well, it's nothing to worry about. I don't need to bore you with the details.

MASON. Great.

MEL. What, uh – what did Susie want?

MASON. Who?

MEL. Susie? The woman who just left. You do know who she is?

MASON. Nope.

MEL. She didn't say?

MASON. Didn't ask.

MEL. She's Susie Spenser – Eddie's sister? She's nothing to do with us, we're not –

MASON. Didn't ask.

MEL. Got it. What did she talk to you about?

MASON. Ronald Reagan.

MEL. Okay.

XANDER. Should we come back later?

MEL. No, let's just plough on. (*To* MASON.) That's okay, isn't it?

MASON (*gesturing off, with a sigh*). Kettle's through there.

MEL. I'm sorry?

MASON. There's a kettle just through there, and some teabags.

MEL. Oh, thank you.

MASON. It's really annoying that you're here. I want it on record that today has been really annoying, but those two got a cup of tea, so you can have one too.

MEL. Right.

MASON. But you'll have to make it yourself.

MEL. Sure.

MEL *starts to leave towards where* MASON *has gestured.*

MASON. I'm not a bad person.

MEL. I'm sorry?

MASON. Because a few things have been said today that have implied that I'm a bad person, and that's not fair. There's just lots to do, and I don't know where anyone else is.

MEL. Right. Yes. I'm sure you're not... I don't think anyone's a bad person, actually. I think we're all trying our best.

MASON. No, plenty of people are bad people, I just get picked on.

MEL. Right. (*Beat.*) So is this where everything gets made now?

MASON. Pretty much.

MEL. And where are all the others? (*Beat.*) You don't know. You just said that.

MASON. Yep.

MEL. Sorry.

XANDER. I'm just going to take a few measurements, if that's okay – as we're here?

MASON *turns back to his work.* XANDER *takes out a laser tape measure and starts making a few notes.*

MEL. It's unloved, but do you think it's all sound?

XANDER. Impossible to tell. I haven't found anything immediately damning.

MEL. Right.

XANDER. But I'm not qualified to answer that really.

MEL. Sure.

MASON. It's not unloved.

MEL. Sorry – I didn't mean –

MASON. It's a shithole. That doesn't mean it's unloved.

MEL. Right.

> ZARA *enters. She sees the others.*

ZARA. Oh.

MEL. Hi.

> MASON *sighs.*

ZARA. Sorry – I thought my dad might be in here. (*To* MASON.) I left you a coffee earlier – did you find it?

> MASON *hammers something.*

You're welcome. (*To* XANDER.) Mr MacIntyre – you found the right Spenser then?

XANDER. Yes, thank you. In the end.

ZARA (*to* MEL). You must be Faye.

MEL. No, I'm Mel – Faye's partner – wife.

ZARA. Zara.

MEL. Oh – you're Mr Sarbani's daughter. I met him earlier.

ZARA. So you're the ones who've come to rob us?

MEL. Excuse me?

> MASON *puts down what he's doing and stops to watch.*

ZARA. You're the ones who broke in earlier?

MEL. No.

ZARA (*to* MASON). Are they?

MASON. Yeah, they are. She is.

MEL. No one broke in anywhere.

MASON. I heard you.

MEL. We had a key.

ZARA. Right.

MEL. We're allowed. We weren't... We don't need permission to be here.

ZARA (*to* XANDER). And what do you make of it – now you've had a proper poke around?

XANDER. It's a beautiful site.

MEL. It's a shame you're getting so little use out of it.

ZARA (*to* MASON). Do you know what they want to do? Has she told you?

MASON. No.

ZARA (*to* MEL). You couldn't be honest with them?

MEL. He didn't seem particularly interested in knowing.

ZARA. Really?

MASON. Yeah, that is true. I've moved past it.

ZARA. Right. Great. No, that's just about the level of commitment I've come to expect from you, Mason.

MASON. What do you want from me?

ZARA. Nothing. Doesn't matter.

MASON. What doesn't?

ZARA. You just keep doing what you're doing.

MASON. Great idea.

ZARA. You know you could be a little more grateful for… (*She stops herself.*) Forget it. It really doesn't matter.

MASON. Okay.

ZARA. Okay.

MASON. Because I raised the alarm, yeah? I said there were intruders, and everyone had a go, and then I tried to engage and talk about my sincere passions, and everyone had a go, so now I'm just trying to filter it all out and crack on, and everyone's still having a go, so I don't really know what you want from me.

ZARA. I didn't realise you had sincere passions.

MASON. Yeah? Well why would I tell you about them?

ZARA. Okay.

MEL. We won't be here much longer. We'll be out of
everyone's way soon.

MASON. Good.

ZARA. And where's everyone else?

With a great sigh, MASON *stands up again.*

MASON. Right. Fuck it. I'm making tea. This is a one-time-
only offer to make you a cup of tea, and I'm not offering to
be nice, and I'm not offering because I find anyone here
attractive, I'm offering because I really don't want to be in
this conversation. Does everyone understand?

ZARA. Okay. Thanks, I'll –

MASON. Not you. Only visitors.

ZARA. I'm a visitor.

MASON. You're an infestation.

ZARA. I bought you coffee this morning.

MASON (*ignoring this, to* MEL *and* XANDER). You two? You
want anything?

MEL. I'm fine, thank you.

XANDER. I could go for a cup of tea.

MASON. Right.

XANDER. Actually could I come with you? Take a look
through – ?

MASON. Knock yourself out. This way. (*To the others.*) Don't
touch anything.

MASON *leads* XANDER *off.*

MEL. Wow.

ZARA. Yeah.

MEL. He is extraordinarily rude.

ZARA. He's… (*Beat.*) No, you're right, he is.

MEL. Are they all like that? From the couple I've met so far –

ZARA. Not all of them. Trent can be quite sweet.

MEL. Where do they come from?

ZARA. What do you mean?

MEL. The apprentices? How do you find them?

ZARA. Oh. They mostly find a way to us. They don't tend to be the kind of people with an awful lot of other options. No offence to anyone.

MEL. Right.

ZARA. Recruitment was always Eddie's thing – gathering up the waifs and strays.

MEL. What was he looking for?

ZARA. God knows. Not manners, or education, or general emotional intelligence.

MEL. Uh-huh.

ZARA. And they get a good deal – they're lucky to be here.

MEL. Yeah?

ZARA. It's skilled work. They get training. They get a qualification. I don't think they realise just how much energy is expended on them.

MEL. What kind of qualification?

ZARA. Oh. I don't know. Something. A certificate, or points towards… Doesn't matter. They're treated well.

MEL. Right.

ZARA. This will be the first summer Dad has to choose a new bunch by himself.

MEL. So he hasn't done that yet then?

ZARA. Not just yet.

MEL. Okay.

Beat.

ZARA. You should talk to him – my dad.

MEL. We have already.

ZARA. But talk properly – find a way to cooperate.

MEL. I don't know if that's going to be possible.

ZARA. It'll be easier for you if you get him onside. You're not the only ones trying to stake a claim. You know Eddie's sister is here too?

MEL. Yes, I'm aware. I don't think anyone needs to take her very seriously.

ZARA (*with a little glance over her shoulder*). Same goes for them.

MEL. The apprentices?

ZARA. Dad feels very beholden to them. They get away with murder.

MEL. Yeah?

ZARA. He does ninety-five per cent of the work anyway, and they'll all be gone in the summer. They don't represent us. They aren't indicative of what we could do here.

MEL. So now's as good a time as any?

ZARA. For what?

MEL. For a change? For a clean break?

ZARA. A change, not a demolition.

MEL. And you'd sell them out, just like that?

ZARA. They're only ever meant to be temporary.

MEL. Right.

ZARA. They come and go – that's the nature of it. I'm not being horrible, but it doesn't really matter what happens to them – none of them were ever going to do this for long. My dad needs to stay though. I don't care what happens to anything else so long as he gets to carry on. He deserves that. It's important.

MEL. He said he worked in the city before coming here.

ZARA. Yeah. In finance.

MEL. Why the change?

ZARA. He wanted to do something with his hands. (*Beat.*)
He gave up a lot – he was earning six figures before he came
here. There were a million things he could've done, but he
chose this.

MEL. And he's happy?

ZARA. As long as he can keep going, he'll be happy. (*Beat.*)
Have you heard about China? Once the next stage goes
through, we could move to new facilities, new equipment,
new staff – actual proper staff who would take it seriously.
Then this site could be repurposed. He wouldn't want to
leave here, but if that became the only option –

Noise of MASON *and* XANDER *coming back.*

MASON (*as they enter*). No, it wouldn't be like a sandwich
made of shit – it wouldn't be shit any more. It'd be turned
back into a sandwich.

XANDER. Right.

ZARA (*a bit louder/more declarative*). My dad will never leave
here without a fight.

MEL. I understand.

ZARA. Good.

XANDER (*to* MEL). The ceilings get a little lower back there,
but there's still plenty of light. You'll need to get a full
survey of the electrics.

MASON. He got a shock off the kettle.

ZARA. Really?

MASON. I told him not to touch it.

ZARA. Are you okay?

XANDER. I'm fine.

MASON. But no one listens, so.

MEL. Right. Well I think we're just about done in here.

FAYE *returns*.

FAYE. Mel? Thank God.

FAYE *flings her arms around* MEL. *She's clearly going through something*.

MEL. Hey – it's okay.

FAYE. Yeah, it's okay. We're okay, aren't we? We're okay.

MEL. Yeah.

FAYE. Hello, Xander. Hello, Mason. (*To* ZARA.) I don't think we've met.

MEL. Omar's daughter.

ZARA. Zara.

FAYE. Oh yes, right – I must've seen you from afar. Hi. Sorry about all the… (*To* MEL.) Can we talk?

MEL. Here?

FAYE. We really need to talk.

MEL. Okay, but –

FAYE. It can't wait. I need you to be emotionally available to me. We need to get a lot of things out in the open. I won't leave until –

MASON *very intentionally starts loudly grinding again*.

MEL. But maybe we could do it somewhere else?

FAYE (*to* MASON). Sorry, we're interrupting.

MASON. Yep.

FAYE (*to* MEL). This boy has the soul of a poet.

MEL. Really?

ZARA. Really?

MASON. No I don't. Fuck off.

FAYE. No, you do – he does.

MEL. We can just go outside for some air. Xander can finish showing us round.

FAYE. Right.

MEL. Is that okay?

FAYE. Yeah, that's fine. But you do know I love you, don't you?

MEL. Yeah, I know.

FAYE. Good.

MEL. I love you too.

More grinding.

FAYE. Yep, yep, we're going. Come on.

MEL (*to* XANDER). Are you coming too, Xander?

XANDER. Yep. Absolutely. Just let me… (*He tries to finish his tea. It's scalding.*) Hot hot hot. Doesn't matter.

XANDER *puts the mug down on a workstation.*

MASON. Er, you can't leave it there – that's how accidents happen.

XANDER. Right. Of course.

MASON. Back in the sink, if you're not drinking it.

XANDER. Yes. One moment.

The others wait awkwardly as XANDER *scurries offstage, gets rid of his mug, and returns a few moments later.*

Okay. Thanks. All set.

MEL. Great. (*To* ZARA.) Thank you. I'm sure we'll talk more soon.

MEL, FAYE *and* XANDER *go. A beat.*

ZARA. I should let you get on.

MASON. Yep.

ZARA. Don't worry about them.

MASON. I won't.

ZARA. Okay.

Before ZARA *can go anywhere,* TRENT *and* LIV *come back in.* LIV *is furious.*

LIV. Fuck's sake!

TRENT. I'm sorry.

LIV. You are such a bell-end though.

TRENT. Okay, but –

MASON. There you are!

LIV (*spotting* ZARA). Oh, and she's back here again. Great.

ZARA. Where have you two been?

LIV. What's it to you?

TRENT (*to* ZARA). Hi, Zee. (*To* MASON.) Alright?

LIV (*still to* ZARA). No actually, I will tell you where we've been. Oh, you'll be dead jealous when I tell you. You won't believe it. You'll lose your shit.

MASON. Everything okay?

LIV. Dunno – why don't you ask Trent?

TRENT. Yeah, fine. Everything's fine.

MASON. Okay.

LIV. No, it isn't.

TRENT. In my defence, I didn't realise straight away.

ZARA. What's happened?

LIV (*to* TRENT). Why is it that even when you're trying to be nice you also have to be such a colossal prick?

ZARA. What's going on?

LIV. Right – so you know how your dad's always going on about *The Star* coming in?

ZARA. Yeah, we were –

LIV. Because apparently he didn't get the memo about print media being dead. Anyway. And the thing is – the important thing is we thought we were saving the factory. We thought we were doing a good deed.

ZARA. Right?

LIV. For us. For your dad. For everyone. You're very welcome.

ZARA. Okay.

LIV. So this photographer rocks up, yeah? We're minding our own business and this photographer walks in, says he's here to take our photo, so we figure that's what it is – it's for this big news story, but it turns out Eddie's sister has hired – (*She interrupts her own train of thought*.) Did any of you know Eddie had a sister?

TRENT. Yeah, I did.

LIV. Okay, but who knew she was in today?

MASON. Yeah, she was in here ten minutes ago.

LIV. Alright, but did anyone know she's hired a band for some reason?

ZARA. Um, yes – yes actually – I did know that.

LIV. Well fuck the lot of you then. I guess I'm the bell-end.

ZARA. So what happened?

LIV. Right – okay, right – yes – so we think he's from *The Star*, but actually he's not, he thinks he's here to shoot a band, so –

MASON. So hold on – you just went off to have your picture taken without me?

LIV. You weren't here.

MASON. Did you try to find me though?

LIV. It wasn't –

MASON. Thanks for that.

TRENT. I didn't think you'd like it.

MASON. That's not the point.

TRENT. You hate having your picture taken.

MASON. It's not about that, it's about being asked.

TRENT. Sorry.

MASON. About being included, y'know?

LIV. You got off lightly.

MASON. Was Ava with you too?

TRENT. I just thought –

MASON. Right. Great.

TRENT. It wasn't –

MASON. So where is she now?

LIV. Gone for some more sanding belts.

MASON. Right.

ZARA. So what actually happened?

LIV. I don't want to talk about it.

ZARA. Okay.

MASON. Good. I don't want to hear about it either.

LIV. But the point is – the point is Trent knew from the start – Trent *recognised* the photographer, because there's no end to the obscurity of his knowledge, but he thought to himself 'oh, there's that music-industry photographer who's dead famous and who takes pictures of all the celebrities and that', only instead of telling us, he decides it's totally normal that he'd be shooting us for a fucking three-paragraph article in *The Star*.

TRENT. I feel like I've already said sorry quite a lot.

LIV. I'd already told my gran, you jizz-sock.

ZARA. Is he still here?

LIV. Who?

ZARA. The photographer?

TRENT. Yeah – over on the old factory floor.

ZARA. Right.

LIV. So that'll be your next stop then, will it?

ZARA. No.

LIV. He won't be interested in you.

ZARA. Yes, thank you, Liv – I know that. I met him already. He's not...

TRENT. You did?

ZARA. Yeah, earlier this morning. Doesn't matter.

MASON. So am I the only one not involved?

ZARA. It's not important. Don't worry about it.

MASON (*to* LIV). What did he make you do then?

LIV. What didn't he make us do?

TRENT (*to* MASON). I'll tell you later.

ZARA. And there's still been no actual band turn up?

TRENT. Don't think so, not yet.

LIV. Why even is there a band coming in?

ZARA. It doesn't matter.

LIV. It's starting to feel like it matters.

ZARA. It's a distraction. You should stay focused on the order.

TRENT. We're on it.

ZARA. Thank you.

TRENT. Ava's been working really hard too – she'll be around somewhere.

ZARA. Okay.

MASON. If she's not been eaten by bears.

ZARA. What?

MASON (*on a separate point*). You'll be wanting to get off now, won't you? Back to your laptop or something? You wouldn't want to distract us any further.

ZARA. Yep. Absolutely. You just... keep it up.

ZARA starts to leave.

LIV. So do we still think *The Star* are coming in today or what?

ZARA. I've no idea.

LIV. Yeah, well you would say that.

ZARA. I don't know anything about it.

TRENT. Can you make sure we get to see the pictures he's taken?

ZARA. Um... I can ask, if I see him?

LIV. And do you know about the lesbians who are trying to shut us down?

ZARA. Yeah. A little bit.

LIV. Course you do.

ZARA. It's nothing to worry about.

LIV. Is Eddie's sister in on it too?

ZARA. No, that's a different... I think Mason's right, actually. It's all just distraction. I think right now if you could all just focus on the work, that'd be fantastic.

TRENT. Okay.

LIV. And what happens next year?

Beat.

ZARA. That isn't anything to do with me.

LIV. But he's your dad. He must've talked about it.

ZARA. I don't know.

LIV. Because this year is different, is it? I get that normally you only keep on apprentices for a year, and that's the deal, that's what we signed up for, but you made an exception for Trent last time –

ZARA. That was –

LIV. And you didn't just keep him because he's a sexy Labrador, it's because you needed him. And now you need us even more.

ZARA. I don't have a say in anything.

LIV. You do. Of course you do. You're his daughter. He worships you. He'll do whatever you tell him, so if you had a word... You could do that.

ZARA. I didn't think you'd want to stay.

LIV. I don't. Who said I wanted to? It's shit here.

ZARA. Okay.

LIV. But maybe some of us do.

ZARA. Right.

LIV. And you need us, don't you? Your dad actually needs all of us. He should be courting us. He can't do it all by himself. And we're overextended right now, and we're behind on the order, and it's make-or-break, isn't it? Fuck up China and we've fucked everything. And if the evil lesbians take us over and shut us down then he's back at square one. So actually we're the most important people here, because we're the only ones who do shit, so if he wants any chance of staying open, he needs to come talk to us and make some reassurances. You love your dad, he loves it here, he needs to show some love to us. You should remind him of that. We might strike. We might unionise. We've been playing nice so far –

ZARA. Have you?

LIV. A workman's nothing without his tools. We're the fucking tools, aren't we? And we demand some respect.

Beat.

ZARA. Right. Okay, right, that's... I'll make sure I pass that on.

ZARA *goes. A beat.*

LIV (*after* ZARA). Yeah, that's what I thought.

MASON. Fuck.

LIV. Yeah, well she needed to be told.

LIV *sits down. After that performance she's a little shaken.*

TRENT. Are you okay?

LIV. Yeah, I've just got the spirits of my ancestors flowing through me.

TRENT. Right.

MASON (*to* LIV). So is that just what happens when you have your picture taken?

LIV. She needed to be told. Ava wants to stay, doesn't she? Always banging on about… I don't care. I don't give a shit about it, but even so… It's fine. Omar needs to hear it.

TRENT. Yeah, it was really good.

MASON. You did call us all tools though.

LIV. It was a metaphor.

MASON. Fair play. I don't trust them.

Beat.

TRENT (*to* MASON). I'm sorry we didn't include you.

MASON. What?

TRENT. In the pictures.

MASON. No, you're right, I wouldn't have liked it.

LIV. She just sets something off in me.

MASON. I noticed.

LIV. Forget it.

TRENT. You will stay though, won't you? When they ask us?

LIV. When?

TRENT. Yeah – once they know what they're doing?

LIV. I'd consider my options.

TRENT. I think we make a really good band. Just saying.

As the scene progresses, they start to fall back into work.

LIV. I still say you're a prick for not telling us – when you
realised who he was.

TRENT. I wanted to see where it was going. (*Beat.*) I had fun.
I think we looked good.

MASON. So what happened?

LIV. They made me play air-drums.

MASON *laughs*.

Yeah, really fucking funny.

MASON. Sounds it.

LIV. Humiliating.

TRENT. He's Billy Gunderson! He's a big deal!

LIV. So what's he doing here? Genuinely what are any of these
people doing here?

TRENT. I don't know! I just know the chances of Billy
Gunderson ever taking my photo again are practically zero,
and I wanted to take advantage of it. Say yes to the universe.

LIV. Dickhead.

TRENT (*to* MASON). I'm sorry, I mean it.

LIV. Why are you still apologising to him? I'm the one you
should be apologising to.

TRENT. Because he needs taking out of his comfort zone
sometimes.

MASON. Uh, no I don't.

TRENT. You do.

MASON. It's a zone of comfort – how is that a bad thing?

TRENT. You do though.

LIV. How did you even know who he was?

TRENT. I follow his Instagram.

LIV. You're on Instagram?

TRENT. Yeah, but I'm private. (*Beat – back to* MASON.) It was an adventure and you should've been a part of it, and I'd like you to accept my apology please.

MASON. Fine. You can owe me one.

LIV. No – wait – I've got it.

TRENT. Got what?

LIV. Yes – fucking seen through it. I was right.

MASON. About what?

LIV. Everything. It's all just a smokescreen. It's a double-bluff. There never was any band! Omar's minted, right? So he's splashed out for some big-shot music photographer to come and do a father-daughter photoshoot, just like I was saying. Because we're being bought out, or sold to China, or to the lesbians, or whatever it is that's going on today – and so Zara's going to take over, and we'll all get fired, and basically everything else is just psychological warfare.

MASON. Right.

TRENT. Why though?

LIV. Mind games.

TRENT. Okay.

LIV. Trust me. It's going to be just like it was fifty years ago with my nana. You give your all to somewhere and then one day, bam – no job, no Picasso, no nothing.

MASON. Oh God, you're not still telling that story about Picasso?

LIV. She was robbed. I'm never going to stop telling it.

MASON. It never happened!

LIV. It did!

MASON. Where's the drawing then?

LIV. You go ask Dylis Ferguson! Evil cow. (*Beat.*) Look, you can all look at me like I'm insane, but she was robbed then and we're being robbed now. People like them are always going to find a way to screw over people like us. Always have, always will do.

MASON. Fair enough.

Beat. LIV *very much isn't working at this point.*

LIV. It's just bullshit, isn't it?

MASON. What is?

LIV. All of it. It's broken. It's like Ava was saying. The deal is they train you – the deal is you work your way up. You make tea. You watch. You do a little bit at a time. Where's Omar? I've seen him for like two minutes today and all he did was yell at me.

TRENT. It's a weird day.

LIV. We shouldn't be doing this. We shouldn't have to. It's fucked. My nana was here for over thirty years, and it fucked her too – it fucked her back, and her eyes, and her lungs – maybe the ciggies fucked her lungs, but… But at least it worked then. You came in, you got trained, you didn't have to do anything until you knew how to do it. This isn't fair. It shouldn't be down to us. And we are – we are the most important people here, of course we fucking are – but we shouldn't be. None of this should be our responsibility. I hate it.

TRENT. I think he is trying his best.

LIV. And it's not enough, is it? (*Beat.*) We're actually all really fucked, aren't we?

TRENT. If they can bring in more people – if they can take some pressure off –

LIV. Yeah.

TRENT. Just got to wait and see.

LIV. I'm not lazy.

TRENT. I know.

LIV. That's not what it's about. I just don't like being bad at things, and I don't know how to get better.

MASON. So what're we going to do?

Beat.

LIV. I want to be outdoors. I'd like to work in a forest. Mostly
I'd just like to live in the forest, but I'd work there too if
I had to. That's a thing, isn't?

TRENT. What is?

LIV. Forestry? Cos I don't want to do prissy stuff – not
gardening, not landscaping, and nothing with other people.
But I could be like – what do they call them – tree doctors?

MASON. Surgeons.

LIV. Tree surgeons, right. I'd do a bit of tree surgery. I'm okay
with heights. But actually there are people whose job is just
to look after the land, aren't there? What are they called?
Sounds like a dessert.

MASON. You what?

LIV. *Custodian.* I'd be a custodian of the land. Like Eddie
always said he was a custodian of here. He was looking after
it, preserving it, only I wouldn't just be looking after a pile
of old bricks, I'd have a whole living, breathing forest. And
that'd be a really worthwhile thing, wouldn't it? More
worthwhile than this. I saw a documentary once about a man
who built himself a house in the middle of the woods, like
this tiny little house made of mud and straw and shit – not
actual shit – or maybe it was – and the deal was he was
allowed to build it there because looking after the woodland
was his job. Why is it only mad posh people who get to do
things like that?

MASON. Cos nobody else wants to.

LIV. I would. Not a shit house. A nice little house. Little log
cabin. Little brick oven outside. And I'd just potter around
like Gandalf, living off the land, whittling shit, making sure
everything was okay. Making sure the right things were
growing.

MASON. Shitting in the woods.

LIV. Why not?

MASON. Wouldn't get Wi-Fi.

LIV. Can't be any worse than in here.

MASON. Wouldn't get hazelnut lattes.

LIV. I'd make my own.

MASON *scoffs*.

Hazel – that's a tree, isn't it? I'd grow a hazel tree. And a coffee tree – in a greenhouse, maybe. And I'd have a cow. No, I wouldn't, that would be a faff. But I'd have a patch of oats – I'd make that sacrifice. So I'd have my hazelnuts and my coffee beans, and I'd… milk my oats somehow. Mix it all up. Bam. Hazelnut latte. Easy.

MASON. Right.

LIV. And I wouldn't have to see Zara to get it.

MASON. Alright. Now I'm sold.

LIV. You weren't invited. Trent? You want to come live in a cabin in the woods with me?

TRENT. Um. I don't think so, but thanks.

LIV. Why not?

TRENT. I'd definitely come visit you though.

LIV. Right.

TRENT. Y'know, bring you news from the city. And Haribo.

LIV. Thanks.

TRENT. Not saying you couldn't make your own Haribo as well, but it might not be worth the effort.

LIV. Yeah, you're right.

TRENT. Gelatine – that's like boiling pig's feet and stuff, isn't it?

AVA *comes back, excited*.

AVA. Oh good, you're all back here.

TRENT. Alright.

AVA. Trent – I need to talk to you. Oh, but you'll never guess who I've just met.

LIV. Who?

AVA. The band. The actual band.

LIV. There's actually a band?

AVA. Oh yeah, and they were really going through something.

TRENT. Did they say why they were here?

AVA. Not really.

MASON. What were they like?

AVA. Intense.

LIV. So what happened?

AVA. Not much – just sent them over to the photographer. Trent –

TRENT. Yeah?

LIV (*still to* AVA). And you're sure it wasn't Zara in a wig?

MASON. Zara doesn't want to take over.

LIV. I know she keeps *saying* that.

MASON. She doesn't.

LIV. She doesn't want to get her hands dirty, but –

MASON. She doesn't want anything to do with us! Are you thick? She hates it here. Loves her dad, hates all this. (*To* AVA.) Why do you think I don't like her? She laughs at us. First time we met, I thought she might be one of us – should've known better, but we were all new – and I asked her, I said 'oh, are you an apprentice too?', and she looked at me like I'd asked if she had herpes. And then I found out who she was, and I'm still trying to be friendly, because I'm a very friendly, sociable person, and I say 'so are you gonna take over from your dad one day then?' and she just *laughed*. She laughed in my face – like uncontrollably – like a reflex.

Because it's beneath her. It's fine for us – she thinks it's
brilliant for us, actually, like they're doing us some massive
favour – but for *her*? Omar has to beg her just to help out –
I've heard him. She's university. She's Westminster. She's
going places. This isn't for her, it's for fuck-ups like us.
Dropouts, young offenders, people who don't have other
options.

LIV. Who's a young offender?

MASON. Nothing. No one. Just an example.

AVA. I'm not a young offender.

MASON. I wasn't –

AVA. Getting a CBO doesn't make me a young offender.

MASON. I know. I wasn't –

AVA. So don't spread shit about me. Because that's my personal
business and it's not –

TRENT. He wasn't –

AVA. Do you always have to take his side?

TRENT. He was talking about me.

Beat.

AVA. Oh.

LIV. What?

MASON (*to* TRENT). I'm sorry.

TRENT. It's okay.

MASON. Sorry, I –

TRENT. It doesn't matter.

MASON. I didn't mean to –

TRENT. Honestly, it's fine. (*To others.*) Anyway. That's where
I was before coming here. Not a big deal.

LIV. What did you do?

TRENT. Something stupid.

LIV. Okay.

TRENT. It's not a big deal. I won't say what, if that's okay.

Beat.

MASON. No.

TRENT. What?

MASON. No, I'm sorry, because it's my fault for bringing it up, but you are actually going to have to tell them what you did now, or you'll sound like a rapist.

TRENT. Shit, really?

LIV. Little bit.

AVA. Yeah. Wouldn't have put it like that, but…

TRENT. Right. Okay. Yeah. Um. Nothing like that. I, um…
I battered my dad. For reasons.

LIV. Oh, okay.

TRENT. Um. The thing is my mum… It wasn't –

LIV. That's okay.

AVA. I can't work on a bar. I see bar jobs going all the time, but I can't work anywhere they sell booze – that's one of the conditions. My options are a bit limited.

TRENT. I don't do any stimulants any more.

AVA. Yeah?

LIV. So hot chocolate?

TRENT. Hot chocolate's just delicious.

LIV. My dad really wanted me to come here – cos it was his side of the family – his grandma who got fired, and plenty of us before then. He was so excited. But my mum still checks my bag every night when I get in, cos it's scissors, and historically speaking I haven't always been the best around sharp things.

MASON. You mean…?

LIV. I've never stabbed anyone! I mean *me*, I mean sometimes I've…

AVA. And your dad still wanted you to work here?

LIV. I don't think he really knows much about it – or pretends like he doesn't. I'm only really here to keep him happy, and I thought 'fine, it'll be fine', cos I spoke to a guy who did it a couple of years ago, back when everything was much quieter, and he was like 'yeah, it's a doss – you just make tea, you run errands, you probably won't touch a blade the whole time you're there', and then Eddie dies, and there's this big new order, and now we're basically unsupervised all the fucking time, and they're really sharp, like really, really sharp, and it'd be really easy to… Sorry.

TRENT. Don't be sorry.

LIV. Wasn't what I signed up for, y'know?

TRENT. Yeah.

LIV. And it's noisy. And it smells. And I want a cabin in the woods.

AVA. Is there anything we can do?

LIV. I'm alright.

AVA. But any time you're not –

LIV. Yeah.

MASON (*mutters almost inaudibly*). I'll do the rumbler.

LIV. What?

MASON. Said I'll do the rumbler for you. Cos it's just a giant bucket full of sharp things, isn't it, so… You don't have to do it. It's not a big deal.

LIV. Thanks.

Beat.

MASON. You know what it is – why I actually can't stand her?

AVA. Oh my God, are you still talking about Zara? You are literally obsessed.

MASON. No, but seriously. It's because of what Eddie's
daughter was saying earlier – it's cos she looks at us like
we're the metaphor.

LIV. What?

MASON. You know – transformation. You see how her eyes lit
up? You take your raw material, you dig it out of the earth
somewhere unpromising, and it's rough, and it's filthy, but
you clean all the crap off it, you purify it, melt it down, bash
it with hammers, sharpen it up until you've got something
that serves a purpose. And there are lots of places that do that
– thousands, millions of ways, probably, that you can do that.
School – bash. College – bash. Prison. Office job. Army.
Whacking you over and over until you look like something
useful. And some of them are better than others. Some are
production lines where it's all just bam-bam-bam, everything
identical. But this place is *bespoke* – this is *artisan*.
Everything we do here is done by hand, by eye, by feel,
because everyone needs to be treated differently. Oh yeah,
I can do the metaphor, I just don't like them. And Eddie –
y'know I thought Eddie was alright, as it goes, but you know
what he called me? 'A diamond in the rough.' Like from
Aladdin. And he meant it as a compliment, but I don't think
it is. Cos he didn't ask his daughter to take over, and Omar
wouldn't want his to either, not really – not forever. Cos
they're not from the rough. They don't need to be ground up
and put through the fire, they're fine to begin with. And he
thought he was saving me. No – you're hiring me to do a
job, so don't... don't... And I still like doing it. I'm getting
alright at it now, and what we make is good, and useful, and
worthwhile, and everything else I said. But no one's saving
me. I'm just here doing a job, same as anyone else, and
metaphors are still for dickheads.

LIV. Amen.

AVA. Don't go to Ikea.

MASON. I'll see.

AVA. Don't. Find something else. If you do have to find
something else, it should still be somewhere you can make
things.

TRENT. She's right.

LIV. Trent, do you want to go get a drink?

TRENT. What, after work?

LIV. Yeah.

MASON *and* AVA *exchange looks.*

Cos who knows how much longer we'll be here. We should get a drink.

TRENT. Yeah. Should be somewhere we can all go though. Like a sober space.

LIV. Right. Yeah, no, totally. Tonight, why don't we all... Anywhere you like. That'd be really nice. But also maybe we could just have a drink just the two of us some time?

TRENT. Oh. Okay. Great.

LIV. Yeah?

TRENT. Yeah, any time. And if you ever want to talk about –

MASON. Trent?

TRENT. Yeah?

MASON. She's asking you out, mate. She just asked you out.

TRENT. Oh. (*To* LIV.) Did you?

LIV. Yeah, I did sort of.

TRENT. Right.

LIV. Is that okay?

TRENT. Right. Uh, thanks, first off. (*To* MASON.) So nobody here – ?

MASON. Why would they?

TRENT. Sorry. Um. So I'm definitely up for any kind of socialising in any combination of people here, would love that, but also I am seeing someone. Um. Romantically.

LIV. Oh.

TRENT. Sorry.

LIV. No, that's… Don't apologise.

AVA. You are?

TRENT. Yeah.

LIV. Right.

AVA (*still to* TRENT). Exclusively, or…?

TRENT. Sorry?

AVA. Doesn't matter. (*Beat.*) Unless you were looking for –

LIV. Ava!

AVA. No, you're right, it doesn't matter.

LIV. I suppose it figures. You are actually quite irritatingly fit.

TRENT. Thanks.

LIV. For a Labrador.

AVA (*to* TRENT). Who is she then?

TRENT. Uh…

AVA. Is it a secret?

LIV. Oh my God, are you fucking Zara? Cos if you're fucking Zara I will absolutely lose my shit.

TRENT. I'm not.

LIV. You swear to me?

TRENT. They're just quite a private person, so –

LIV. International man of mystery over here.

MASON *smirks*.

AVA. And why does Mason know about her, and we don't? Aren't we bros too?

At this point, MASON *bursts into giggles.*

MASON. Sorry.

LIV. Is it someone we know? Cos who else even is there that we all know?

MASON. Fuck it.

    MASON *takes* TRENT*'s head in his hands and gently kisses him on the lips.*

AVA. Oh. Oh!

LIV. Fuck!

MASON. If we're all doing big confessions about shit.

LIV. Wow.

AVA. Do you feel better about being rejected now?

LIV. Actually no.

AVA. Nah, me neither.

LIV. I mean standards, come on.

MASON. Right – everyone happy?

AVA. How long has this been going on for?

TRENT (*casually*). Few months.

LIV. Jesus Christ. (*To* AVA, *opening her arms up*.) What do you say? Run away with me to the forest?

AVA. You're alright.

LIV. Two for two. Striking out.

MASON. Just don't go spreading it around, yeah?

AVA. To who?

TRENT. It's not a big deal.

LIV. Uh, yes it is.

TRENT. And here is fine – you two knowing is fine, but…

AVA. Yeah, of course.

MASON. Did you really have no idea? Haven't you noticed how much happier I've been?

TRENT. I have.

LIV. Oh God, just don't get all mushy now.

TRENT. We won't.

LIV. And you're way out of his league.

TRENT *and* MASON (*together*). Thanks.

AVA. Right, any more revelations? Can we just get on?

> BILLY *enters. He carries a mop, broom and an old briefcase, along with some of his other photography gear.*

BILLY. Hi – sorry. Don't mind me – just left my tripod. And returning your props.

AVA. Oh, Billy! Mason, this is Billy.

MASON. Hiya.

BILLY. Hi.

LIV. You missed him earlier, but Mason's actually a really big part of the band.

BILLY. Oh, okay.

MASON. No –

AVA. He is.

TRENT (*to* BILLY). Do you think you could take a couple more of us?

BILLY. Uh –

MASON. It doesn't matter.

TRENT. No, it does. (*Back to* BILLY.) Please? There was just a mix-up before. He should always have been a part of it. Can we just do a couple in here?

BILLY. Sure, why not?

TRENT. Thanks.

LIV. You're a legend, Billy.

> BILLY *takes a few photos. Smiles, silly poses, the group are at ease.*

BILLY. A nice one now, for your gran.

LIV. And one more for my Tinder?

BILLY. I think that's enough.

The shoot ends.

We're going to have some nice ones here. Stick your email down?

TRENT *puts his email into* BILLY's *phone.*

TRENT. Thanks. And you're following me now on Insta.

BILLY. Thanks for that. Good luck with it all. I'll send them on.

AVA (*gesturing to the briefcase*). Oh, that isn't from in here.

BILLY. No?

AVA. Nah, it'll be from the office – just across the yard.

BILLY. Right.

BILLY *picks up the briefcase again along with his tripod and goes.*

AVA. I think I'm a bit in love with Billy.

LIV. Me too.

MASON. Not really my type.

TRENT. I bet you look great. I bet we all do.

MASON. We are still going to have to get this done though. We do have to finish the order.

TRENT. I know. We will.

COCO *and* MOLLY, *two would-be popstars in ludicrous customised boiler suits, walk in.*

MOLLY. I'm telling you it's not this way!

COCO (*seeing everyone*). Oh – sorry.

LIV (*taking them in*). Amazing.

COCO. Sorry, we're just trying to find our way out.

LIV. The band!

AVA. This is the real band.

MOLLY. Um. Hi.

LIV. We could be a real band too, if we wanted.

AVA. Hello again.

TRENT. You're the band?

COCO. I'm Coco, this is Molly.

MOLLY (*taking in* TRENT). Hi, I'm Molly.

LIV. Wouldn't waste your time there.

COCO. We were just leaving.

AVA. How did your shoot go?

MOLLY. Not great. Got kicked out.

AVA. Really? Why?

COCO. Creative differences.

AVA. Shit. Sorry.

COCO. It happens.

TRENT. Yeah, different artistic temperaments, in't it? Must be hard.

MOLLY. Do you all work here?

LIV. For now.

MASON. Right. Okay, right – hello, Mason, nice to meet you, et cetera. I think we do all actually need to know why you're here though. Like I've been trying not to involve myself, but I might actually go insane if no one tells us why you're here.

MOLLY. Photoshoot.

MASON. Yeah, but why?

MOLLY. Don't you know?

MASON. No, I'm fully clued up, that's why I'm asking.

COCO. For publicity shots. For when they turn it into a club.

MASON. What?

COCO. We didn't know people were still working here. This all feels a bit rude now. We were just told they're turning this old factory into an epic music venue, and –

LIV. Who told you that?

COCO. The woman – the one who's just inherited it. Susie? Her brother just died?

LIV. Right.

MOLLY. But who fucking knows, because no one seems to know anything, and we're not even getting paid, but they've had us dicking around and holding scissors like they were microphones and… (*Looking around.*) Do you make these?

AVA. Yeah.

MOLLY. From scratch?

AVA. More or less.

MOLLY. That's amazing. I don't know how to make anything. (*To* COCO.) Do you?

COCO. I know how to make music.

MOLLY. Yeah, but anything real?

COCO. I can do a mean lemon drizzle cake.

TRENT. How did you get together?

MOLLY. At uni.

LIV. Course they did.

MOLLY. So how does all this work?

COCO. I thought you wanted to get food.

MOLLY. Yeah, but look at it all. When are we going to be here again?

AVA (*to* MASON). Why don't you show her? (*Beat.*) You're not talking to anyone so you might as well.

MASON. You can watch. I'm not explaining anything.

MOLLY. Okay.

MASON. And I've got a boyfriend. Just so you know.

MOLLY (*a bit thrown*). Good for you?

MASON *starts working*.

MASON. Anyone else is very welcome to do some work too.

AVA. Yeah, okay.

Maybe some of the other apprentices do bits and pieces as they talk.

TRENT (*to* COCO). What did you study?

COCO. English Lit.

LIV. So you just sit around reading all day?

MOLLY. She didn't even read.

COCO. I did! Sometimes.

AVA. And what do you do with an English Lit degree?

COCO. Start a band.

LIV. Are you famous?

COCO. No.

LIV. Do you make money?

COCO. Not yet.

MOLLY. But we will. I keep telling her – you've got to invest in your future. Speculate to accumulate.

LIV. You're both rich then?

COCO. No.

LIV. No?

MOLLY. It's not about money. It's not even about ability. It's all about attitude. All the great artists get where they are because they want it more. (*More for* COCO *than anyone else*.) You just have to keep going, and believe, and… manifest.

AVA. Right.

MOLLY. If you believe you'll succeed, your success becomes inevitable.

TRENT. Right. Except it's probably also about structural advantages, isn't it?

MOLLY. What?

TRENT. Just saying. Without judgement.

COCO. You don't know us.

TRENT. No, you're right, I don't. Sorry.

COCO. So don't mansplain to us.

TRENT. Yep, absolutely. Totally fair. It's just… It's interesting, isn't it? Because it feels like a really nice thing to be able to say 'I just wanted it more.' Y'know, 'I stuck at it, I gave it everything.' But ultimately that might be an ideological justification of privilege that fails to take into account the complexity of individual circumstance. (*Beat.*) But I'm not having a go. Just something to think about.

COCO. What's your name?

TRENT. I'm Trent.

COCO. Go fuck yourself, Trent.

TRENT. Okay.

AVA. Now hang on –

TRENT. I'm sorry.

LIV. Don't say sorry. (*To* COCO.) We're the only people who are allowed to tell Trent to go fuck himself.

AVA. Exactly.

COCO. You have no fucking clue who we are.

MOLLY. It's alright.

COCO. No it isn't. You don't know us. You don't know our situation. And I'm not going to be lectured to about structural privilege by some spotty gimp with a five-pound haircut.

MASON *slams down whatever he's doing.*

MASON. Right – off you fuck then.

COCO. Yeah, we're going.

MASON. His skincare routine is on point.

COCO. Whatever.

MOLLY. Sorry.

COCO. Come on.

MOLLY. Thanks. Sorry. Bye.

COCO *and* MOLLY *go.*

TRENT. Sorry.

AVA. You alright?

TRENT. Yeah, I'm fine.

LIV. You sure?

TRENT. Yeah. (*Beat.*) I feel bad now.

LIV. Don't. She was awful. They're all awful.

AVA. Everyone's awful.

MASON. Everything's awful.

LIV. Forever and ever, amen.

Beat.

AVA. A club?

LIV. Yeah, as if.

AVA. You don't think – ?

MASON. No one's ever going to come to a club here.

AVA. Are we ever going to finish this?

TRENT. We will.

AVA. And then what?

LIV. Another order, right? Another massive order from China, so they have to keep us open, they have to hire us permanently, no one gets to leave.

AVA. Yeah?

LIV. Isn't that what you've been *manifesting*?

AVA. That's right.

MASON. Pretty boring thing to manifest, if you ask me. I'd manifest a… a Lamborghini. Or a Snickers.

TRENT. You can't drive.

MASON. So I'd manifest a license.

AVA. I don't think you know what 'manifest' means.

Beat.

LIV (*to* TRENT). Why don't you freak out? (*Beat.*) None of us know what's going on, but it's clearly something, and it's nothing good, but you're still channelling this 'I'm a feather on the breeze' Zen bullshit and if you say it's all just because of a meditation app or something I will end you.

TRENT. I've got coping mechanisms in place.

LIV. Right.

TRENT. It's something I've had to work on.

AVA. Like the breathing? Is that why you're so good at breathing?

MASON. That's not generally something people have to work at.

AVA. Not just regular breathing, dickhead. Counting and breathing! You know what I mean.

TRENT. Yeah, that's one of them.

AVA. Right.

TRENT. Anyway, nothing's happened yet.

LIV. Yeah, but –

TRENT. So I'm not going to freak out about the bad thing until the bad thing happens. I freaked out last year, before I met any of you. I freaked out because my year was almost up, and I didn't have anything else, and I panicked, but the panic didn't make anything better. And then they kept me on, so…

AVA. But have you really not made any plans?

TRENT. What if Liv was right? What if Eddie's changed his will and left everything to us? He might've done. We don't know that he hasn't. And imagining that makes me much happier than imagining us getting shut down, so until I know something for certain, I'll go with that.

LIV. Fucking Labrador.

AVA. No, I'm with him. Team Labrador.

LIV. Fuck it – Team Labrador, on three. Hands in.

MASON. Jesus Christ.

LIV. Come on!

They put their hands in, MASON *more reluctantly than most.*

AVA. One, two, three –

ALL. Labrador!

General laughter.

TRENT. I feel like I'm being mocked.

LIV. Yeah, that's cos you are.

More giggles.

AVA. And it would sort of make sense, wouldn't it?

LIV. What would?

AVA. If Eddie had left everything to us? Why not? He wanted things to keep going.

LIV. He did love us. Well, he loved the boys.

AVA. Can you imagine? Factory owners.

LIV. I'd buy a monocle.

AVA. And a fur coat.

LIV. I'd get corrupted so quickly.

MASON. I thought you wanted to piss off to the forest anyway?

LIV. Nah, sod that. Not if we were in charge. I'd *buy* a forest, for like corporate getaways. We could get proper Wi-Fi, and a proper breakroom, and a fridge just for water.

TRENT. Sure. Hydration – important.

AVA. And we could, um, we could hire a bunch of old, a bunch of retired… Because there must still be people knocking around who used to do this, who were made redundant, or… and when the next batch of the China order comes through, wages won't be an issue. We can bring in whoever we want. Get trained properly.

MASON. Red Bull.

LIV. What?

MASON. We'll not have a fridge just for water, that's a shit idea. We'll have one for Red Bull.

AVA. We'll have one of each.

TRENT. So you'll all stay then?

MASON. Dunno. I'll have to weigh up my options.

AVA. Yeah, me too. I'm also being headhunted by Rolls-Royce, so.

MASON. Same. I start at Gucci next week.

LIV. Got a big interview lined up at Fabergé.

Beat.

AVA. You what?

LIV. Y'know, the egg people.

This sends the others into hysterics.

What?

AVA. That was the fanciest thing you could think of?

LIV. Have you seen those eggs?

MASON. How is that a job?

LIV. They come from somewhere.

AVA. Just vajazzling an ostrich, on the daily.

LIV. No, I'd feed the crystals to the chickens who lay the eggs –
that's how you do it.

AVA. Right, of course.

TRENT. Classic Liv.

MASON. Incredible.

*All four are in absolute fits of giggles now. They don't really
notice OMAR enter. He seems very serious.*

AVA. Omar!

LIV. There he is!

AVA. We are getting on, I promise.

OMAR. Can we talk?

AVA. It's all under control.

TRENT. Is everything okay?

OMAR. Can you all sit down so we can talk?

LIV. What's happened?

OMAR. Please.

*A bit stiffly, the four apprentices pull themselves together and
sit at their stations.*

Thank you. Um… I know today has been…

OMAR *is struggling to engage all of them at once, shuffling
awkwardly.*

I know there's been a lot of distraction – and some
speculation too. I know you all want to know where we
stand. Uh. I'd like to try and tell you where we stand.

TRENT. Here.

TRENT *finds an old wooden stool, moves a box off it, and
places it down for OMAR to sit on.*

OMAR. Thank you.

MASON. Go on then.

OMAR. I'm very thankful for everything you've been doing.
I know it hasn't been easy. I hope you've all benefitted from
it in some way. I know Eddie believed – sincerely believed –
he wasn't just providing a job, he was giving you
something –

LIV. What's happened?

OMAR. Something more important –

LIV. Are you letting us go? Is this a 'you're fired' speech?

OMAR. I wanted to talk to you about the work you've been
doing – the order you've been putting together for China.
I know we've talked a lot about how important it is – how
it's the only thing, really, keeping us afloat.

TRENT. And it'll be finished soon.

OMAR. If anything we've put far too much pressure on you –
too much responsibility.

MASON. Is it not good enough?

OMAR. What?

MASON. It's not good enough, is it? I've been telling them.
China isn't all mass-produced shit – they'll be able to tell.

OMAR. It isn't about that.

MASON. You must've known – Eddie must've known.

AVA. Is that true?

MASON. Is that why nothing's been sent out yet?

OMAR. No. It's nothing to do with your work.

AVA. Have they cancelled it? They've not cancelled the order?

Beat.

LIV. Omar?

OMAR. This is no reflection on your abilities.

AVA. So they have?

OMAR. That isn't the entire story.

MASON. So what is?

OMAR. All I can tell you right now is that there won't be any
more orders from China.

AVA. Why?

OMAR. There are all sorts of... of... global, economic factors –

LIV. And you've just found out today?

OMAR. New information has come to light today, yes. We need
to take careful stock of our position. There's still a lot that
we don't know.

LIV. What aren't you telling us?

AVA. What about the batch we're making now?

OMAR. There is no buyer for any of this order. Not any more.
We are extremely overextended. The raw materials alone –

AVA. But they must have paid for what they've ordered
already?

OMAR. No, it doesn't appear they have.

MASON. What the fuck?

OMAR. I don't have a firm grasp on the numbers.

MASON. What the actual fuck?

LIV. You're lying. You're just trying to find a way to get rid of us.

OMAR. I promise you I'm not.

LIV. Oh, if you 'promise'.

OMAR. We are in debt. The reality is we are hundreds of
thousands of pounds in debt, in raw material costs, in
amenities, wages, mortgage repayments, and we no longer
have a buyer for our product – for an order of this scale –

AVA. So you gambled?

OMAR. No.

AVA. You gambled and you got it wrong?

OMAR. I had assurances. I was led to believe… I'm deeply sorry – truly very sorry. There needs to be a thorough examination – I have a very incomplete picture of the facts at the moment, and I have a lot to get to grips with. But from what we know right now it's very hard to imagine a way forward where we can remain operational. I wanted you all to know that as soon as I did.

MASON. Fuck's sake.

LIV (*to* OMAR). But you'll be okay, won't you? You'll just go and do something else.

OMAR. Any remaining assets will go to ensuring any outstanding wages are paid. Any references you need, any letters of recommendation, anything at all that might help you going forward –

Suddenly TRENT *stands, picks up something – a hammer, a bit of wood, whatever might be lying around – and starts attacking his workstation violently with it. He's not able to do any real damage to anything, it's just an expression of frustration.* MASON *is immediately out of his seat and wraps his arms around* TRENT, *trying to pin his arms down.*

MASON. Hey, hey, it's alright.

TRENT *calms a little.*

You're alright.

MASON *kisses* TRENT*'s neck or cheek.*

Not here. You're okay. Not this.

TRENT. Sorry.

MASON. It's okay.

TRENT. I'm stupid. I'm so sorry.

MASON. You're not.

OMAR. You should all go home. Leave everything and go home. Don't come in on Monday, wait until you hear from me. I'll try to find out everything I can and call you all when I know more. Go on.

A beat. MASON *sits back down at his station. He starts to work.*

Mason – I said go home.

MASON. Someone's going to want them.

OMAR. I'll call you when there's news.

MASON. As long as the product's good. It's not good enough yet, but it will be.

AVA. What are you doing?

MASON. Doesn't matter who put the order in. Once it's good enough, someone's gonna want it. Right?

AVA nods and turns back to her station.

AVA. Okay.

LIV does the same.

LIV. I still say these new blanks are wank.

MASON (*to* OMAR). You cutting corners on the steel? Cheap bastard.

OMAR (*struggling to hold it together, but playing along*). No, it's the same it's always been.

LIV. Molecularly identical?

OMAR. That's right.

LIV. Then why is it so shit?

OMAR. I'll take a look.

AVA (*holding something up*). Omar – how does this look to you?

OMAR. Good – that's good.

MASON. It's not.

OMAR. It's getting there. Let me see.

AVA. So what're you all doing at the weekend?

MASON. Not talking to you.

AVA. Fuck off, flat pack.

LIV. Gonna see my gran, tell her about my photoshoot.

AVA. Oh yeah?

LIV. Yeah, she'll love it. So will Dad.

Throughout this, TRENT *has just been standing numbly, watching them.*

MASON (*to* TRENT, *gently*). Sit down, you're making me nervous.

TRENT (*quietly*). Yeah.

TRENT *sits, picks up his tools. His hands are still shaking.*

LIV. Omar, I'm fucking this right up – can you show me?

OMAR *goes over to* LIV*'s station and sits with her.*

All apprentices are now back engrossed in their work. They fall into a rhythm. It builds as the lights slowly fade on them.

End.

www.nickhernbooks.co.uk

facebook.com/nickhernbooks

twitter.com/nickhernbooks